D1301192

COMMUNICATION RESEARCH
IN LIBRARY
AND INFORMATION SCIENCE

Communication Research
in Library
and Information Science

A Bibliography on Communication

in the Sciences, Social Sciences, and Technology

Thomas J. Waldhart
and
Enid S. Waldhart

Libraries Unlimited, Inc.

Littleton, Colo.

1975

LIBRARIES UNLIMITED, INC.
P.O. Box 263
Littleton, Colorado 80120

Library of Congress Cataloging in Publication Data

Waldhart, Thomas J   1940—
    Communication research in library and information
science.

    Includes index.
    1. Communication in science—Bibliography.
2. Communication in the social sciences—Bibliography.
3. Communication of technical information—Bibliography.
I. Waldhart, Enid S., 1942—   joint author.
II. Title.
Z7405.C6W35   016.029   75-5551

ISBN 0-87287-111-8

TABLE OF CONTENTS

INTRODUCTION 7

GENERAL. 13
BIBLIOGRAPHIES AND SURVEYS 13
METHODS OF STUDY 17
SOCIAL ORGANIZATION 20
MISCELLANEOUS 24

STRUCTURES OF COMMUNICATION 28
DATA ACTIVITIES 28
INFORMATION SYSTEMS 33
International 33
National 36
General, 36; Sciences, 39; Social sciences, 42;
Technology, 46
NATIONAL AND INTERNATIONAL MEETINGS 47
PUBLICATION PATTERNS 55
General 55
Bibliometric Analysis 56
Author Collaboration 60
Economics 61
Literature Growth and Obsolescence 65
Microforms 67
Primary Sources 70
Journals—Manuscript processing, 70; Journals—Role and
development, 74; Technical reports, 77
Secondary Sources 78
Abstracting and indexing journals, 78; Citation and title
derivative indexes, 82
Tertiary Sources 85

DISCIPLINE ORIENTED STUDIES 88

  SCIENCES 88
    General 88
    Biological Sciences 91
    Chemistry 94
    Geosciences 96
    Mathematics 97
    Physics 98

  SOCIAL SCIENCES 102
    General 102
    Anthropology 105
    Communication Sciences 105
    Economics 106
    Education 107
    Language Sciences 109
    Political Science and Law 110
    Psychology 111
    Sociology 114

  TECHNOLOGY 115
    General 115
    Agriculture 117
    Engineering 118
    Medicine 125

**COMMUNICATION BARRIERS—LANGUAGE, MESSAGE
STRUCTURE AND SECURITY** 131

COMMUNICATION INNOVATIONS 135
  GENERAL 135
  INFORMATION EXCHANGE GROUPS 136
  METHODS, MEDIA, AND PUBLICATION FORMS 137

AUTHOR INDEX 143

SUBJECT INDEX 153

INTRODUCTION

PURPOSE

The ability to manage the communication system of the sciences, social sciences and technology, an ability which is essential if the performance of the system is to be systematically improved, requires first an understanding of the communication behavior of scientists, social scientists, and technologists. Lacking such understanding, changes in the communication system tend to be made with little capability of accurately predicting their probable success, or with little awareness of how these changes may influence the performance or operation of the broader communication system.

Since the mid-1960s a significant part of the research activities of the library and information science community has been devoted to the study of communication patterns in the sciences, social sciences and technology in an attempt to gain such understanding. Through the support of the federal government, the efforts of individual researchers and research centers, and the information programs of a number of professional societies, a partial view of the communication system of the sciences, social sciences, and technology has begun to emerge.

While interest in communication patterns remains relatively high to date, within the last few years there appears to have been a noticeable shift in emphasis from the study of communication patterns *per se* to efforts directed at improving the performance of communication systems, based on the knowledge accumulated over the last decade of research and experimentation. The quantity of research is substantial and is generally of high quality, and yet, at least three factors have tended to limit its impact on the design and operation of communication systems. First, since much of the research on communication behavior was supported by the federal government and professional societies, the results have often been made available to the general public only through the medium of technical reports whose distribution is generally limited. Second, the research reported in the open literature, primarily journals, is widely dispersed throughout the journals of library and information science as well as the literature of specific disciplines under investigation. For example, research on communication in psychology is as likely to be published in *American Psychologist*, as in the *Journal* of the American Society for Information Science. And third, traditional indexing and abstracting services, with their own discipline orientations, are unable to provide comprehensive access to information related to communication behavior in the sciences, social sciences, and technology.

Thus, it is the purpose of this bibliography to increase the usefulness of research on communication in the sciences, social sciences and technology by making it more accessible to researchers, educators, students and other professionals responsible for the design and operation of communication systems. While the primary audience of concern is the library and information science community, it is hoped that the bibliography will also serve as a useful source of information to individuals within specific substantive disciplines (e.g., chemistry, physics, psychology, sociology, engineering, etc.), who are responsible for the management of communication systems.

COVERAGE

The 1964-1973 time frame was selected for this bibliography because it represents a period during which not only the quantity of research on communication in the sciences, social sciences, and technology reached a particularly high level, but also the research methodologies employed achieved a degree of sophistication that was not common to much of the research conducted during the 1950s and early 1960s. Individuals who are interested in pre-1964 research can gain access to this literature through the use of the bibliographies and surveys that are found in the first section (General—Bibliographies and Surveys) of this compilation.

A modified version of the Research Information Cycle, originally developed by Redmond, Sinclair, and Brown, is presented on page 9, in an attempt to delineate those aspects of the communication system of the sciences, social sciences, and technology that have received emphasis in the development of this reference. In general, only those studies whose subjects were scientists, social scientists, or technologists were selected for inclusion, while the analysis, design, and operation of information storage and retrieval systems, although important to the overall communication process, were considered outside the scope of this bibliography.

ORGANIZATION AND BIBLIOGRAPHIC STRUCTURE

The body of the bibliography is organized on a topical basis with author and subject access provided through the indexes. Because of the number of references and the expected wide range in interest and expertise of the intended audience, "mini-indicators" (bracketed information following the citation) were employed when the subjects discussed in the references were not clearly defined by either the topical headings or the titles of the publications. These indicators are not standardized terms, but are rather terms or descriptive phrases that the

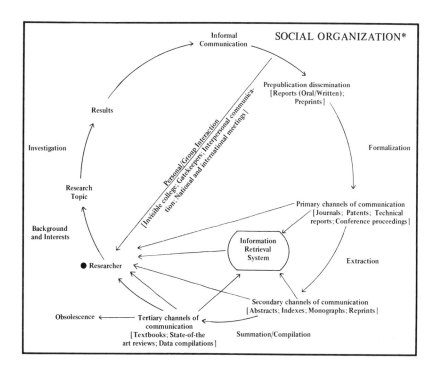

*Donald A. Redmond, Michael P. Sinclair, and Elinore Brown, "University Libraries and University Research," *College & Research Libraries* 33(6):447-453, November 1972.

user may find helpful in establishing the scope or emphasis of the reference. To assist those individuals who are generally unfamiliar with this field of research, we have flagged with an asterisk those references of high quality that provide surveys of particular topics.

An effort was made to ensure that the references were both as complete and accurate as possible. Technical reports that are available from the National Technical Information Service include the AD- , PB- , N- , or other report series code; those available from the ERIC Document Reproduction Service include the ED- number; and dissertations that are available from the Xerox University Microfilms, Inc., have order numbers appended. Full titles for periodicals were included in the bibliographic citation to make it easy for the reader to identify any unfamiliar titles.

METHOD OF COMPILATION

In the process of compilation we relied on examination of indexing and abstracting services, existing bibliographic sources, and tracing of references cited in previously identified documents. In addition, journals that were found to publish most often the results of research on communication in the sciences, social sciences, and technology were systematically reviewed from 1964 to 1973 for any references which might have previously escaped detection. The sources examined were:

Abstracting and Indexing Services

Dissertation Abstracts International
Government Reports Announcements
Information Science Abstracts
Library and Information Science Abstracts
Research in Education

Bibliographies/Surveys

Annual Review of Information Science and Technology
Jacqueline Hills. A Review of the Literature on Primary Communications in Science and Technology. London, Aslib Occasional Publication No. 9, 1972. 36p.

Journals

American Behavioral Scientist
American Journal of Sociology
American Psychologist
American Scientist
American Society for Information Science Journal
American Society for Information Science Proceedings
American Sociological Review
American Sociologist
Aslib Proceedings
Australian Library Journal
College & Research Libraries
Federation Proceedings
Impact of Science on Society
Information
Information Scientist
Information Storage and Retrieval
IEEE Transactions on Education
IEEE Transactions on Engineering Management
IEEE Transactions on Professional Communication
International Federation for Documentation Proceedings
International Library Review
International Science and Technology
International Social Science Journal
Journal of Applied Psychology
Journal of Chemical Documentation
Journal of General Psychology
Journal of Librarianship
Library Quarterly
Medical Library Association Bulletin
Methods of Information in Medicine
Minerva
Nature
Physics Today
Science
Social Science Information
Special Libraries
Technology and Culture
Technology and Society
Technology Review
UNESCO Bulletin for Libraries

The worth of any bibliographic compilation lies in its use by those for whom it was intended. If this reference reveals a body of knowledge that has heretofore gone largely unrecognized by many librarians, information scientists, and other communication specialists, and if that knowledge results in the development of improved communication systems, then the long hours of work in its preparation will represent time well spent.

GENERAL

BIBLIOGRAPHIES AND SURVEYS

*0001 Allen, T. J. "Information Needs and Uses," In: Annual Review of Information Science and Technology. Edited by C. A. Cuadra. Chicago, Encyclopaedia Britannica, 1969, Vol. 4, pp. 3-30. [Scientists and engineers as information processors; Influence of work team on communication; Influence of the organization on communication; Role of professional society; Invisible college.]

0002 Atkin, P. Bibliography of Use Surveys of Public and Academic Libraries, 1950–November, 1970. London, The Library Association, 1971, 84p.

0003 Barnes, R. C. M. "Information Use Studies: Part II–Comparison of Some Recent Surveys," In: Journal of Documentation, 21(3): 169-176, September, 1965. [British surveys.]

0004 Bates, M. J. Use Studies: A Review for Librarians and Information Scientists. March, 1971, 60p. ED 047 738. [Information use; Library use; Information-seeking patterns of scientists.]

0005 Boyer, C. J. The Doctoral Dissertation as an Information Source: A Study of Scientific Information Flow. Metuchen, N. J., Scarecrow, 1973, 129p.

*0006 Crane, D. "Information Needs and Uses," In: Annual Review of Information Science and Technology. Edited by C. A. Cuadra. Chicago, Encyclopaedia Britannica, 1971, Vol. 6, pp. 3-39. [Social organization of research area; Development of research area; Diffusion of information; Information-seeking patterns; Innovations in formal communication; Communication in technology.]

0007 Crawford, S. Y. Informal Communication among Scientists: Proceedings of a Conference on Current Research. Chicago, American Medical Association, February 22, 1971, 50p. ED 056 697. [Invisible college; A social scientist's view of communication research; Summaries of current research.]

0008   Davis, R. A., and C. A. Bailey. Bibliography of Use Studies. Philadelphia, Drexel Institute of Technology, Graduate School of Library Science, 1964, 98p.

0009   DeWeese, L. C. "A Bibliography of Library Use Studies," In: A Statistical Study of Book Use. By A. K. Jain and L. C. DeWeese. Lafayette, Ind., Purdue University, Library Operations Research Project, 1967, pp. 128-199. PB 176 525.

0010   Farr, R. S., and S. Pingree. Research Utilization: An Annotated Bibliography, Palo Alto, Calif., Stanford University, ERIC Clearinghouse on Educational Media and Technology, July, 1970, 72 p. ED 039 777.

0011   Fishenden, R. M. "Information Use Studies: Part I—Past Results and Future Needs," In: Journal of Documentation, 21(3): 163-168, September, 1965.

0012   Frohman, M. A. The Impact of the Characteristics of the Organization on Information Flow. Ann Arbor, Mich., University of Michigan, August, 1969, 93p. ED 049 427. [Characteristics of an organization which influence information flow.]

*0013   Graham, W. R., et. al. Exploration of Oral/Informal Technical Communications Behavior. Silver Springs, Md., American Institutes for Research, August, 1967, 179p. AD 669 586. [Review of research; Social psychology of informal communication; Informal communication behavior of researchers.]

*0014   Griffith, B. C., and A. J. Miller. "Networks of Informal Communication among Scientifically Productive Scientists," In: Communication among Scientists and Engineers. Edited by C. E. Nelson and D. K. Pollock. Lexington, Mass., Heath Lexington Books, 1970, pp. 125-140.

0015   Hanson, C. W. "Research on Users' Needs: Where Is It Getting Us?" In: Aslib Proceedings, 16(2): 64-78, February, 1964. [Summary of research.]

0016   Havelock, R. G. Bibliography on Knowledge Utilization and Dissemination. Ann Arbor, Mich., University of Michigan, Institute for Social Research, 1972, 250p. ED 061 466.

0017   Havelock, R. G., et. al. A Comparative Study of the Literature on the Dissemination and Utilization of Scientific Knowledge. Ann Arbor, Mich., University of Michigan, Center for Research on Utilization of Scientific Knowledge, July, 1969, 507p. ED 029 171.

*0018   Havelock, R. G., et. al. Planning for Innovations through Dissemination and Utilization of Knowledge, Ann Arbor, Mich., University of Michigan, Institute for Social Research, 1971, 533p.

*0019   Herner, S., and M. Herner. "Information Needs and Uses in Science and Technology," In: Annual Review of Information Science and Technology. Edited by C. A. Cuadra. New York, Interscience, 1967, Vol. 2, pp. 1-34. [Evaluation of survey methodologies; Diaries; Interviews; Observations; Questionnaires; Indirect studies; Solution development records.]

0020   Hills, J. A Review of the Literature on Primary Communications in Science and Technology. London, Aslib, Aslib Occasional Paper No. 9, 1972, 36p. [Preliminary communication; Authors and editors; Economics; Journals; Publication methods; Information transfer; Secondary publications.]

0021   Jahoda, G. "Information Needs of Science and Technology—Background View," In: Proceedings of the 1965 Congress of the International Federation for Documentation. Washington, Spartan, 1966, pp. 137-142.

*0022   Ladendorf, J. M. "Information Flow in Science, Technology, and Commerce; A Review of the Concepts of the Sixties," In: Special Libraries, 61(5): 215-222, May-June, 1970.

*0023   Lin, N., and W. D. Garvey. "Information Needs and Uses," In: Annual Review of Information Science and Technology. Edited by C. A. Cuadra. Washington, American Society for Information Science, 1972, Vol. 7, pp. 5-38. [Phases in communication process; Factors influencing information needs; Patterns of information exchange; Use of primary publications; Innovations.]

*0024   Lipetz, B. "Information Needs and Uses," In: Annual Review of Information Science and Technology. Edited by C. A. Cuadra. Chicago, Encyclopaedia Britannica, 1970, Vol. 5, pp. 1-32. [Scientists and engineers as information processors; The research environment; Professional societies; Invisible colleges; Formal information system.]

*0025   Lorenz, J. G. "International Transfer of Information," In: Annual Review of Information Science and Technology. Edited by C. A. Cuadra. Chicago, Encyclopaedia Britannica, 1969, Vol. 4, pp. 379-402. [Historical review; International governmental organizations; International non-governmental organizations; U.S. government agencies; U.S. professional associations.]

0026   Massey, R. J. Information Requirements for Contract, Defense, Mission-Oriented Basic Research Investment Decisions. Ph.D. Dissertation,

Washington, The American University, 1967, 228p. (University Microfilms, Inc., Order No. 68-5519)

0027   Menzel, H. "Informal Communication in Science: Its Advantages and Its Formal Analogues," In: The Foundations of Access to Knowledge. Edited by E. B. Montgomery. Syracuse, N.Y., Syracuse University, 1968, pp. 153-163.

*0028   Menzel, H. "Information Needs and Uses in Science and Technology," In: Annual Review of Information Science and Technology. Edited by C. A. Cuadra. New York, Interscience, 1966, Vol. 1, 1966, pp. 41-69. [Methods of study; Preference, demand, and experimental studies; Use studies; Dissemination studies.]

*0029   Paisley, W. J. "Information Needs and Uses," In: Annual Review of Information Science and Technology. Edited by C. A. Cuadra. Chicago, Encyclopaedia Britannica, 1968, Vol. 3, pp. 1-30. [The scientist within his work team, a formal organization, an invisible college, his reference group, a membership group, a formal information system, a political system, his culture, and his own head.]

0030   Parker, E. B. Oral and Informal Scientific Communication. Washington, Committee on Scientific and Technical Information, Seminar on Oral and Informal Communication, 1966.

0031   Porter, L. W., and K. H. Roberts. Communication in Organizations, Irvine, Calif., University of California at Irvine, Graduate School of Administration, July, 1972, 99p. AD 747 305. [A critical review of communication literature published from 1962-1972.]

*0032   Rogers, E. M., and F. Shoemaker. Communication of Innovations: A Cross-Cultural Approach. New York, The Free Press, 2d ed., 1971. [Communication channels in the diffusion of innovations.]

0033   Rutgers—The State University, Bureau of Information Science Research, Graduate School of Library Science. Bibliography of Research Relating to the Communication of Scientific and Technical Information. New Brunswick, N. J., Rutgers University Press, 1967, 732p. [Information systems; Information exchange groups; Economics; Invisible college; Preprints; Serials; Use of information; Editing; Microforms.]

0034   Schlessinger, B. S., ed. Proceedings of the Scientific and Technical Information Seminar (5th), April 9, 1970. New Haven, Conn., Southern Connecticut State College, March 8, 1971, 102p. AD 722 463. [Technological gatekeepers; Information needs of science and technology; Activities of government agencies.]

0035   Short, E. C. A Review of Studies on the General Problem of Knowledge
       Production and Utilization. 1970, 70p. ED 055 022. [Relation of
       research to practice; Nature of knowledge production; Nature of
       knowledge utilization.]

*0036 Vavrek, B. F. Communication and the Reference Interface. Ph.D. Disser-
       tation, Pittsburgh, University of Pittsburgh, 1971, 136p. (University
       Microfilms, Inc., Order No. 72-4247) [Question negotiation; Reference
       interface; Information seeking in libraries.]

0037   Westley, B. H. "Communication and Social Change," In: American
       Behavioral Scientist, 14(5): 719-743, May-June, 1971. [Review of liter-
       ature on relationship between communication and social change.]

*0038 Wood, D. N. "User Studies: A Review of the Literature from 1966-1970,"
       In: Aslib Proceedings, 23(1): 11-23, January, 1971.

0039   Ziman, J. M. "Information, Communication and Knowledge," In:
       Nature, 224(5217): 318-324, October 25, 1969.

*0040 Ziman, J. M. Public Knowledge; An Essay Concerning the Social Dimen-
       sion of Science. Cambridge, England, Cambridge University Press, 1968,
       154p. [Study of the process by which scientific information becomes
       public knowledge.]

METHODS OF STUDY

0041   Barber, A. S. "A Critical Review of the Surveys of Scientists' Use of
       Libraries," In: The Provision and Use of Library and Documentation
       Services. Edited by W. L. Saunders. London, Pergamon, 1966, pp. 145-
       179. [Evaluating use surveys.]

0042   Bernier, C. L. "Measurement of How Well Professional People Keep Up
       with Their Technical Literature," American Society for Information
       Science Journal, 22(4): 292-293, July, 1971.

0043   Berul, L., and A. Karson, "An Evaluation of the Methodology of the
       DoD User Needs Study," In: Proceedings of the 1965 Congress of the
       International Federation for Documentation. Washington, Spartan,
       1966, pp. 151-157.

0044   Borenius, G., and S. Schwarz. "Remarks on the Use of Citation Data in
       Predictive Models of Scientific Activity," In: Information Storage and
       Retrieval, 8(4): 171-175, August, 1972.

0045   Brittain, J. M., and M. B. Line. "Sources of Citations and References for Analysis Purposes: A Comparative Assessment," In: Journal of Documentation, 29(1): 72-86, March, 1973. [Abstracting and indexing journals; Bibliographies; Primary publications.]

*0046   Chernyi, A. I., ed. Problems of Information Science: Collection of Papers. Hague, Netherlands, International Federation for Documentation, Report FID-478, 1972, 241p. [Studies of information needs; Informal communication; Social aspects of formal communication; Literature obsolescence; Secondary services.]

0047   Cole, J. R., and S. Cole. "Measuring the Quality of Sociological Research: Problems in the Use of the Science Citation Index," In: American Sociologist, 6(1): 23-29, February, 1971.

0048   Coover, R. W. "User Needs and Their Effect on Information Center Administration," In: Special Libraries, 60(7): 446-456, September, 1969. [Evaluating use surveys.]

0049   Garfield, E. "Citation Analysis as a Tool in Journal Evaluation," In: Science, 178(4060): 471-478, November 3, 1972.

0050   Garfield, E. "Citation Indexing for Studying Science," In: Nature, 227(5259): 669-671, August 15, 1970. [Sociology of science.]

0051   Garfield, E. "Citation Indexing, Historio-Bibliography, and the Sociology of Science," In: Proceedings of the 3rd International Congress of Medical Librarianship, Amsterdam, May 5-9, 1969. Amsterdam, Excerpta Medica, 1970, pp. 187-204.

*0052   Hall, A. M. The Use and Value of Citations: A State of the Art Report. London, England, INSPEC, November, 1970, 32p. (Report No. R70/4)

0053   Landau, H. B. "Methodology of a Technical Information Use Study," In: Special Libraries, 60(6): 340-346, July-August, 1969. [Questionnaire; Informal interviews.]

0054   Lehigh University, Center for the Information Sciences. Methods of Studying Use by Scientists and Engineers: Questionnaire Model, Appendix. Bethlehem, Pa., Lehigh University, March, 1965, 105p. PB 167 972.

0055   Leyman, E., S. Thomas, and G. Huden. A Study of Library Users' Needs in the Savannah District, Corps of Engineers, Final Report. Washington, Herner and Co., July, 1969, 162p. AD 728 700. [Questionnaire.]

0056   Margolis, J. "Citation Indexing and Evaluation of Scientific Papers," In: Science, 155(3767): 1213-1219, March 10, 1967.

0057   May, K. O. "Abuses of Citation Indexing," In: Science, (Letter),
        156(3777): 890, 892, May 19, 1967.

*0058   Menzel, H. "Can Science Information Needs be Ascertained Empiri-
        cally?" In: Communication: Concepts and Perspectives. Edited by L.
        Thayer. Washington, Spartan Books, 1967, pp. 279-295.

0059   North American Aviation, Inc., Space and Information Systems Division.
        Scientific and Technical Information in the Defense Industry: Interview
        Guide Handbook, DoD User-Needs Study, Phase II. Downey, Calif.,
        North American Aviation, Inc., Space and Information Systems Division,
        August 1, 1965, 121p. AD 655 297.

*0060   Parker, E. B., W. J. Paisley, and R. Garrett. Bibliographic Citations as
        Unobtrusive Measures of Scientific Communication. Palo Alto, Calif.,
        Stanford University, Institute for Communication Research, October,
        1967, 126p. PB 177 073. [Bibliometric analysis.]

0061   Pritchard, A. Statistical Bibliography, Interim Bibliography. London,
        England, North-Western Polytechnic School of Librarianship, May,
        1969, 70p. PB 184 244. [Bibliometric analysis.]

0062   Rosenberg, V. The Application of Psychometric Techniques to Deter-
        mine the Attitudes of Individuals Toward Information Seeking. Bethle-
        hem, Pa., Lehigh University, Center for the Information Sciences, July,
        1966, 46p. AD 637 713.

0063   Rothman, H., and M. Woodhead. "The Use of Citation Counting to
        Identify Research Trends," In: Journal of Documentation, 27(4):
        287-294, December, 1971. [Economic entomology; Pest control; Man-
        power trends.]

0064   Shirey, D. "Critical Incident Technique," In: Encyclopedia of Library
        and Information Science. New York, Dekker, 1971, Vol. 6, pp. 286-291.

0065   Sieber, H. F., Jr. "The Methodology of the DoD Scientific and Techni-
        cal Information Use Study," In: Proceedings of the American Documen-
        tation Institute. Washington, American Documentation Institute, 1964,
        Vol. 1, pp. 235-242.

0066   Slater, M., and S. Keenan. "Methods of Conducting a Study of Physicist's
        Requirements in Current Awareness in the U.S. and the U.K.," In:
        Proceedings of the American Documentation Institute. Washington,
        Thompson, 1967, Vol. 4, pp. 63-69. [American Institute of Physics;
        Current Papers in Physics; Physics Abstracts.]

0067   Van Valen, L. "Citation and Distinction," In: Nature, (Letter),
        243(5405): 250, May 25, 1973. [*Science Citation Index.*]

0068 Velke, L. "The Use of Citation Patterns in the Identification of 'Research Front' Authors and 'Classic' Papers," In: Proceedings of the American Society for Information Science. Washington, American Society for Information Science, 1970, Vol. 7, pp. 49-52.

0069 Vickery, B. C. "Indicators of the Use of Periodicals," In: Journal of Librarianship, 1(3): 170-182, July, 1969. [Advantages and disadvantages of citation analysis.]

*0070 Wood, D. N. "Discovering the User and His Information Needs," In: Aslib Proceedings, 21(7): 262-270, July, 1969.

0071 Wuest, F. J. Studies in the Methodology of Measuring Information Requirements and Use Patterns: Questionnaire. Bethlehem, Pa., Lehigh University, Center for the Information Sciences, May, 1965, 41p. PB 167 971.

*0072 Wysocki, A. "Study of Users' Information Needs: Subject and Methods," In: International Federation for Documentation, On Theoretical Problems of Informatics. Moscow, All-Union Institute for Scientific and Technical Information, 1969, pp. 80-92.

SOCIAL ORGANIZATION

0073 Barnes, S. B., and R. G. A. Dolby. "The Scientific Ethos: A Deviant Viewpoint," In: European Journal of Sociology, 11(1): 3-25, 1970. [Scientific values; Scientific norms; Effects on communication patterns and innovation in science.]

*0074 Blau, J. R. The Structure of Science, Final Report. Ph.D. Dissertation, Evanston, Ill., Northwestern University, June, 1972, 253p. (Also as PB 208 970) [Reward system; Social stratification; Communication networks; Subdivision of disciplines.]

0075 Blume, S. S., and R. Sinclair. "Chemists in British Universities: A Study of the Reward System in Science," In: American Sociological Review, 38(1): 126-137, February, 1973.

0076 Boalt, G. The Sociology of Research. Carbondale, Ill., Southern Illinois University Press, 1969, 161p. [Scientific values; Social interaction; Research role.]

0077   Cole, J. R. "Patterns of Intellectual Influence in Scientific Research,"
In: Sociology of Education, 43(4): 377-403, Fall, 1970. [Physics;
Social stratification.]

*0078   Cole, J. R., and S. Cole. Social Stratification in Science. Chicago, Uni-
versity of Chicago Press, 1973, 283p. [Patterns of stratification; Stratification and the communication process.]

0079   Cole, S. "Professional Standing and the Reception of Scientific Dis-
coveries," In: American Journal of Sociology, 76(2): 286-306, September, 1970. [Matthew effect; Social stratification; Physics.]

0080   Cole, S., and J. R. Cole. "Scientific Output and Recognition: A Study
in the Operation of the Reward System in Science," In: American
Sociological Review, 32(3): 377-390, June, 1967. [Physics; Scientific
role performance.]

0081   Cole, S., and J. R. Cole. "Visibility and the Structural Basis of Awareness of Scientific Research," In: American Sociological Review, 33(3):
397-412, June, 1968. [Social stratification.]

0082   Corwin, R. G., and M. Seider. "Patterns of Educational Research:
Reflections on Some General Issues," In: The Educational Research
Community: Its Communication and Social Structure. Edited by R. A.
Dershimer. Washington, Office of Education, April, 1970, pp. 17-68.
ED 057 275.

*0083   Crane, D. Invisible Colleges: Diffusion of Knowledge in Scientific
Communities. Chicago, University of Chicago Press, 1972, 213p.
[Social organization of the research area; Scientific growth.]

0084   Crane, D. "Scientists at Major and Minor Universities: A Study of Productivity and Recognition," In: American Sociological Review, 30(5):
699-714, October, 1965. [Role of publication in social system; Reward
system.]

0085   Crane, D. "Social Structure in a Group of Scientists: A Test of the
'Invisible College' Hypothesis," In: American Sociological Review,
34(3): 335-353, June, 1969. [Social organization of the research area;
Measurement of social ties.]

0086   Crawford, E. T., ed. "The Sociology of the Social Sciences: An International Bibliography," In: Social Sciences Information, 9(1): 79-93,
February, 1970; 9(4): 137-149, August, 1970; 10(2): 121-134, April,
1971; 10(5): 73-84, October, 1971; 11(1): 99-112, February, 1972;
11(6):99-107, December, 1972; 12(2): 113-121, April, 1973. [Commu-
nication patterns.]

0087 Echols, H. "Scientific Community," In: Nature, (Letter), 239(5373): 476-477, October 20, 1972.

0088 Eyring, H. B. Continuity and Openness in High Energy Physics Groups. Cambridge, Mass., Massachusetts Institute of Technology, Sloan School of Management, Working Paper No. 142-1965, 1965.

0089 Farris, G. F. Colleague Roles and Innovation in Scientific Teams. Cambridge, Mass., Massachusetts Institute of Technology, Sloan School of Management, July, 1971. 25p. N71-36373.

*0090 Friedrichs, R. W. A Sociology of Sociology. New York, Free Press, 1970, 429p.

0091 Gaston, J. C. Big Science in Britain: A Sociological Study of the High Energy Physics Community. Ph.D. Dissertation, New Haven, Conn., Yale University, 1969, 397p.

*0092 Gaston, J. C. Originality and Competition in Science; A Study of the British High Energy Physics Community. Chicago, University of Chicago Press, 1973, 234p. [Organization of basic research; Reward system; Competition in science; Communication patterns.]

0093 Gaston, J. C. "The Reward System in British Science," In: American Sociological Review, 35(4): 718-732, August, 1970.

*0094 Griffith, B. C., and N. C. Mullins. "Coherent Social Groups in Scientific Change," In: Science, 177(4053): 959-964, September 15, 1972. [Invisible college; Leadership roles.]

0095 Hagstrom, W. O. "Anomy in Scientific Communities," In: Social Problems, 12(2): 186-195, Fall, 1964. [Social stratification; Consequences of stratification; Development of stratification.]

0096 Hagstrom, W. O. Competition and Teamwork in Science, Final Report to the National Science Foundation. Madison, Wisc., University of Wisconsin, Department of Sociology, 1967.

0097 Hagstrom, W. O. "Educational Researchers, Social Scientists, and School Professionals," In: The Educational Research Community: Its Communication and Social Structure. Edited by R. A. Dershimer. Washington, Office of Education, April, 1970, pp. 143-158. ED 057 275. [Review of roles and relationship between educational researchers, social scientists and school professionals.]

*0098 Hagstrom, W. O. The Scientific Community. New York, Basic Books, 1965, 304p. [Social control; Competition in science; Teamwork; Priority of discovery.]

*0099   Hagstrom, W. O. "Traditional and Modern Forms of Scientific Team-
         work," In: Administrative Science Quarterly, 9(3): 241-263, December,
         1964. [Collaboration; Professional peers; Teachers and students.]

0100   Hargens, L. L. The Social Contexts of Scientific Research. Ph.D. Disser-
         tation, Madison, Wisc., University of Wisconsin, 1971, 357p. (University
         Microfilms, Inc., Order No. 71-16,080) [Process of research; Mathe-
         matics; Chemistry; Political science.]

0101   Hirsch, W. Scientists in American Society. New York, Random House,
         1968, 194p. [Sociology of science; Institutional environment; Opera-
         tional problems; Scientists and social action.]

0102   Kadushin, C. "Power, Influence and Social Circles: A New Methodology
         for Studying Opinion Leaders," In: American Sociological Review,
         33(5): 685-699, October, 1968.

*0103   Kuhn, T. S. The Structure of Scientific Revolutions. 2nd. ed. Chicago,
         University of Chicago Press, 1970, 210p. [Process of science; Growth of
         science; Changes in the structure of science.]

0104   Merton, R. K. "Behavior Patterns of Scientists," In: American Scientist,
         57(1): 1-23, Spring, 1969.

0105   Merton, R. K., and R. Lewis. "The Competitive Pressures (I): The Race
         for Priority," In: Impact of Science on Society, 21(2): 151-162, April-
         June, 1971. [Competition in science; Changes in the structure of
         science.]

0106   Merton, R. K. "The Matthew Effect in Science; The Reward and Com-
         munication Systems of Science Are Considered," In: Science, 159(3810):
         56-63, January 5, 1968. [Reward system; Publication patterns.]

*0107   Merton, R. K. The Sociology of Science; Theoretical and Empirical
         Investigations. Chicago, University of Chicago Press, 1973. 616p.
         [Reward system; Sociology of knowledge.]

0108   Oromaner, M. J. "Comparison of Influentials in Contemporary and
         British Sociology: A Study of the Internationalization of Sociology,"
         In: British Journal of Sociology, 21(3): 324-331, September, 1970.

0109   Paisley, W. "The Role of Invisible Colleges," In: The Educational
         Research Community: Its Communication and Social Structure. Edited
         by R. A. Dershimer. Washington, Office of Education, April, 1970,
         pp. 105-122. ED 057 275. [Information flow models.]

*0110   Pelz, D. C., and F. M. Andrews. Scientists in Organizations: Productive
         Climates for Research and Development. New York, Wiley, 1966. 318p.

0111   Price, D. J. S. "Research on Research," In: Journeys in Science (Small Steps—Great Strides). Edited by D. L. Arm. Albuquerque, N. M., University of New Mexico Press, 1967, pp. 1-21. [Interaction of science and technology.]

0112   Price, D. J. S. "Some Remarks on Elitism in Information and the Invisible College Phenomena in Science," In: American Society for Information Science Journal, 22(2): 74-75, March-April, 1971.

0113   Smith, C. G. "Scientific Performance and the Composition of Research Teams," In: Administrative Science Quarterly, 16(4): 486-495, December, 1971.

0114   Storer, N. W. "The Hard Sciences and the Soft: Some Sociological Observations," In: Bulletin of the Medical Library Association, 55(11): 75-84, January, 1967.

0115   Storer, N. W. "The Internationality of Science and the Nationality of Scientists," In: International Social Science Journal, 22(1): 80-93, 1970.

0116   Storer, N. W. "The Organization and Differentiation of the Scientific Community: Basic Disciplines, Applied Research, and Conjunctive Domains," In: The Educational Research Community: Its Communication and Social Structure. Edited by R. A. Dershimer. Washington, Office of Education, April, 1970, pp. 123-142. ED 057 275.

*0117   Storer, N. W. The Social System of Science. New York, Holt, 1966, 180p. [Scientific norms; Scientific values; Consequences of publication explosion.]

0118   Swatez, G. M. "The Social Organization of a University Laboratory," In: Minerva, 8(1): 36-58, January, 1970.

*0119   Zuckerman, H. "Stratification in American Science," In: Sociological Inquiry, 40(2): 235-257, Spring, 1970. [Reward system.]

MISCELLANEOUS

0120   Chapanis, A. "The Communication of Factual Information Through Various Channels," In: Information Storage and Retrieval, 9: 215-231, April, 1973. [Problem solving; Oral channels *vs.* hardcopy channels of communication.]

*0121   Crane, D. "The Nature of Scientific Communication and Influence," In: International Social Science Journal, 22(1): 28-41, 1970. [Social organization of the research area; Invisible college; Structure of formal and informal communication.]

0122   Cravens, D. W. An Exploratory Study of Individual Information-Processing and Decision-Making, Final Report. Bloomington, Ind., Indiana University, Aerospace Research Applications Center, August 15, 1967, 213p. N68-15996. [Decision-making process; Individual thinking process; Information processing behavior.]

0123   Fairthorne, R. A. "Morphology of 'Information Flow'," In: Association for Computing Machinery Journal, 14(4): 710-719, October, 1967. [Communication model.]

0124   Griffith, B. C., M. J. Jahn, and A. J. Miller. "Informal Contacts in Science: Probabilistic Model for Communication Processes," In: Science, 173(3992): 164-166, July 9, 1971. [Distribution of social contacts; Poisson distribution; Invisible college.]

0125   Guerrero, J. L. The Influence of Pre-Decisional and Interpersonal Communication Variables on Information Exchange Behavior. Ph.D. Dissertation, Madison, Wisc., University of Wisconsin, 1970, 105p. (University Microfilms, Inc., Order No. 70-15,893)

0126   Hagstrom, W. O. "Inputs, Outputs, and Prestige of University Science Departments," In: Sociology of Education, 44: 375-397, Fall, 1971. [Informal communication; Departmental morale.]

0127   Harmon, G. "Information Need Transformation during Inquiry: A Reinterpretation of User Relevance," In: Proceedings of the American Society for Information Science. Washington, American Society for Information Science, 1970, Vol. 7, pp. 41-43. [Information need model; Information-seeking.]

0128   Hillis, R. E. Some Effects of Socio-Economic-Educational Similarity on the Interpersonal Communication Process. Ph.D. Dissertation, Los Angeles, Calif., University of California, 1968, 222p. (University Microfilms, Inc., Order No. 69-1109)

0129   Holland, W. E. "Characteristics of Individuals with High Information Potential in Government Research and Development Organizations," In: IEEE Transactions on Engineering Management, 19(2): 38-44, May, 1972.

0130   Jordan, M. P. "Expanding the Invisible College," In: Proceedings of the American Society for Information Science. Westport, Conn., Greenwood, 1973, Vol. 10, pp. 103-104. [Relation of libraries to invisible college.]

*0131   Katz, E. "The Two-Step Flow of Communication: An Up-to-Date Report of an Hypothesis," In: Dimensions of Communication. Edited by L. Richardson. New York, Appleton-Century-Crofts, 1969, pp. 246-262.

0132   Lanzetta, J. T., and J. M. Driscoll. "Effects of Uncertainty and Importance of Information Search in Decision Making," In: Journal of Personality and Social Psychology, 10(4): 479-486, December, 1968.

0133   Levine, J. M., and R. E. Brahlek. Parameters of Information-Seeking Behavior, Interim Report, January 1–December 31, 1972. Silver Springs, Md., American Institutes for Research, December, 1972, 10p. AD 754 226. [Decision-making.]

*0134   Lin, N. "A Comparison Between the Scientific Communication Model and the Mass Communication Model: Implications for the Transfer and Utilization of Scientific Knowledge," In: IEEE Transactions on Professional Communication, PC 15(2): 34-39, June, 1972. [Characteristics; Participants; Content; Channels; Reward system.]

0135   Lin, N. "Information Flow, Influence Flow, and the Decision Making Process," In: Journalism Quarterly, 48: 33-40, Spring, 1971. [Two-step flow hypothesis.]

0136   Martyn, J., and M. Slater. "Characteristics of Users and Non-Users of Scientific Information," In: Looking Forward in Documentation: Papers and Discussion of the Aslib 38th Conference. London, Aslib, 1964, pp. 4-6–4-11.

0137   Menzel, H. "Planning the Consequences of Unplanned Action in Scientific Communication," In: Communication in Science: Documentation and Automation. Edited by A. DeReuck and J. Knight. Boston, Little, Brown & Co., 1967, pp. 57-71. [Function of informal communication; Relative performance of formal and informal communication.]

0138   Murdock, J. W., and D. M. Liston, Jr. "A General Model of Information Transfer: Theme Paper 1968 Annual Convention," In: American Documentation, 18(4): 197-208, October, 1967.

0139   Paisley, W. J. Extent of Information-Seeking as a Function of Subjective Certainty and the Utility of the Information. Ph.D. Dissertation, Palo Alto, Calif., Stanford University, 1965, 95p. (University Microfilms, Inc., Order No. 65-12,831)

0140   Robbins, J. C. "Communication Among Scientists and Engineers: A Commentary," IEEE Transactions on Professional Communication, PC 15(2): 65-67, June, 1972. [Communication models; Information theory; Research needs.]

0141   Streufert, S., and C. H. Castore. "Effects of Increasing Success and
        Failure on Perceived Information Quality," In: Psychonomic Science,
        11(2): 63-64, 1968. (Also as AD 668 529)

0142   Sutton, H. The Grapevine: A Study of Role Behavior within an Informal
        Communication System. Ph.D. Dissertation, Berkeley, Calif., University
        of California, 1969, 89p. (University Microfilms, Inc., Order No.
        70-6235) [Communication in organizations; Informal communication;
        Management personnel.]

0143   Tagliacozzo, R., M. Kochen, and W. Everett. "The Use of Information
        by Decision-Makers in Public Service Organizations," In: Proceedings
        of the American Society for Information Science. Westport, Conn.,
        Greenwood, 1971, Vol. 8, pp. 53-57.

*0144   Taylor, R. S. "Question-Negotiation and Information Seeking in
        Libraries," In: College and Research Libraries, 29(3): 178-194, May,
        1968. (Also as AD 659 468) [Information needs.]

0145   Upton, A. "Communication and the Problem Solving Process," In:
        Communication: Concepts and Perspectives. Edited by L. Thayer.
        Washington, Spartan, 1967, pp. 373-396.

*0146   Van Den Ban, A. W. "A Revision of the Two-Step Flow of Communica-
        tions Hypothesis," In: Dimensions of Communication. Edited by L.
        Richardson. New York, Appleton-Century-Crofts, 1969, pp. 263-274.

0147   Wallace, J. F. "Can Information Be Available Too Early in a Project?"
        In: Institute of Information Scientists, Proceedings of the 1st Conference,
        Oxford, July, 1964. Orpington, Kent, The Institute of Information
        Scientists, 1966, pp. 11-14.

0148   Wittmore, B. J., and M. C. Yovits. "A General Conceptual Development
        for the Analysis and Flow of Information," In: American Society for
        Information Science Journal, 24(3): 221-231, 1973. (Also as
        PB 215 530/7 or ED 071 684) [Information defined; Communication
        models; Decision-making.]

*0149   Wolek, F. W. "Preparation for Interpersonal Communication," In:
        American Society for Information Science Journal, 23(1): 3-10,
        January-February, 1972. (Also as PB 190 828)

STRUCTURES OF COMMUNICATION

DATA ACTIVITIES

0150   Adams, M. O., and J. Dennis. "Creating Local Social Science Data Archives," In: Social Science Information, 9(2): 51-60, April, 1970.

0151   Aines, A. A. "Data Banking—Rx. for Future Science and Technology," In: Innovations in Communications Conference. Washington, Office of Science and Technology, April, 1970, pp. 5-13. PB 192 294.

*0152   Alt, F. L. Information Handling in the National Standard Reference Data System, Technical Note. Washington, National Bureau of Standards, Office of Standard Reference Data, July 1, 1966, 30p. NBS-TN-290.

0153   Bell, C. G. "The Joys and Sorrows of Secondary Data Use," In: Data Bases, Computers, and the Social Sciences. Edited by R. L. Bisco. New York, Wiley, 1970, pp. 52-60.

0154   Bisco, R. L. "Information Retrieval from Data Archives: The ICPR System," In: American Behavioral Scientist, 7(10): 45-48, June, 1964. [Interuniversity Consortium for Political Research.]

*0155   Bisco, R. L. "Social Science Data Archives: Progress and Prospects," In: Social Science Information, 6(1): 39-74, February, 1967.

0156   Bisco, R. L. "Social Science Data Archives: A Review of Developments," In: American Political Science Review, 60(1): 93-109, March, 1966.

0157   Blackman, S., and K. M. Goldstein. An Introduction to Data Management in the Behavioral and Social Sciences. New York, Wiley, 1971, 104p.

0158   Brady, E. L., and M. B. Wallenstein. National Standard Reference Data System: Plan of Operation. Washington, National Bureau of Standards, 1964. NSRDS-NBS-1.

0159   Brady, E. L. "The National Standard Reference Data System," In: Journal of Chemical Documentation, 7(1): 6-9, February, 1967.

0160   Brady, E. L., and M. B. Wallenstein. "The National Standard Reference
        Data System," In: Science, 156(3776): 754-762, May 12, 1967.

0161   Brady, E. L., ed. National Standard Reference Data System, Status
        Report. Washington, National Bureau of Standards, 1968. NBS-TN-448.

*0162   Brown, H. "International Cooperation: The New ICUS Program on
        Critical Data," In: Science, 156(3776): 751-754, May 12, 1967. [Inter-
        national Council of Scientific Unions, Committee on Data for Science
        and Technology.]

0163   Bryum, J. D., and J. S. Rowe. "An Integrated User-Oriented System for
        the Documentation and Control of Machine-Readable Data Files." In:
        Library Resources and Technical Services, 16(3): 338-346, 1972.

0164   Campbell, A. "Some Questions about the New Jerusalem," In: Data
        Bases, Computers, and the Social Sciences. Edited by R. L. Bisco. New
        York, Wiley, 1970, pp. 42-51.

0165   Campbell, H. C. "A Canadian Social Science Data Clearinghouse," In:
        UNESCO Bulletin for Libraries, 26(4): 188-192, July-August, 1972.

0166   Converse, P. E. "The Availability and Quality of Sample Survey Data
        Archives within the United States," In: Comparing Nations: The Use of
        Quantitative Data in Cross-National Research. Edited by R. L. Merritt
        and S. Rokkan. New Haven, Conn., Yale University Press, 1966, pp.
        419-440.

0167   Converse, P. E. "A Network of Data Archives for the Behavioral
        Sciences," In: Public Opinion Quarterly, 28: 273-286, 1964.

0168   Dennis, J. "The Relation of Social Science Data Archives to Libraries
        and Wider Information Networks," In: Conference on Inter-Library
        Communications and Information Networks. Edited by J. Becker.
        Chicago, American Library Association, 1971, pp. 117-120.

*0169   Deutsch, K. W. "The Impact of Complex Data Bases on the Social
        Sciences," In: Data Bases, Computers, and the Social Sciences. Edited
        by R. L. Bisco. New York, Wiley, 1970, pp. 19-41.

0170   Fairbairn, R. E. "Progress with Data Centers," In: Aslib Proceedings,
        20(11): 496-501, November, 1968. [Office of Scientific and Technical
        Information; International Council of Scientific Unions, Committee on
        Data for Science and Technology.]

0171   Funkhouser, G. R. "Data Management in the Social Sciences," In: The
        Proceedings of the 15th International Technical Communications Con-
        ference. Los Angeles, Society of Technical Writers and Publishers, 1968.

*0172   Garrison, W. A., and C. V. Ramamrorthy. Privacy and Security in Data Banks. Austin, University of Texas, November, 1970, 120p. AD 718 406.

0173   Glaser, W., and R. L. Bisco. "Plans of the American Council of Social Science Data Archives," In: Social Sciences Information, 5(4): 71-96, December, 1966.

0174   Glenn, N. D. "The Social Scientific Data Archives: The Problem of Underutilization," In: American Sociologist, 8(1): 42-45, February, 1973.

0175   Gulick, M. C. "Nonconventional Data Sources and Reference Tools for Social Science and Humanities," In: College and Research Libraries. 29(3): 224-234, May, 1968.

0176   Hastings, P. K. "The Roper Public Opinion Research Center: International Archive of Sample Survey Data," In: International Social Science Journal, 16(1): 90-97, 1964.

0177   Ivanov, K. Quality-Control of Information: On the Concept of Accuracy of Information in Data-Banks and in Management Information Systems. Stockholm, Sweden, Royal Institute of Technology, Department of Information Processing Computer Science, March, 1972, 264p. PB 219 297/9.

0178   Jones, S. D., and J. D. Singer. Beyond Conjecture in International Politics; Abstracts of Data-Based Research. Itasca, Ill., Peacock, 1972, 432p.

0179   Karlow, N., and J. I. Vette. Flow and Use of Information at the National Space Science Data Center. Greenbelt, Md., National Aeronautics and Space Administration, January, 1969, 45p. N69-17410.

0180   Kramer, D. A. Lange's Handbook of Chemistry: A Study of the Cultural Influence on the Design of a Data Compilation. Ph.D. Dissertation, Cleveland, Ohio, Case Western Reserve University, 1972. (University Microfilms, Inc., Order No. 72-26,174)

0181   Maron, M. E. "Large Scale Data Banks," In: Special Libraries, 60(1): 3-9, January, 1969.

0182   Miller, W. E. "The Development of Archives for Social Science Data," In: Quantitative Ecological Analysis in the Social Sciences. Edited by M. Dogan and S. Rokkan. Cambridge, Mass., Massachusetts Institute of Technology Press, 1969, pp. 521-531.

0183   Miller, W. E., and P. E. Converse. "The Inter-University Consortium for Political Research," In: International Social Science Journal, 16(1): 70-76, 1964.

*0184   Mountstephen, B., A. Osborn, and M. Slater. Quantitative Data in Science and Technology. London, Aslib, Aslib Occasional Publication No. 7, 1971, 24p.

0185   Nasatir, D. "The International Data Library and Reference Service," In: Public Opinion Quarterly, 32: 688-690, 1968/1969.

*0186   Rokkan, S. C. Conference on Data Archives in the Social Sciences. Paris, Mouton, 1966, 213p.

0187   Rokkan, S. C. "International Efforts to Develop Networks of Data Archives," In: Social Sciences Information, 4(3): 9-13, September, 1965.

*0188   Rossini, F. D. "Historical Background of Data Compiling Activities," In: Journal of Chemical Documentation, 7(1): 2-6, February, 1967. [Chemistry; National Standard Reference Data Program; International Council of Scientific Unions, Committee on Data for Science and Technology.]

0189   Rossini, F. D. "The ICSU Committee on Data for Science and Technology (CODATA)," In: Journal of Chemical Documentation, 10(4): 261-264, November, 1970.

*0190   Rossmassler, S. A. Critical Evaluation of Data in the Physical Sciences— A Status Report of the National Standard Reference Data System— June 1972. Washington, National Bureau of Standards, November, 1972, 80p. NBS-TN-747. [History; Data evaluation program; Information services.]

0191   Ruggles, R., and N. Ruggles. "Data Files for a Generalized Economic Information System," In: Social Sciences Information, 6(4): 187-196, August, 1967.

0192   Salomonsson, O. "Data Banking Systems for Urban Planning," In: Proceedings of the Conference on Information and Urban Planning, London, 1969. London, Centre for Environmental Studies, 1969, Vol. 2, pp. 7-48.

0193   Sarett, L. H. "The Scientist and Scientific Data," In: American Documentation, 19(3): 299-304, July, 1968.

0194   Sawyer, J., and H. Schechter. "Computers, Privacy, and the National Data Center: The Responsibility of Social Scientists," In: American Psychologist, 23(11): 810-818, November, 1968.

0195   Schoenfeldt, L. F. "Data Archives as Resources for Research, Instruction, and Policy Planning," In: American Psychologist, 25(7): 609-616, July, 1970.

*0196   Science Communication, Inc. Study of Scientific and Technical Data Activities in the United States. 3 Vols. Washington, National Technical Information Service, April, 1968. AD 670 606—AD 670 608. [National data systems; Aerospace sciences; Engineering; Agriculture; Biomedical sciences; Pharmacology; Social sciences; Environmental sciences; Geosciences; Oceanography.]

*0197   Slater, M., A. Osborn, and A. Presanis. Data and the Chemist. Aslib, Aslib Occasional Publication No. 10, 1972, 82p.

0198   Speight, F. Y. "Numerical Data Activities of Engineering Societies," In: Journal of Chemical Documentation, 7(1): 26-30, February, 1967.

0199   Squires, D. F. An Information Storage and Retrieval System for Biological and Geological Data, Interim Report. Washington, Smithsonian Institution, January, 1969, 37p. ED 029 672. [Museum specimen data.]

0200   Thompson, J. E. Data Editing. Cleveland, Ohio, NASA, Lewis Research Center, April, 1971. 13p. N71-22575.

0201   Vette, J. I., et. al. Report of the Ad Hoc Group on Data Centers. Greenbelt, Md., National Aeronautics and Space Administration, Goddard Space Flight Center, September, 1969, 20p. PB 195 523. [Information flow; Characteristics of data centers; Problems confronting data centers.]

0202   Waddington, G. "CODATA—Its Organization, Activities, and Goals," In: Journal of Chemical Documentation, 9(9): 174-177, August, 1969.

0203   Way, K. "Free Enterprise in Data Compilation," In: Science, 159(3812): 280-282, January 19, 1968.

*0204   Weisman, H. M. "A Survey of the Use of National Standard Reference Data System Publications," In: Journal of Chemical Documentation, 12(4): 211-216, November, 1972.

INFORMATION SYSTEMS

International

0205 Adams, S., et. al. "UNISIST: A Forum," In: Aslib Proceedings, 24(2): 111-122, February, 1972.

0206 Adams, S. "UNISIST: A Progress Report," In: Symposium on Handling of Nuclear Information. Vienna, International Atomic Energy Agency, 1970, pp. 599-606. [World Science Information System.]

0207 Bree, R. "World Cooperation in Nuclear Science Information," In: Special Libraries, 61(5): 229-232, May-June, 1970.

0208 Brown, H. "UNISIST: Growing Interest in a Worldwide Science Information System," In: American Society for Information Science Journal, 22(4): 288-289, July-August, 1971.

0209 Campbell, H. C. "Possibilities of International Diffusion and Documentation of Scientific Innovations by Communication Satellites," In: International Library Review, 1(1): 21-34, January, 1969.

0210 Chemical Abstracts Service. Preliminary Development of a Cooperative International Computer-Based Chemical Information Network, Annual Report No. 1. Columbus, Ohio, Chemical Abstracts Service, February, 1970, 44p. PB 195 259. [Cost estimates; American Chemical Society; Information centers.]

0211 Coblans, H. "Control and Use of Scientific Information," In: Nature, 226(5243): 319-321, April 25, 1970. [UNISIST; World Science Information System.]

0212 Crane, D. "Transnational Networks in Basic Science," In: International Organization, 25(3): 585-601, Summer, 1971. [Social organization; International scientific community.]

0213 El-Hadidy, A. R. "World-Wide Cooperation in Scientific Information— INIS," In: Symposium on the Handling of Nuclear Information. Vienna, International Atomic Energy Agency, 1970, pp. 623-630. [Nuclear science; International Nuclear Information System.]

0214 Glass, G. "Pugwash Interest in Communications!" In: Science, 159 (3821): 1328-1331, March 22, 1968. [UNISIST; World Science Information System.]

*0215   Information. "ICSU/UNESCO World Science Information System (UNISIST) Recommendations; Comments by U.S. Info. Leaders," In: Information, Pt. 1, 3(4): 113-133, May-June, 1971.

0216   Information. "UNISIST (World Science Information System) Concept Approved at Inter-Governmental Conference," In: Information, Pt. 1, 3(6): 279-285, November-December, 1971.

0217   Irick, P. "International Aspects of Transportation Research Information Services," In: Innovations in Communications Conference, April 9-10, 1970. Washington, Highway Research Board, April 1970, pp. 72-85. PB 192 294.

0218   Judge, A. J. N. The Improvement of Communication within the World-System. Brussels, Belgium, Union of International Associations. September, 1969, 64p. ED 056 719. [Data bases; Information centers; Information networks.]

0219   Kitagawa, T. Information Science Approaches to Scientific Information Systems and Their Implications to Scientific Researchers. Fukuoka, Japan, Kyushu University, March, 1969, 42p. ED 050 766. [World science information network system.]

0220   Komurka, M. "International Nuclear Information System," In: Proceedings of the American Society for Information Science. Westport, Conn., Greenwood, 1969, Vol. 6, pp. 441-446.

*0221   Pelzer, C. W. "The International Nuclear Information System," In: Aslib Proceedings, 24(1): 38-55, January, 1972. [Products; System cost; Operational policies.]

0222   Perez-Vitoria, A. "Towards a World Science Information System: An ICSU-UNESCO Joint Venture," In: UNESCO Bulletin for Libraries, 23(1): 1-7, January-February, 1969. [UNISIST.]

0223   Salton, G. "Thoughts on the UNISIST Feasibility Study," In: American Society for Information Science Journal, 23(1): 68-70, January-February, 1972. [Review of proposal; Impact on scientific community.]

*0224   Samuelson, K. "International Information Transfer and Network Communication," In: Annual Review of Information Science and Technology. Edited by C. A. Cuadra. Chicago, Encyclopaedia Britannica, 1971, Vol. 6, pp. 277-324. [Network structures; UNISIST.]

*0225   Samuelson, K. "World-Wide Information Networks," In: Conference on Interlibrary Communications and Information Networks (CICIN). Chicago, American Library Association, 1971, pp. 317-328. [Goal orientation; Current programs.]

0226 Smith, J. R. "The Feasibility of a World System: UNISIST by ISCU out of UNESCO," In: Aslib Proceedings, 22(8): 395-398, August, 1970.

0227 Tocatlian, J. T. "UNISIST Implementation Plans," In: Proceedings of the American Society for Information Science. Westport, Conn., Greenwood, 1972, Vol. 9, pp. 9-14. [Management; Financing; Implementation.]

0228 Turkov, Z. "The International Nuclear Information System (INIS)— Practical and Political Aspects of International Cooperation in Information Exchange," In: Proceedings of the American Society for Information Science. Westport, Conn., Greenwood, 1972, Vol. 9, pp. 15-22. [Structure of system; Operational goals; Operational policies.]

*0229 UNESCO. Primary Scientific Publication: A Report Prepared (with Special Reference to Physics) for the UNESCO Ad Hoc Sub-Committee on Methods of Primary Scientific Publication and the ICSU-UNESCO Joint Study on the Communication of Scientific Information and on the Feasibility of a Worldwide Science Information System. Paris, UNESCO, October, 1967, 105p. ED 061 953. [UNISIST; Manufacturing, distribution and processing of scientific information; Growth of primary journals; Evaluation of science information problems.]

0230 UNESCO. UNISIST: Study Report on the Feasibility of a World Scientific Information System. New York, UNIPUB, Inc., 1971, 171p. ED 054 808. [History; Recommendations; Implementation; Program priorities; Benefits and values of UNISIST.]

*0231 U.S. National Academy of Sciences. Proceedings of the Study of the Feasibility of a World Scientific Information System (UNISIST). Washington, National Academy of Sciences, 1971. 207p. PB 204 746.

0232 U.S. National Science Foundation. An Overview of Worldwide Chemical Information Facilities and Resources. Washington, National Science Foundation, September, 1967, 255p. PB 176 160. [Primary journals; Secondary information services; Libraries.]

0233 Woolston, J. E., et. al. "The Design and Implementation of an International Nuclear Information System (INIS)," In: Symposium on the Handling of Nuclear Information. Vienna, International Atomic Energy Agency, 1970, pp. 607-619.

0234 Woolston, J. E. "The Future of International Information Systems," In: Proceedings of the American Society for Information Science. Westport, Conn., Greenwood, 1972, Vol. 9, pp. 23-24. [International Nuclear Information System; Political structure; Agricultural Science and Technology Information System.]

0235   Woolston, J. E. "The International Nuclear Information System (INIS),"
        In: UNESCO Bulletin for Libraries, 23(3): 135-138, May-June, 1969.
        [Scope; Organization; Utilization.]

0236   Wysocki, A. Educational and Training Issues in UNISIST. Paris, UNESCO,
        November, 1971, 12p. ED 084 779. [World Science Information System.]

0237   Wysocki, A., and J. Tocatlian. "A World Science Information System:
        Necessary and Feasible," In: UNESCO Bulletin for Libraries, 25(2):
        62-66, March-April, 1971.

0238   Wysocki, A. "World Science Information System: UNISIST," In: Pro-
        ceedings of the International Conference on Information Science,
        1971. Tel Aviv, Israel, 1972, pp. 17-25.

National

General

0239   Arutjunov, N. B. "The Requirements To Be Met by National Scientific
        and Technical Information Systems," In: UNESCO Bulletin for
        Libraries, 27(5): 246-249, September-October, 1973. [Functions and
        requirements of national systems; UNISIST.]

0240   Aines, A. A. "The Promise of National Information Systems," In:
        Library Trends, 16(3): 410-418. January, 1968. [Factors favoring
        development of national systems.]

0241   Beaulnes, A. Science Policy and STI in Canada. Ottawa, (Ontario)
        Canada, Ministry of State for Science and Technology, May 15, 1973,
        40p. ED 083 989.

0242   Brown, J. E. The Canadian National Scientific and Technical Informa-
        tion (STI) System; A Progress Report. 1972 Miles Conrad Memorial
        Lecture, Report 4. Philadelphia, Pa., National Federation of Science
        Abstracting and Indexing Services, 1972, 26p.

*0243 Carter, L. F., et. al. National Document-Handling Systems for Science
        and Technology. New York, Wiley, 1967, 344p. (Also as PB 168 267 or
        AD 624 560) [System requirements; Alternative systems; Review of
        user studies, existing proposals, and legislation.]

0244   Carter, L. F. "National Document-Handling Systems in Science and Technology," In: Science, 154(3754): 1299-1303, December 9, 1966. [Summary of recommendations.]

*0245   Hammer, D. P. "National Information Issues and Trends," In: Annual Review of Information Science and Technology. Edited by C. A. Cuadra. New York, Interscience, 1967, Vol. 2, pp. 385-417. [Governmental activities; Copyright law.]

0246   Heaps, D. M., and G. A. Cooke. "National Policies, National Networks, and National Information Studies in Canada," In: Proceedings of the American Society for Information Science. Westport, Conn., Greenwood, 1970, Vol. 7, pp. 199-203.

0247   Henderson, M. M., et. al. Cooperation, Convertibility, and Compatibility among Information Systems: A Literature Review. Washington, National Bureau of Standards, June 15, 1966, 144p. NBS Misc. Pub.-276. [Government agencies; Scientific and technical information.]

0248   Hookway, H. T. "Some Problems in Developing National Systems for Science Information," In: Communication in Science: Documentation and Automation. Edited by A. DeReuck and J. Knight. Boston, Little, Brown & Co., 1967, pp. 165-170.

0249   Hoshovsky, A. G. "COSATI Information Studies—What Results," In: Proceedings of the American Society for Information Science. Westport, Conn., Greenwood, 1969, Vol. 6, pp. 401-410. [Technical information problems; Review of proposals for national systems.]

*0250   Hoshovsky, A. G., and H. H. Album. "Toward a National Technical Information System," In: American Documentation, 16(4): 313-322, October, 1965. (Also as AD 625 496) [Review of proposals for national systems.]

0251   Judge, P. J. "The User-System Interface Today: National and International Information Systems," In: Communication in Science: Documentation and Automation. Edited by A. DeReuck and J. Knight. Boston, Little, Brown & Co., 1967, pp. 37-51.

0252   Kirson, B. L. "Scientific and Technological Information Systems in the Soviet Union," In: American Society for Information Science Journal, (Brief Communication), 24(4): 306-307, July-August, 1973. [VINITI, All-Union Institute of Scientific and Technological Information.]

0253   Knox, W. T. "Planning for National Information Networks," In: Proceedings of the 2d National Symposium on Engineering Information. New York, Engineers Joint Council, 1965, pp. 5-8. [Engineering.]

0254   Knox, W. T. Recommendations for National Document Handling Systems in Science and Technology. Washington, Committee on Scientific and Technical Information, 1965. [Proposal.]

0255   Knox, W. T. "Systems for Technological Information Transfer," In: Science, 181(4098): 415-419, August 3, 1973.

*0256   Library Trends. "Development in National Document and Information Services," In: Library Trends, 17(3): 227-338, January, 1969. [India; Latin America; Japan; South Africa; Canada; Scandinavia; United Kingdom; United States; Soviet Union.]

*0257   Licklider, J. C. R., et. al. A Report of the Office of Science and Technology Ad Hoc Panel on Scientific and Technical Communication. Washington, Office of Science and Technology, February, 1965, 41p. ED 048 895. [Governmental role in communication process; Assessment of scientific and technical communication activities.]

0258   Liston, D. M., Jr., and M. L. Schoene. Basic Elements of Planning and Design of National and Regional Information Systems. Columbus, Ohio, Battelle Memorial Institute, May, 1971, 39p.

*0259   Myatt, D. O., and S. I. Jorer. Compilation of Major Recommendations from Five Studies Relating to National Scientific and Technical Information Systems, Final Report. McLean, Va., Science Communication, Inc., April 16, 1970, 147p. PB 193 345. [Management concepts for national programs; Role of organizations generating information; Role of scientific and technical community; Education; Standardization; Informal communication; Summary recommendation.]

0260   Organization for Economic Cooperation and Development. Review of National Scientific and Technical Information Policy–Canada. Washington, Organization for Economic Cooperation and Development, 1971, 161p.

0261   Penna, C. V. "Seminar on Planning of National Scientific and Technical Information Structures," In: UNESCO Bulletin for Libraries, 25(4): 186-190, July-August, 1971.

0262   Rajagopalan, T. S. "The Soviet Scientific Information System," In: Annals of Library Science and Documentation, 15(3): 125-154, September, 1968.

0263   Rubinoff, M., ed. Toward a National Information System. Washington, Spartan, 1965, 242p. [Proposals; Review.]

0264   Salton, G. "Some Thoughts on Scientific Information Dissemination," In: Journal of the Association for Computing Machinery, 18(1): 1-3, January, 1971. [Critique of proposals for national systems.]

0265 Sawamoto, T. "Toward a National Science Information Network in Japan," In: Annals of Library Science and Documentation, 17 (3/4): 81-104, September-December, 1970.

0266 Simpson, G. S. "The Evolving U.S. National Scientific and Technical Information System," In: Battelle Technical Review, 17: 21-28, May-June, 1968.

0267 Stevens, M. E. "Compatibility Problems of Network Interfacing," In: Conference on Interlibrary Communications and Information Networks (CICIN). Chicago, American Library Association, 1971, pp. 202-214.

*0268 U.S. Federal Council for Science and Technology, Committee on Scientific and Technical Information. Legal Aspects of Computerized Information Systems. Washington, Committee on Scientific and Technical Information, September, 1972, 89p. PB 223 496/1GA. [Right of entry and access to information systems; Freedom of Information Act; Right of privacy; Anti-trust issues; Property rights; Copyright.]

*0269 U.S. Federal Council for Science and Technology, Committee on Scientific and Technical Information. The Copyright Law as It Relates to National Information Systems and National Programs. Washington, Committee on Scientific and Technical Information, July, 1967, 82p. PB 175 618. [Problems of ready access to copyrighted materials, making computer input an infringement, and exemptions for nonprofit use.]

*0270 U.S. National Academy of Sciences. Libraries and Information Technology: A National System Challenge. Washington, National Academy of Sciences, 1972, 83p. [Economics; Libraries; Proprietary interests.]

0271 Warren, S. L. The National Library of Science System and Network for Published Scientific Literature; A Memorandum for the President. Washington, February 17, 1964. [Proposal.]

0272 Wigington, R. L., and J. L. Wood. "Standardization Requirements for a National Program for Information Transfer," In: Library Trends, 18(4): 432-447, April, 1970.

Sciences

*0273 Alt, F. L., and A. Herschman. Plans for a National Physics Information System. New York, American Institute of Physics, Information Division, ID-68-6, March, 1968, 58p. PB 178 745. [Data storage system; Astronomy; Physics.]

*0274   American Geological Institute, Committee on Geoscience Information. "A Concept of an Information System for the Geosciences," In: Information, 3(2): 57-61, March-April, 1971. [Geoscience citation study; Literature needs; Scope and characteristics of literature.]

 0275   American Geological Institute, Committee on Geoscience Information. A Concept of an Information System for the Geosciences. Washington, American Geological Institute, December, 1970, 25p. ED 046 429. [Proposal.]

*0276   American Institute of Physics, Information Division. A Program for a National Information System for Physics, 1970-1972. New York, American Institute of Physics, Information Division, August, 1969, 183p. PB 185 388. [Physics; Astronomy; American Institute of Physics; System requirements; Proposal.]

*0277   American Institute of Physics, Information Division. A Program for a National Information System for Physics and Astronomy, 1971-1975. New York, American Institute of Physics, Information Division, ID-70-P, June, 1970, 127p. PB 192 717 or ED 033 731. [System goals, priorities, and strategy; Information channels in physics and astronomy; Pilot operation of stage 1.]

*0278   American Institute of Physics, Information Division. A National Information System for Physics and Astronomy, 1972-1976. Annual Report. New York, American Institute of Physics, Information Division, ID-71-P, June, 1971, 74p. PB 200 991 or ED 051 849.

 0279   Caless, T. W. Plan for Implementing an Information System for Marine Science Literature. Washington, George Washington University, Biological Sciences Communication Project, November, 1968, 12p. AD 678 837. [Proposal; Organization; Operation; Cost estimates.]

 0280   Carlson, W. M. "Toward a National Chemical Information Network," In: Journal of Chemical Documentation, 5(1): 1-3, February, 1965.

 0281   Carroll, K. D. "Development of a National Information System for Physics," In: Special Libraries, 61(4): 171-179, April, 1970.

 0282   Gordon, R. E. "Toward an Information System for Biology-Community Activity," In: BioScience, 19(7): 628-629, July, 1969. [American Institute of Biological Sciences.]

 0283   Herschman, A. "An Integrated Information System for Physics and Astronomy," In: Proceedings of the International Conference on Information Science. Edited by L. Vilentchuk and G. Haimovic. Tel Aviv, Israel, 1971, pp. 147-156.

*0284   Herschman, A. "A Program for a National Information System for Physics," In: Communication among Scientists and Engineers. Edited by C. E. Nelson and D. K. Pollock. Lexington, Mass., Heath Lexington Books, 1970, pp. 307-323. [Criteria for a national system; Communication in physics.]

*0285   Information Management, Inc. System Development Plan for a National Information System. Burlington, Mass., Information Management, Inc., April, 1967, 35p. PB 174 438 or AD 650 900. [System management; Resource requirements; Developmental plans; Scheduling.]

 0286   Information Management, Inc. System Performance Specification for a National Chemical Information System. Burlington, Mass., Information Management, Inc., April, 1967, 129p. PB 174 484 or AD 650 901. [Policy decisions; Funding; Cost estimates; Manpower; Implementation.]

 0287   Koch, H. W. "A National Information System for Physics," In: Physics Today, 21(4): 41-49, April, 1968. [American Institute of Physics; Characteristics of physicists; Characteristics of national system.]

*0288   Koch, H. W., and A. Herschman. A Network for Physics Information. New York, American Institute of Physics, Information Division, AIP-ID-68-13, October, 1968, 17p. PB 180 209 or ED 039 006. [Characteristics; Functions; Operation.]

 0289   Lerner, R. G., and K. D. Carroll. "Future Plans for Information System for Physicists," In: Innovations in Communications Conference, April 9-10, 1970. New York, American Institute of Physics, April, 1970, pp. 60-71. PB 192 294.

 0290   Libbey, M. A., and A. R. Blum. A Study of Information Elements for the National Information System for Physics. New York, American Institute of Physics, Information Division, June, 1968, 62p. PB 180 208 or ED 025 273. [Bibliographic data elements.]

 0291   Lloyd, J. J. "Design and Building of an Information System for Geoscience," In: Proceedings of the American Society for Information Science. Westport, Conn., Greenwood, 1971, Vol. 8, pp. 121-123. [Communication problems in the geosciences.]

 0292   Moody, D., and O. Kays. "Development of the U.S. Geological Survey Bibliographic System Using GIPSY," In: American Society for Information Science Journal, 23(1): 39-49, January-February, 1972. [Geosciences literature; Generalized Information Processing System.]

 0293   Olsen, W. C. A Library Network for the Geosciences. Washington, ERIC, November, 1971, 8p. ED 056 733. [American Geological Institute; Role of libraries in national system.]

*0294   Phelps, C. R., ed. Proceedings of a Conference on a National Information System in the Mathematical Sciences, January 18-20, 1970, Glen Cove, New York. Washington, Conference Board of the Mathematical Sciences, July, 1970, 58 p. ED 043 524.

0295   Physics Today. "Toward National Information Networks," In: Physics Today, 19(1): 38-60, January, 1966. [Governmental role; Physics.]

0296   Resnikoff, H. L. On Information Systems, With Emphasis on the Mathematical Sciences. Washington, Conference Board of the Mathematical Sciences, January 1971, 31p. [Communication problems in mathematics.]

0297   Smith, F. D., Jr., and W. A. Creager. Developing a Coordinated Information Program for Geological Scientists in the United States. Washington, American Geological Institute, December, 1967, 56p. PB 177 290. [Communication problems; Role of professional societies; System requirements; Role of libraries; Data activities.]

0298   Vallee, J. Scientific Information Networks: A Case Study. Palo Alto, Calif., Stanford University, Computation Center, September, 1970, 72p. ED 050 767. [Astronomy; Data system.]

0299   Wilkinson, W. A., and W. H. Waldo. "A Decentralized National Chemical Information System," In: American Documentation, 18(1): 47-48, January, 1967.

0300   Williams, V. Z., E. Hutchisson, and H. C. Wolfe. "Considerations of a Physics Information System," In: Physics Today, 19(1): 45-49, January, 1966.

Social Sciences

0301   Banks, E. "Quick Publication Schemes," In: Science (Letter), 168(3928): 194-195, April 10, 1970. [Preprint exchange; National Information System for Psychology.]

0302   Boffey, P. M. "Psychology; Apprehension Over a New Communication System," In: Science, 167(3922): 1228-1230, February 17, 1970. [National Information System for Psychology; Preprint exchange; Tape cassettes; Films; Editor/referee system.]

0303   Booz-Allen and Hamilton, Inc. Economic Analyses Related to the Future Market for Psychological Information. Washington, American Psychological Association, Office of Communication Management and

Development, OCMD-5/70-TR#5, 1970. [National Information System for Psychology.]

*0304   Borgeson, E. C., and P. Freeman. "Network Prospects for Legal Profession," In: Conference on Interlibrary Communications and Information Networks (CICIN). Chicago, American Library Association, 1971, pp. 288-293.

0305   Brayfield, A. H. "Perspective on NISP," In: American Psychologist, 26(4): 337-338, April, 1971. [National Information System for Psychology.]

*0306   Burchinal, L. G. "The Educational Resources Information Center: An Emergent National System," In: Journal of Educational Data Processing, 7(2): 55-67, April, 1970.

*0307   Center for Applied Linguistics. An Information System Program for the Language Sciences, Final Project Report. Washington, Center for Applied Linguistics, Language Information Network and Clearinghouse System, December, 1971, 82p. PB 206 505.

*0308   Clark, K. E. "A Critical Examination of the National Information System for Psychology—Introduction," In: American Psychologist, 26(4): 325-329, April, 1971.

0309   Creager, W. A. Methodological Bases for the Design of a Language Information Network and Clearinghouse System. Washington, Center for Applied Linguistics, December, 1969, 42p. PB 195 713.

0310   Grant, D. A. "Psychology: Apprehension Over a New Communication System." In: American Psychologist, 26(4): 329-330, April, 1971. [National Information System for Psychology.]

*0311   Greenwood, P. W., and D. M. Weiler. Alternative Models for the ERIC Clearinghouse Network. Santa Monica, Calif., Rand Corp., January, 1972, 92p. ED 058 508. [Educational Resources Information Centers.]

0312   Holt, R. R. "Some Neglected Assumptions and Problems in Psychology's Information Crisis," In: American Psychologist, 26(4): 331-334, April, 1971. [National Information System for Psychology.]

0313   Jenkins, J. J. "The NISP Controversy: A Version from the Board of Scientific Affairs," In: American Psychologist, 26(4): 334-335, April, 1971. [National Information System for Psychology; American Psychological Association.]

0314   King, D. W., and N. W. Caldwell. Cost-Effectiveness of Retrospect Search Systems. Washington, American Psychological Association,

Office of Communication Management and Development, OCMD-3/71-TR#14, 1971. [National Information System for Psychology.]

*0315 Kinkade, R. G. Desirable Characteristics of a Scientific Publication System. Washington, American Psychological Association, Office of Communication Management and Development, OCMD-4/70-TR#3, April, 1970, 19p. ED 038 995. [National Information System for Psychology.]

0316 Kinkade, R. G. "The Experimental Publication System: An Aid to Information System Planning," In: American Psychologist, 25(10): 925-936, October, 1970. [National Information System for Psychology.]

0317 Kinkade, R. G. "Long Range Plans for a National Information System for Psychology," In: Innovations in Communications Conference, April 9-10, 1970. Washington, American Psychological Association, Inc., April, 1970, pp. 197-203. PB 192 294.

0318 Kinkade, R. G. Results of a Questionnaire Evaluating the Goals of Professional Psychology. Washington, American Psychological Association, Office of Communication Management and Development, OCMD-10/70-TR#9, 1970. [National Information System for Psychology.]

0319 Kinkade, R. G., and J. A. Whittenberg. The Results of Operating an Experimental Publication System: An Interim Report. Washington, American Psychological Association, OCMD-1/70-TR#2, January, 1970, 26p. [National Information System for Psychology.]

0320 Kurke, M. I. "Defense of Quick Publication," In: Science, 168(3935): 1041, May 29, 1970. [Preprint exchange; National Information System for Psychology.]

0321 Loevinger, J. "The Philosophical Issues," In: American Psychologist, 26(4): 338, April, 1971. [National Information System for Psychology.]

0322 Loevinger, J. "Quick Publication Schemes," In: Science, (Letter), 168(3928):194, April 10, 1970. [Preprint exchange; National Information System for Psychology.]

0323 Miller, G. A. "The Real Heart of NISP," In: American Psychologist, 26(4): 335-336, April, 1971. [National Information System for Psychology.]

0324 Orr, D. B. The APA Journal Program: A Summary of Its Status. Washington, American Psychological Association, Office of Communication Management and Development, OCMD-12/70-TR#13, 1970. [National Information System for Psychology.]

0325 Prescott, S., and B. C. Griffith. A Descriptive Study of Information Needs and Practices of Clinical Psychologists. Washington, American Psychological Association, Office of Communication Management and Development, OCMD-5/70-TR#4, 1970, 83p. [National Information System for Psychology.]

0326 Prescott, S. Impact of Workshops on Practitioners: A Current Evaluation. Washington, American Psychological Association, Office of Communication Management and Development, OCMD-6/70-TR#6, 1970. [National Information System for Psychology.]

0327 Prescott, S. Psychologist's Interest in Audiotapes and Other Audiovisual Media; Survey Reports. Washington, American Psychological Association, Office of Communication Management and Development. OCMD-10/70-TR#10, 1970, 30p. [National Information System for Psychology.]

0328 Sasmor, R. M. National Information System for Psychology: Support to Informal Communications. Washington, American Psychological Association, 1970, 13p.

0329 Seashere, S. E. "Psychology: Apprehension Over a New Communication System—An Alternative View," In: American Psychologist, 26(4): 330-331, April, 1971. [National Information System for Psychology.]

0330 Sender, J. W. "The Hierarchy of Publication Forms," In: American Psychologist, 26(4): 336-337, April, 1971. [National Information System for Psychology.]

0331 Van Cott, H. P. APA's Communication Program. Washington, American Psychological Association, Office of Communication Management and Development, OCMD-11/70-TR#12, 1970. [National Information System for Psychology.]

0332 Van Cott, H. P. "Innovations in the Transfer of Psychological Information: The Communications Programme of the American Psychological Association," In: Bulletin of the British Psychological Society, 25: 193-196, 1972. [National Information System for Psychology.]

*0333 Van Cott, H. P. "National Information System for Psychology: A Proposed Solution for a Pressing Problem," In: American Psychologist, 25(5): i-xx, May, 1970.

0334 Whittenburg, J. A. "An Experimental Publication System in Psychology," In: Innovations in Communications Conference, April 9-10, 1970. Washington, American Psychological Association, Inc., April, 1970, pp. 36-45. PB 192 294. [National Information System for Psychology.]

0335 Whittenburg, J. A., and G. L. Baker. Exploratory Investigation of Information Needs of Individuals and Institutions. Washington, American Psychological Association, Office of Communication Management and Development, OCMD-11/70-TR#11, 23p., November, 1970. ED 046 408. [National Information System for Psychology.]

Technology

0336 Bracken, M. C. An Analysis of the Evolution of the National Library of Medicine: Implications for the Development of Scientific and Technical Information Networks. Ph.D. Dissertation, Washington, American University, 1971, 312p. (University Microfilms, Inc., Order No. 71-25,285) [Biomedical communication; Role of user needs studies; Future developments.]

0337 Clayton, F. W. "The Toxicology Information Program of the National Library of Medicine," In: Clinical Toxicology, 5(5): 283-294, 1972.

*0338 Davis, R. M. "National Biomedical Network," In: Conference on Interlibrary Communications and Information Networks (CICIN). Chicago, American Library Association, 1971, pp. 294-309. [History; Biomedical communications; Structure of medical community.]

*0339 EDUCOM. Agricultural Sciences Information Network Development Plan: Research Report. Boston, Mass., EDUCOM, August, 1969, 98p. PB 185 978. [Libraries; Information analysis centers; Telecommunications.]

0340 EDUCOM. A Master Technical Plan for the National Mental Retardation Information and Resource Center. Boston, Mass., EDUCOM, April, 1969, 75p. ED 055 613.

0341 Engineering Education. "Action Plan for the Establishment of a United Engineering Information Service," In: Engineering Education, 60(5): 371-374, January, 1970.

0342 Farquhar, J. A. Biomedical Information Dissemination: Alternative Systems. Santa Monica, Calif., Rand Corp., March, 1970, 50p. ED 047 734. [National Library of Medicine; MEDLARS.]

0343 Herner, S., et. al. A Recommended Design for the United States Medical Library and Information System. Volume I: System Design, Implementation, and Cost. Washington, Herner & Co., July, 1966, 115p. PB 172 923.

*0344   Liston, D. M., Jr., et. al. Development of an Engineered Plan for a
        United Engineering Information Service (UEIS), Volume I: Final
        Report. Columbus, Ohio, Battelle Memorial Institute, July 21, 1969,
        81p. PB 188 052.

*0345   Liston, D. M., Jr., et. al. Development of an Engineered Plan for a
        United Engineering Information Service (UEIS), Volume II: Appendix.
        Columbus, Ohio, Battelle Memorial Institute, July 21, 1969, 283p.
        PB 188 053.

 0346   Liston, D. M., Jr., et. al. "United Engineering Information System Study."
        In: Proceedings of the National Engineering Information Conference.
        New York, Engineers Joint Council, 1969, pp. 69-81.

 0347   National Agricultural Library. A Progress Report on the Agricultural
        Sciences Information Network. Washington, National Agricultural
        Library, August, 1971, 15p. ED 078 859.

 0348   National Agricultural Library. Report of Task Force ABLE (Agricul-
        tural Biological Literature Exploitation); A Systems Study of the
        National Agricultural Library and Its Users. Washington, Government
        Printing Office, 1965, 477p.

 0349   Rice, C. N. "Toward a National Systems Resource in Toxicology," In:
        Journal of Chemical Documentation, 9(3): 181-183, August, 1969.

 0350   Wall, E. Cooperative Potential in Agricultural Information Utilization,
        Technical Report. Philadelphia, Pa., Auerbach Corp., September 15,
        1970, 37p. PB 195 458.

 0351   Weinstock, M. J., et. al. A Recommended Design for the United States
        Medical Library and Information System, Volume II: Background
        Studies. Washington, Herner & Co., January, 1966, 374p. PB 172 924.

NATIONAL AND INTERNATIONAL MEETINGS

 0352   American Psychological Association. "Information Exchange at the
        American Psychological Association Annual Convention and the Func-
        tion of the Convention Proceedings in Such Exchange," In: APA's Pro-
        ject on Scientific Information Exchange in Psychology. Washington,
        American Psychological Association, Report No. 18, April, 1968, Vol.
        3, pp. 99-160. PB 182 962. [Effects of presentations on subsequent
        research; Role of convention in establishing informal contacts.]

0353   American Psychological Association. Scientific Communication at the XVIII International Congress of Psychology, 1966, and Some Implications for the Design and Operation of International Meetings—Moscow. Washington, American Psychological Association, Report No. 20, April, 1968.

0354   Baum, H. "Documentation of Technical and Scientific Meetings," In: Proceedings of the American Documentation Institute. Washington, American Documentation Institute, 1964, Vol. 1, pp. 243-246.

0355   Baum, H. "Scientific and Technical Meeting Papers: Transient Value or Lasting Contribution," In: Special Libraries, 56(9): 651-653, November, 1965.

0356   Compton, B. E. "Communication and the Scientific Conference," In: Technology and Society, 4(3): 39-42, 1968. [Psychology.]

0357   Compton, B. E. "The Convention Presentation: Interim or Ultimate Type of Dissemination?" In: American Psychologist, 20(4): 300-302, April, 1965.

0358   Compton, B. E., and W. D. Garvey. "Information Functions of an International Meeting: Attendants at the 18th International Congress of Psychology in Moscow Evaluate Its Effectiveness," In: Science, 155(3770): 1648-1650, March 31, 1967.

0359   Compton, B. E. "A Look at Conventions and What They Accomplish," In: American Psychologist, 21(2): 176-183, February, 1966. [Characteristics of convention presentations; Pre- and post-conference dissemination practices.]

*0360   Garvey, W. D., et. al. "A Comparison of Scientific Communication Behavior of Social and Physical Scientists," In: International Social Science Journal, 23(2): 256-272, 1971. [Communication delays; Informal networks; Prepublication dissemination; Transfer of information from informal to formal domain.]

0361   Garvey, W. D., and B. C. Griffith. "The Effect of Convention Presentation on Information Exchange Behavior and Subsequent Research," In: Proceedings of the American Documentation Institute. Washington, American Documentation Institute, 1964, Vol. 1, pp. 201-213. [Psychology.]

*0362   Garvey, W. D., et. al. "An Overview of the Information Exchange Associated with National Scientific Meetings in Relation to the General Process of Communication," In: The Role of the National Meeting in Scientific and Technical Communication. Baltimore, Md., Johns Hopkins University, Center for Research on Scientific Communication, June,

1970, Vol. 1, pp. 1-47. PB 202 367. [Sciences; Social Sciences; Technology.]

0363 Garvey, W. D., et al. "Research Studies in Patterns of Scientific Communication: I. General Description of Program," Information Storage and Retrieval, 8(3): 111-122, June, 1972. [Center for Research in Scientific Communication.]

*0364 Garvey, W. D., et al. "Research Studies in Patterns of Scientific Communication: II. Role of National Meetings in Scientific and Technical Communication," In: Information Storage and Retrieval, 8(4): 159-169, August, 1972.

0365 Garvey, W. D., N. Lin, and K. Tomita. "Research Studies in Patterns of Scientific Communication: III. Information-Exchange Processes Associated with the Production of Journal Articles," In: Information Storage and Retrieval, 8(5): 207-221, October, 1972. [Prepublication dissemination; Preprint distribution; Postpublication dissemination.]

0366 Garvey, W. D., N. Lin, and K. Tomita. "Research Studies in Patterns of Scientific Communication: IV. Continuity of Dissemination of Information by Productive Scientists," In: Information Storage and Retrieval, 8(6): 265-276, December, 1972.

*0367 Garvey, W.D., N. Lin, and C. E. Nelson. "Some Comparisons of Communication Activities in the Physical and Social Sciences," In: Communication among Scientists and Engineers. Edited by C. E. Nelson and D. K. Pollock. Lexington, Mass., Heath Lexington Books, 1970, pp. 61-84. [Communication delays; Prepublication dissemination; Pre-meeting dissemination; Post-meeting publication.]

0368 Griffith, B. C., and W. D. Garvey. "The National Scientific Meeting in Psychology as a Changing System," In: American Behavioral Scientist, 9(6): 3-8, February, 1966.

0369 Griffith, B. C., W. D. Garvey, and B. E. Compton. "Scientific Information Exchange at the XVIIIth International Congress of Psychology, Moscow," In: International Journal of Psychology, 3(2): 123-128, 1968.

0370 Johns Hopkins University. Communication Cohesiveness of Scientific Activities and the Development of Science. Baltimore, Md., Johns Hopkins University, Center for Research in Scientific Communication, JHU-CRSC-Report 13, April, 1970. PB 192 121.

0371 Johns Hopkins University. A Comparison of the Dissemination of Scientific and Technical Information, Informal Interaction, and the Impact of Information Associated with Two Meetings of the American Institute of Aeronautics and Astronautics. Baltimore, Md., Johns

Hopkins University, Center for Research in Scientific Communication, JHU-CRSC-Report 1, August, 1967, 71p. PB 176 495. (Also in PB 202 367)

0372 Johns Hopkins University. A Comparison of the Dissemination of Scientific Information, Informal Interaction, and the Impact of Information Received from Two Meetings of the American Meteorological Society. Baltimore, Md., Johns Hopkins University, Center for Research in Scientific Communication, JHU-CRSC-Report 6, November, 1967, 46p. PB 176 906. (Also in PB 202 367)

0373 Johns Hopkins University. A Comparison of the Utility of Information Contained in Copies of Papers Presented at the October, 1966, Meeting of the American Sociological Association with Journal Articles Based on the Same Material. Baltimore, Md., Johns Hopkins University, Center for Research in Scientific Communication, JHU-CRSC-Technical Note 11, February, 1969. PB 202 341-U.

0374 Johns Hopkins University. Description of a Machine-Readable Data Bank on the Communication Behavior of Scientists and Technologists. Baltimore, Md., Johns Hopkins University, Center for Research in Scientific Communication, JHU-CRSC-Report 20, October, 1971.

0375 Johns Hopkins University. Dissemination and Assimilation of Materials Presented in Journals on Metallurgy. Baltimore, Md., Johns Hopkins University, Center for Research in Scientific Communication, JHU-CRSC-Report 16, September 1970, 56p. PB 194 401.

0376 Johns Hopkins University. The Dissemination of Scientific Information, Informal Interaction, and the Impact of Information Associated with the 48th Annual Meeting of the American Geophysical Union. Baltimore, Md., Johns Hopkins University, Center for Research in Scientific Communication, JHU-CRSC-Report 5, October, 1967, 41p. PB 202 367.

0377 Johns Hopkins University. The Dissemination of Scientific Information, Informal Interaction, and the Impact of Information Received from Two Meetings of the Optical Society of America. Baltimore, Johns Hopkins University, Center for Research in Scientific Communication, JHU-CRSC-Report 3, September, 1967, 68p. PB 176 493 (Also in PB 202 367)

0378 Johns Hopkins University. The Dissemination of the Program Material from Two Meetings of the American Institute of Aeronautics and Astronautics. Baltimore, Johns Hopkins University, Center for Research in Scientific Communication, JHU-CRSC-Technical Note 2, March, 1968, 27p. PB 184 216.

0379 Johns Hopkins University. The Information-Dissemination Process Associated with Journal Articles Published by Heating, Refrigerating, and

Air-Conditioning Engineers. Baltimore, Johns Hopkins University, Center for Research in Scientific Communication, JHU-CRSC-Report 19, April, 1971, 40p. PB 198 651.

0380   Johns Hopkins University. The Information-Dissemination Process Associated with the Production of Journal Articles on Geophysics. Baltimore, Johns Hopkins University, Center for Research in Scientific Communication, JHU-CRSC-Report 14, May, 1970, 61p. PB 192 126.

0381   Johns Hopkins University. The Journal Publication Fate of Work Reported at Two 1967 Meetings of the American Meteorological Society. Baltimore, Johns Hopkins University, Center for Research in Scientific Communication, JHU-CRSC-Technical Note 5, June 28, 1969, 30p. PB 186 140.

0382   Johns Hopkins University. Journal Publication of Material Presented at the 1967 Annual Meeting of the American Geophysical Union during the Year Following the Meeting. Baltimore, Johns Hopkins University, Center for Research in Scientific Communication, JHU-CRSC-Technical Note 6, 1968, 25p. PB 184 968.

0383   Johns Hopkins University. Journal Publication of Material Presented at the 1967 Annual Meeting of the Association of American Geographers. Baltimore, Johns Hopkins University, Center for Research in Scientific Communication, JHU-CRSC-Technical Note 7, June 28, 1968, 22p. PB 186 139.

0384   Johns Hopkins University. The Journal Publication of Material Presented at the 96th Annual Meeting of the American Institute of Mining, Metallurgical and Petroleum Engineers: 2 Years After the Meeting. Baltimore, Johns Hopkins University, Center for Research in Scientific Communication, JHU-CRSC-Technical Note 16, June, 1969. (In PB 185 469)

0385   Johns Hopkins University. The Journal Publication of Papers Presented at the 1966 Meeting of the American Sociological Association: 2 Years after the Meeting. Baltimore, Md., Johns Hopkins University, Center for Research in Scientific Communication, JHU-CRSC-Technical Note 12, February, 1969. (In PB 185 469)

0386   Johns Hopkins University. Journal Publication of Papers Presented at the October, 1966, Meeting of the Optical Society of America; 27 Months after the Meeting. Baltimore, Johns Hopkins University, Center for Research in Scientific Communication, JHU-CRSC-Technical Note 10, February, 1969. (In PB 185 469)

0387   Johns Hopkins University. The Journal Publication of Papers Presented at Two Meetings of the American Institute of Aeronautics and Astronautics; 2 Years after the Meetings. Baltimore, Johns Hopkins University,

Center for Research in Scientific Communication, JHU-CRSC-Technical Note 14, April, 1969. (In PB 185 469)

0388   Johns Hopkins University. The Journal Publication of the Main Content of Papers Presented at Two Meetings of the American Meteorological Society: 2 Years after the Meetings. Baltimore, Johns Hopkins University, Center for Research in Scientific Communication, June, 1969. (In PB 185 469)

0389   Johns Hopkins University. The Nature of Program Materials and the Results of Interaction at the February, 1968, Semiannual Meeting of the American Society of Heating, Refrigerating and Air-Conditioning Engineers. Baltimore, Johns Hopkins University, Center for Research in Scientific Communication, JHU-CRSC-Report 8, April, 1968, 33p. PB 179 674. (Also in PB 202 367)

0390   Johns Hopkins University. The 1966 International Congresses of Psychology and Sociology: A Study of Information Exchange and Meeting Effectiveness. Baltimore, Johns Hopkins University, Center for Research in Scientific Communication, Series 2, Report 1, February, 1968, 82p.

0391   Johns Hopkins University. The Postmeeting Dissemination in Scholarly Journals of Material Presented at the 1968 Annual Meeting of the American Educational Research Association. Baltimore, Johns Hopkins University, Center for Research in Scientific Communication, JHU-CRSC-Technical Note 8, April, 1969, 47p. PB 184 218.

0392   Johns Hopkins University. The Postmeeting Publication of Material Presented at the February, 1968, Semiannual Meeting of the American Society of Heating, Refrigerating, and Air-Conditioning Engineers. Baltimore, Johns Hopkins University, Center for Research in Scientific Communication, JHU-CRSC-Technical Note 9, April, 1969, 17 p. PB 184 219.

0393   Johns Hopkins University. The Production, Dissemination, and Assimilation of Information Contained in Journal Articles in Geography. Baltimore, Johns Hopkins University, Center for Research in Scientific Communication, JHU-CRSC-Report 18, March, 1971, 64p. PB 198 650 or ED 048 875.

0394   Johns Hopkins University. Production, Exchange, and Dissemination of Information in Journal Articles on Sociology. Baltimore, Johns Hopkins University, Center for Research in Scientific Communication, JHU-CRSC-Report 17, January, 1971, 72p. PB 197 641.

0395   Johns Hopkins University. Production, Exchange, and Dissemination of Information Presented in Journal Articles on Meteorology. Baltimore,

Johns Hopkins University, Center for Research in Scientific Communication, JHU-CRSC-Report 15, June, 1970, 68p. PB 199 477.

0396   Johns Hopkins University. The Publication Efforts of Authors of Presentations at the 1966 Annual Meeting of the American Sociological Association during the Year Following the Meeting. Baltimore, Johns Hopkins University, Center for Research in Scientific Communication, JHU-CRSC-Technical Note 3, April, 1968, 23p. PB 179 675.

0397   Johns Hopkins University. The Publication Fate of Material Presented at the October, 1966, Annual Meeting of the Optical Society of America. Baltimore, Johns Hopkins University, Center for Research in Scientific Communication, JHU-CRSC-Technical Note 1, February, 1968, 23p. PB 184 215.

0398   Johns Hopkins University. Scientific Information-Exchange Behavior at the 1966 Annual Meeting of the American Sociological Association. Baltimore, Johns Hopkins University, Center for Research in Scientific Communication, JHU-CRSC-Report 4, September, 1967, 43p. PB 176 492. (Also in PB 202 367)

0399   Johns Hopkins University. A Study of Scientific Information Exchange at the 1968 American Educational Research Association Meeting. Baltimore, Johns Hopkins University, Center for Research in Scientific Communication, JHU-CRSC-Report 9, May, 1969, 44p. (In PB 202 367)

0400   Johns Hopkins University. A Study of Scientific Information Exchange at the 96th Annual Meeting of the American Institute of Mining, Metallurgical, and Petroleum Engineers. Baltimore, Johns Hopkins University, Center for Research in Scientific Communication, JHU-CRSC-Report 2, August, 1967, 74p. PB 176 494. (Also in PB 202 367)

0401   Johns Hopkins University. A Study of Scientific Information Exchange at the 63rd Annual Meeting of the Association of American Geographers. Baltimore, Johns Hopkins University, Center for Research in Scientific Communication, JHU-CRSC-Report 7, November, 1967, 37p. PB 176 900. (Also in PB 202 367)

0402   Johns Hopkins University. The Subsequent Dissemination of Material Presented in Sessions of the Metallurgical Society of the 96th AIME Annual Meeting. Baltimore, Johns Hopkins University, Center for Research in Scientific Communication, JHU-CRSC-Technical Note 4, April, 1968, 22p. PB 179 676.

0403   Johns Hopkins University. A Survey of Authors on the Publication Practices in Meteorology. Baltimore, Johns Hopkins University, Center for Research in Scientific Communication, JHU-CRSC-Preliminary Report-3 (Rev.), September, 1968, 27p. PB 184 217.

0404   Lin, N., W. D. Garvey, and C. E. Nelson. "Publication Fate of Material Presented at an Annual ASA Meeting: Two Years after the Meeting," In: The American Sociologist, 5(1): 22-25, February, 1970. [Sociology.]

*0405   Lin, N., W. D. Garvey, and C. E. Nelson. "A Study of the Communication Structure of Science," In: Communication among Scientists and Engineers. Edited by C. E. Nelson and D. K. Pollock. Lexington, Mass., Heath Lexington Books, 1970, pp. 23-60. [Primary journals; Pre-publication dissemination; Engineering sciences; Physical sciences; Social sciences.]

0406   Mills, P. R. "Characteristics of Published Conference Proceedings," In: Journal of Documentation, 29(1): 36-50, March, 1973. [Publication delays; Format; Subjects; Publishers; Languages.]

0407   Nelson, C. E., and K. Tomita. "Impact of the Proceedings of the Annual Meeting of the Association of American Geographers: A Comparison of Scientific Information Exchange at the 1967 and 1969 Annual Meeting." In: The Professional Geographer, 22(4): 221-226, July, 1970.

0408   Paisley, W. J., and E. B. Parker. "The AAPOR Conference as a Communication Medium," In: Public Opinion Quarterly, 32(1): 65-72, Spring, 1968. [American Association of Public Opinion Research.]

*0409   Paisley, W. J., and M. B. Paisley. Communication at Scientific and Professional Meetings. Palo Alto, Calif., Stanford University, Institute for Communication Research, April, 1971, 74p.

0410   Paisley, W. J., and E. B. Parker. Scientific Information Exchange at an Interdisciplinary Behavioral Science Convention. Palo Alto, Calif., Stanford University, Institute for Communication Research, March, 1967, 46p. PB 177 073. [American Association for Public Opinion Research.]

0411   Paul, E. "Acquisition and Announcement of Conference Paper Literature," In: Symposium on the Handling of Nuclear Information. Vienna, International Atomic Energy Agency, 1970, pp. 527-542. [Nuclear Science; Zentralstelle fur Atomkernenergie-Dokumentation.]

0412   Sherrill, P. N. Information Acquisition in Scientific Specialties Differing in Age, Size, and Theoretical Status. Ph.D. Dissertation, Palo Alto, Calif., Stanford University, 1968, 107p. (University Microfilms, Inc., Order No. 69-8265)

0413   UNESCO Bulletin for Libraries. "The Flow of Information from International Scientific Meetings: Report of the UNESCO Ad Hoc Sub-Committee," In: UNESCO Bulletin for Libraries, 24(2): 88-97, March-April, 1970.

0414 Van Cott, H. P. Functions and Forms of International Congresses of Psychology. Washington, American Psychological Association, Office of Communication Management and Development, 1971, 12p. (TR-16)

PUBLICATION PATTERNS

General

0415 Cook, E. B. "Biology Editor's Definition of Primary Literature," In: Science, (Letter), 168(3937): 1286, June 12, 1970.

*0416 Doebler, P. D. "Publication and Distribution of Information," In: Annual Review of Information Science and Technology. Edited by C. A. Cuadra. Chicago, Encyclopaedia Britannica, 1970, Vol. 5, pp. 223-257. [Technological tools of publishing; Multimedia publishing trends; Operating patterns in publishing; National information transfer systems.]

*0417 Freeman, R. R., et. al. "Techniques for Publication and Distribution of Information," In: Annual Review of Information Science and Technology. Edited by C. A. Cuadra. New York, Wiley, 1967, Vol. 2, pp. 339-384. [Primary journal publication; Secondary publication; New publication techniques; Current awareness; Selective dissemination of information; Invisible colleges; Preprints; Report literature.]

*0418 Gannett, E. K. "Primary Publication Systems and Services," In: Annual Review of Information Science and Technology. Edited by C. A. Cuadra. Washington, American Society for Information Science, 1973, Vol. 8, pp. 243-275. [Generation and production of primary publications; The journal as a communication medium; Alternative modes of dissemination; Economics of primary publication.]

0419 Hagstrom, W. O. "Factors Related to the Use of Different Modes of Publishing Research in Four Scientific Fields," In: Communication among Scientists and Engineers. Edited by C. E. Nelson and D. K. Pollock. Lexington, Mass., Heath Lexington Books, 1970, pp. 85-124. [Mathematics; Physics; Chemistry; Biology; Collaboration; Preprints; Reprints.]

0420 Hurd, E. A. "Patent Literature: Current Problems and Future Trends," In: Journal of Chemical Documentation, 10(3): 167-173, August, 1970. [Growth of patent literature; U.S. Patent Office.]

0421 Kilgour, F. G. "Publication of Scientific Discovery: A Paradox," In: Proceedings of the American Documentation Institute. Los Angeles, Adrianne Press, 1966, Vol. 3, pp. 427-430.

*0422 Kuney, J. H. "Publication and Distribution of Information," In: Annual Review of Information Science and Technology. Edited by C. A. Cuadra. Chicago, Encyclopaedia Britannica, 1968, Vol. 3, pp. 31-59. [The journal as a communication medium; Quality control; Journal format; Scientific meetings; Information exchange groups; Index and abstract preparation; Microform publication.]

*0423 Metzner, A. W. K. "Integrating Primary and Secondary Journals: A Model for the Immediate Future," In: IEEE Transactions on Professional Communication, PC 16(3): 84-91, 175-176, September, 1973. [American Institute of Physics; Current Physics Information Program.]

0424 Price, D. J. S. "Ethics of Scientific Publication," In: Science, 144(3619): 655-657, May 8, 1964. [Reward system; Freedom to publish.]

*0425 Price, D. J. S. "The Structures of Publication in Science and Technology," In: Factors in the Transfer of Technology. Edited by W. H. Gruber and D. G. Marquis. Cambridge, Mass., Massachusetts Institute of Technology Press, 1969, pp. 91-104. [Social organization; Invisible colleges; Models of communication; Role of publications; Interaction of science and technology.]

0426 Rowlett, R. J., Jr., F. A. Tate, and J. L. Wood. "Relationships between Primary Publications and Secondary Information Services," In: Journal of Chemical Documentation, 10(1): 32-37, February, 1970. [Chemical Abstracts Service; American Chemical Society; the Chemical Society (London); Trends in primary publication; Institutional cooperation.]

0427 Shank, R. Physical Science and Engineering Societies in the United States as Publishers, 1939-1964. D. L. S., New York, Columbia University, 1966, 447p. (University Microfilms, Inc., Order No. 67-5836)

0428 Shilling, C. W., et al. Scientific Literature for Newly Developing Countries. Washington, George Washington University, Biological Sciences Communication Project, BSCP-17-64, January, 1964, 24p. PB 170 721.

Bibliometric Analysis

0429 Brookes, B. C. "Bradford's Law and the Bibliography of Science," In: Nature, 224(5223): 953-956, December 6, 1969. [Applications; Zipf distribution; Theoretical problems.]

0430   Brookes, B. C. "The Complete Bradford-Zipf 'Bibliograph'," In: Journal of Documentation, 25(1): 58-60, March, 1969.

*0431   Brookes, B. C. "The Derivation and Application of the Bradford-Zipf Distribution," In: Journal of Documentation, 24(4): 247-265, December, 1968. [Historical review.]

0432   Brookes, B. C. "Library Zipf," In: Journal of Documentation, (Letter), 29(2): 155, June, 1969. [Library applications.]

0433   Buckland, M. K., and A. Hindle. "Library Zipf," In: Journal of Documentation, 25(1): 52-57, March, 1969. [Applications.]

0434   Buckland, M. K., and A. Hindle. "Library Zipf," In: Journal of Documentation, (Letter), 25(2): 154, June, 1969. [Applications.]

0435   Cawkell, A. E. "Citation Practices," In: Journal of Documentation, 24(4): 299-303, December, 1968. [Law of constant citation.]

*0436   Donohue, J. C. Understanding Scientific Literatures: A Bibliometric Approach. Cambridge, Mass., The MIT Press, 1973, 101p. [Bradford distribution; Citation tracing; Epidemic theory.]

0437   Douglas, I. A. "Science Libraries," In: Nature, (Letter), 239(5373): 477, October 20, 1972. [Bradford's law; Applications.]

*0438   Fairthorne, R. A. "Empirical Hyperbolic Distributions (Bradford-Zipf-Mandelbrot) for Bibliometric Description and Prediction," In: Journal of Documentation, 24(4): 319-343, December, 1969. [Lotka distribution.]

0439   Fairthorne, R. A. "Library Zipf," In: Journal of Documentation, (Letter), 25(2): 152-153, June, 1969. [Applications.]

0440   Goffman, W., and T. G. Morris. "Bradford's Law and Library Acquisitions," In: Nature, 226(5249): 922-923, June 6, 1970. [Applications.]

0441   Goffman, W., and V. A. Newill. "Communication and Epidemic Processes," In: Royal Society of London, Proceedings A, 298(5223: 316-334, 1967. [Diffusion of ideas; Mathematical models.]

0442   Goffman, W., and K. S. Warren. "Dispersion of Papers among Journals Based on a Mathematical Analysis of Two Diverse Medical Literatures," In: Nature, 221(5187): 1205-1207, March 19, 1969. [Schistosomiasis; Mast cell research.]

0443   Goffman, W. "An Epidemic Process in an Open Population," In: Nature, 205(4973): 831-832, February 20, 1965. [Diffusion of ideas; Mathematical models.]

0444   Goffman, W., and V. A. Newill. "Generalization of Epidemic Theory: An Application to the Transmission of Ideas," In: Nature, 204(4955): 225-228, October 17, 1964. [Mathematical models.]

0445   Goffman, W., and G. Harmon. "Mathematical Approach to the Prediction of Scientific Discovery," In: Nature, 229(5280): 103-104, January 8, 1971. [Symbolic logic; Mathematical models.]

0446   Goffman, W. "Mathematical Approach to the Spread of Scientific Ideas—The History of Mast Cell Research," In: Nature, 212(5061): 449-452, October 29, 1966. [Epidemic process.]

*0447   Goffman, W. Mathematical Foundations for Measuring Information Transfer and Flow, Final Report. Cleveland, Ohio, Case Western Reserve University, January, 1972, 9p. AD 736 536 or ED 068 138. [Diffusion of ideas; Epidemic theory; Symbolic logic.]

*0448   Goffman, W. "A Mathematical Model for Analyzing the Growth of a Scientific Discipline," In: Journal of the Association for Computing Machinery, 18(2): 173-185, April, 1971. [Epidemic theory; Symbolic logic; Diffusion of ideas.]

0449   Goffman, W. "Stability of Epidemic Processes," In: Nature, 210(5038): 786-787, May 21, 1966. [Diffusion of ideas; Mathematical models.]

*0450   Gomperts, M. C. "The Law of Constant Citation for Scientific Literature," In: Journal of Documentation, 24(2): 113-117, June, 1968. [Literature growth.]

0451   Groos, O. V. "Bradford's Law and the Keenan-Atherton Data," In: American Documentation, 18(1): 46, January, 1967. [Physics.]

0452   Krevitt, B., and B. C. Griffith. "A Comparison of Several Zipf-Type Distributions in Their Goodness of Fit to Language Data," In: American Society for Information Science Journal, 23(3): 220-221, May-June, 1972. [Log-linear distributions; Whitworth distribution; Hyperbolic distributions.]

0453   Lawani, S. M. "Bradford's Law and the Literature of Agriculture," In: International Library Review, 5(3): 341-350, July, 1973.

0454   Leimkuhler, F. F. "The Bradford Distribution," In: Journal of Documentation, 23(3): 197-207, September, 1967.

0455   Leimkuhler, F. F. The Distribution of References in Serials. Lafayette, Ind., Purdue University, September, 1966, 44p. PB 174 392. (Bradford distribution; Mathematical models.]

0456   Line, M. B., et. al. Patterns of Citations to Articles within Journals: A Preliminary Test of Scatter, Concentration, and Obsolescence. England, Bath University of Technology, University Library, October, 1972, 37p. ED 076 197. [Journal obsolescence.]

0457   Murphy, L. J. "Lotka's Law in the Humanities," In: American Society for Information Science Journal, 24(6): 461-462, November-December, 1973. [Lotka's law of productivity.]

0458   Naranan, S. "Bradford's Law of Bibliography of Science: An Interpretation," In: Nature, 227(5258): 631-632, August 8, 1970.

*0459   Naranan, S. "Power Law Relations in Science Bibliography—A Self-consistent Interpretation," In: Journal of Documentation, 27(2): 83-97, June, 1971. [Bradford's law; Mathematical derivation.]

0460   O'Neill, E. T. Journal Usage Patterns and Their Implications in the Planning of Library Systems. Ph.D. Dissertation, Lafayette, Ind., Purdue University, 1970, 419p. (University Microfilms, Inc., Order No. 70-18,704) [Bradford distribution; Yule distribution; Borle distribution; Fisher distribution.]

0461   O'Neill, E. T. "Limitations of the Bradford Distributions," In: Proceedings of the American Society for Information Science. Westport, Conn., Greenwood, 1973, Vol. 10, pp. 177-178. [Zipf distribution.]

*0462   Pritchard, A. "Statistical Bibliography or Bibliometrics?" In: Journal of Documentation, 25(4): 348-349, December, 1969. [Definitions.]

*0463   Saracevic, T., and L. J. Perk. "Ascertaining Activities in a Subject Area through Bibliometric Analysis," In: American Society for Information Science Journal, 24(2): 120-134, March-April, 1973. [Library science; Bradford distribution.]

0464   Schreider, Y. A. "Theoretical Derivation of Text Statistical Features (A Possible Proof of Zipf's Law)," In: Problems of Information Transmission, 3(1): 45-49, 1967.

0465   Smith, D. A. "Library Zipf," In: Journal of Documentation, (Letter), 25(2): 153-154, June, 1969. [Applications.]

0466   Wilkinson, E. A. "The Ambiguity of Bradford's Law," In: Journal of Documentation, 28(2): 122-130, June, 1972.

*0467   Worthen, D. B. "The Epidemic Process and the Contagion Model," In: American Society for Information Science Journal, 24(5): 343-346, September-October, 1973. [Diffusion of ideas; Goffman's epidemic theory; Menzel's contagion theory.]

Author Collaboration

0468   Chaison, G. N. "Changes in Authorship, Affiliation, and Research Support Patterns of *Journal of Applied Psychology* Articles," In: Journal of Applied Psychology, 55(5): 484-486, October, 1971.

0469   Clarke, B. L. "Communication Patterns of Biomedical Scientists: I. Multiple Authorship of Federation Program Volunteer Papers," In: Federation Proceedings, 26: 1288-1292, September-October, 1967.

*0470   Clarke, B. L. "Multiple Authorship Trends in Scientific Papers," In: Science, 143(3608): 822-824, February 21, 1964. [Biomedical sciences.]

*0471   Crane, D. Collaboration: Communication and Influence. A Study of the Effects of Formal and Informal Collaboration among Scientists. Baltimore, Johns Hopkins University, 1968.

0472   Guyer, L., and L. Fidell. "Publications of Men and Women Psychologists: Do Women Publish Less?" In: American Psychologist, 28(2): 157-160, February, 1973.

0473   Hirsch, W., and J. Singleton. Research Support, Multiple Authorship, and Publication in Sociological Journals, 1936-1964. Lafayette, Ind., Purdue University, 1964, 10p.

0474   Katzin, L. I. "Multiple Authorship: Other Interpretations," In: Science, (Letter), 144(3620): 798, May 15, 1964.

0475   Moscatelli, E. A. "Multiple Authorship: Other Interpretations," In: Science, (Letter), 144(3620): 798, May 15, 1964.

*0476   Over, R., and S. Smallman. "Maintenance of Individual Visibility in Publication of Collaborative Research by Psychologists," In: American Psychologist, 28(2): 161-166, February, 1973.

*0477   Price, D. J. S., and D. B. Beaver. "Collaboration in an Invisible College," In: American Psychologist, 21(11): 1011-1018, November, 1966.

0478   Schmid, R. "Multiple Authorship," In: Nature, (Letter), 229(5284): 436, February 5, 1971. [Weighting system for individual contributions.]

0479   Spiegel, D., and P. Keith-Spiegel. "Assignment of Publication Credits: Ethics and Practices of Psychologists," In: American Psychologist, 25(8): 738-747, August, 1970.

*0480   Zuckerman, H. "Nobel Laureates in Science: Patterns of Productivity, Collaboration, and Authorship," In: American Sociological Review, 32(3): 391-403, June, 1967.

Economics

0481   Andrade, C. A Report on the Page Charge Policies and Practices of 51 Primary Mathematics Journals. Providence, R. I., American Mathematical Society, December, 1968, NP68-1, 15p. PB 182 554.

*0482   American Mathematical Society. Report of Committee on Publication Costs. Providence, R. I., American Mathematical Society, 1970, 28p. PB 196 558. [Revenue sources; Mathematics; Statistical data; Periodical publishing.]

*0483   Baumol, W. J. A Cost Benefit Approach to Evaluation of Alternative Information Provision Procedures. Princeton, N. J., Mathematica, January, 1971.

*0484   Berg, S. V. "An Economic Analysis of the Demand for Scientific Journals," In: American Society for Information Science Journal, 23(1): 23-29, January-February, 1972. [Model of journal market; Pricing journals; Page charges; Journal demand.]

0485   Berg, S. V. "Increasing the Efficiency of the Economics Journal Market," In: Journal of Economic Literature, 9(3): 798-813, September, 1971. [Communication patterns of economists; Experimental program.]

0486   Berg, S. V. Structure, Behavior, and Performance in the Scientific Journal Market. Ph.D. Dissertation, New Haven, Conn., Yale University, 1970, 115p. (University Microfilms, Inc., Order No. 70-25,239) [Economics; Model of journal market; Pricing journals; Page charges; Journal demand.]

0487   Berg, S. V., D. Campion, and L. Okreglak. Toward a Model of Journal Economics in the Language Sciences. Washington, Center for Applied Linguistics, Language Information Network and Clearinghouse System,

1971, 31p. PB 206 498 [Model of journal market; Demand analysis; Supply analysis.]

0488   Bilboul, R. "The Economics of Concurrent Microfiche Editions of Published Periodicals," In: NRCD Bulletin, 3(1): 5-6, Winter, 1969/1970.

0489   Boffey, P. M. "Journals Fear Damaging Decline in Page Charge Revenues," In: Science, 162(3856): 884, November 22, 1968. [Federal support of research.]

0490   Bourne, C. P., J. B. North, and M. S. Kasson. Abstracting and Indexing Rates and Costs: A Literature Review. Washington, ERIC Clearinghouse for Library and Information Science, May, 1970, 9p. ED 043 798. [Publication costs; Secondary sources; Unit costs.]

0491   Crowder, T. "Scientific Publishing," In: Science, 144(3619): 633-637, May 8, 1964. [Publishing economics; Advertising revenue.]

*0492   Crum, J. K. "Financing a Multijournal System in the 1970's," In: IEEE Transactions on Professional Communication, PC 16(3): 71-72, 173, September, 1973. [Publishing economics; Revenue sources; Page charges; Advertising; Reprint sales; Back-issue sales; Subscriptions; Membership dues.]

0493   Culliton, B. J. "AMA: Specialty Journals Must Lure Paying Subscribers," In: Science, (News), 178(4065): 1070-1071, December 8, 1972.

*0494   George Washington University. Biological Sciences Communication Project. Scientific Journal Page Charge Practice. Washington, George Washington University, 1968, 269p. PB 180 089. [Historical review; Science; Social sciences; Technology.]

0495   Goudsmit, S. A. "Important Announcement: Page Charge Problem," In: Physical Review Letters, (Editorial), 21(18): 1301-1302, October 28, 1968. [Federal support of research.]

0496   Grundfest, H. "Page Charges and Tight Budgets," In: Science, (Letter), 164(3882): 905-906, May 23, 1969. [Federal support of research.]

*0497   Gushee, D. E. "Problems of the Primary Journal," In: Journal of Chemical Documentation, 10(1): 30-32, February, 1970. [American Chemical Society; Page charges; Advertising; Subsidy.]

0498   Hamelman, P. W., and E. M. Mazze. "Of Models and Scientific Markets," In: IEEE Transactions on Professional Communication, PC 16(3): 120-125, 177, September, 1973. [Economics journals; Citation analysis.]

0499   Hamelman, P. W., and E. M. Mazze. "Toward a Cost/Utility Model for
       Social Science Periodicals," In: Socio-Economic Planning Sciences,
       6(5): 465-475, October, 1972. [Citation analysis.]

0500   Harte, R. A. "Page Charge Practice Survey," In: CBE Newsletter, Sep-
       tember, 1969. [Biological sciences.]

*0501 Heilprin, L. B. Effects of Copyright and of Journal Economics on Com-
       munication in Science and Education. East Lansing, Mich., American
       Society for Engineering Education, 1967.

*0502 Herring, C., V. J. Danilov, and D. J. Hillman. Report of the Panel on
       Economics of the Science Information Council. Washington, National
       Science Foundation, February 9, 1973, 115p.

*0503 Herring, C. "A Study of Primary Journal Economics," In: Report of
       the Task Group on the Economics of Primary Publication. Washington,
       National Academy of Sciences–National Academy of Engineering,
       1970, pp. 26-250. PB 194 400. [Role of journals; Value of journals;
       Production costs; Sources of revenue; Page charges; Federal support.]

0504   Herwald, S. W. "Society Publications: Their Financial Problems," In:
       Engineering Societies and Their Literature Problems. New York, Engi-
       neers Joint Council, 1967, pp. 33-36.

0505   Industrial Research. "Publishing: Task Force Report Fans 'Page
       Charges' Dispute," In: Industrial Research, 12(10): 26, October, 1970.

*0506 King, D. W., and A. M. Brown. Some Comments on Marketing AIP Infor-
       mation Products and Services. Bethesda, Md., Westat Research Company,
       July, 1970, 79p. ED 046 447. [Cost demands; Price demands.]

*0507 Koch, H. W. Economics of Primary Journals in Physics. New York,
       American Institute of Physics, Information Division, AIP-ID-69-5,
       December, 1969, 27p. PB 190 490 or ED 038 990. [Publication costs;
       Page charges; Restructuring of primary journals.]

0508   Koch, H. W. "Publication Charges and Financial Solvency," In: Physics
       Today, 21(12): 126-127, 1968. [Page charges; Physics.]

0509   Kuney, J. H. "Impact of Microfilms on Journal Costs," In: IEEE Trans-
       actions on Professional Communication, PC 16(3): 80-81, 175, Septem-
       ber, 1973. [Page charges; Subscription prices; American Chemical
       Society.]

0510   Landau, H. B. "The Cost Analysis of Document Surrogation: A Litera-
       ture Review." In: American Documentation, 20(4): 302-310, October,
       1969. [Classification; Cataloging; Indexing; Abstracting.]

0511   Matarazzo, J. M. "Scientific Journals: Page or Price Explosion?" In: Special Libraries, 63(2): 53-58, February, 1972. [Physics; Page charges; Subscription prices.]

0512   Nature. "Page Charges for Scientific Journals," In: Nature, 202(4936): 956, June 6, 1964. [Royal Society of London.]

0513   Olsen, H. A. "The Economics of Information: Bibliography and Commentary on the Literature," In: Information, Part 2, 1(2): 31p., March-April, 1972.

0514   Paige, L. J., W. T. Martin, and A. Rosenberg. Means of Financing Mathematical Journals, Special Report. Providence, R. I., American Mathematical Society, 1964, 94p. PB 177 569. [Revenue sources; Page charges; Federal support of journals.]

0515   Patil, M. B., and G. J. Narayana. "Price Trends in Mathematical Journals," UNESCO Bulletin for Libraries, 27(3): 171-175, May-June, 1973.

0516   Physics Today. "Page Charges," In: Physics Today, (Letter), 22(7): 15-17, July, 1969.

0517   Prosser, R. T. "An Inquiry into the Problem of Page Charges," In: Notices of the American Mathematical Society, 15(3): 449-450, April, 1968. [Mathematics.]

*0518   Scal, M. "The Page Charge," In: Scholarly Publishing, 3(1): 62-69, October, 1971. [Historical review.]

0519   Sophar, G. J. "The Determination of Legal Facts and Economic Guideposts with Respect to the Dissemination of Scientific and Educational Information as It Is Affected by Copyright—A Status Report," In: American Documentation, 19(3): 317-321, July, 1968. (Also as PB 178 463 or ED 014 621)

0520   U.S. House of Representatives, 89th Congress, 1st Session, 1965. Committee to Investigate Copyright Problems Affecting Communication in Science and Education (CICP), Statement by H. A. Meyerhoff before House Committee on the Judiciary, Subcommittee #3, June 30, 1965.

0521   Woodford, F. P. "Inflexible Page Charges," In: Science, 168(3937): 1285-1286, June 12, 1970. [Microform editions.]

Literature Growth and Obsolescence

0522 Baker, D. B. "Communication or Chaos," In: Science, 169(3947): 739-742, August 21, 1970. [Chemical Abstracts Service; Secondary services; Primary literature.]

0523 Barr, K. P. "Estimates of the Number of Currently Available Scientific and Technical Periodicals," In: Journal of Documentation, 23(2), 110-116, June, 1967.

0524 Baughman, J. C. "Federal Aid and the Growth of a Subject Literature," In: American Society for Information Science Journal, (Brief Communication), 23(2): 129-130, March-April, 1972. [Education; *Education Index*; Elementary and Secondary Education Act of 1965.]

0525 Beck, L. N. "Soviet Discussion of the Exponential Growth of Scientific Publications," In: Proceedings of the American Society for Information Science. Washington, American Society for Information Science, 1970, Vol. 7, pp. 5-17. [Price's exponential growth model; Unified Lotka-Bradford- Zipf law.]

0526 Boutry, G. A. "Quantity versus Quality in Scientific Research (II): The Paper Explosion," In: Impact of Science on Society, 20: 195-206, 1970. [Physics.]

*0527 Brookes, B. C. "The Growth, Utility, and Obsolescence of Scientific Periodical Literature," In: Journal of Documentation, 26(4): 283-294, December, 1970.

*0528 Brookes, B. C. "Obsolescence of Special Library Periodicals: Sampling Errors and 'Utility Contours'," In: American Society for Information Science Journal, 21(5): 320-329, September-October, 1970. [Measuring obsolescence rates; Graphical applications.]

0529 Bryan, H. "The Explosion in Published Information—Myth or Reality," In: Australian Library Journal, 17(11): 389-401, December, 1968. [Factors favoring exponential growth.]

0530 Crane, D. "Fashion in Science: Does It Exist?" In: Social Problems, 16(4): 433-441, Spring, 1969.

*0531 Emrich, B. R. Scientific and Technical Information Explosion, Technical Report. Wright-Patterson Air Force Base, Ohio, Air Force Materials Laboratory, November, 1970, 35p. AD 717 654.

0532 Green, J. C. "The Information Explosion—Real or Imaginary." In: Science, 144(3619): 646-648, May 8, 1964.

0533   Krauze, T. K., and C. Hillinger. "Citation, References, and the Growth of Scientific Literature: A Model of Dynamic Interaction," In: American Society for Information Science Journal, 22(5): 333-336, September-October, 1971. [Mathematical model.]

0534   Licklider, J. C. R. "A Crux in Scientific and Technical Communication," In: American Psychologist, 21(11): 1044-1051, November, 1966. [Proposed systems for handling exponential growth.]

*0535   Line, M. B. "The 'Half-life' of Periodical Literature: Apparent and Real Obsolescence," In: Journal of Documentation, 26(1): 46-54, March, 1970.

*0536   London, G. "The Publication Inflation," In: American Society for Information Science Journal, 19(2): 137-141, April, 1968. [Multiple publication; Quality filters.]

0537   Lukasiewicz, J. "Ignorance Explosion—Contribution to Study of Confrontation of Man with Complexity of Science Based on Society and Environment," In: Transaction of the New York Academy of Science, 34(5): 373-391, May, 1972. [Obsolescence of information; Exponential growth.]

0538   MacRae, D., Jr. "Growth and Decay Curves in Scientific Citations," In: American Sociological Review, 34(5): 631-635, October, 1969. [Sociology.]

0539   Maddox, J. "Journals and the Literature Explosion," In: Nature, (Editorial), 221(5176): 128-130, January 11, 1969. [*Nature* editorial practices.]

0540   Mantell, L. H. "On Laws of Special Abilities and the Production of Scientific Literature," In: American Documentation, 17(1): 8-16, January, 1966. [Estimating literary productivity.]

0541   Newman, E. S. "Sorcerer's Apprentice Crisis," In: Science, 170(3960): 807-808, November 20, 1970. [Control of publication growth.]

*0542   Piganiol, P. "The Competitive Pressures (II): The Effects of 'Publish or Perish'," In: Impact of Science on Society, 21(2): 163-172, April-June, 1971. [Science.]

*0543   Sandison, A. "The Use of Older Literature and Its Obsolescence," In: Journal of Documentation, 27(3): 183-199, September, 1971.

0544   Scott, J. T. "The New Journals," In: Physics Today, 23(8): 54-55, August, 1970. [Growth of specialized journals.]

*0545   Searle, S. R. "The Publish-or-Perish Syndrome," In: IEEE Transactions on Professional Communication, PC 16(3): 136-139, 180, September, 1973. [Effects of 'publish-or-perish' on scientific community.]

0546   Shipman, J. "The Mounting Crisis in Primary Literature," In: Engineering Societies and Their Literature Programs. New York, Engineers Joint Council, 1967, pp. 25-28. [Journal effectiveness.]

0547   Storer, N. W. "The Literature of Science and the Publication Explosion," In: American Sociological Association Annual Meeting, Montreal, August, 1964.

0548   Urquhart, D. J. "Statistics of Scientific and Technical Articles," In: Journal of Documentation, (Letter), 25(1): 63-64, March, 1969.

0549   Vickery, B. C. "Statistics of Scientific and Technical Articles," In: Journal of Documentation, 24(3): 192-195, September, 1968.

*0550   Voos, H. "Information Explosion: Or Redundancy Reduces the Charge," In: College and Research Libraries, 32(1): 7-14, January, 1971. [Multiple publication.]

Microforms

0551   Baldwin, T. S., and L. J. Bailey. "Readability of Technical Training Materials Presented on Microfiche versus Offset Copy," In: Journal of Applied Psychology, 55(1): 37-41, February, 1971.

0552   Bovee, W. G. "Microform Publishing: Salvation for Short-Run Periodicals?" Paper presented at the Annual Meeting of the Association for Education in Journalism, 1973, 18p. ED 084 557.

*0553   Bovee, W. G. "Scientific and Technical Journals on Microfiche," In: IEEE Transactions on Professional Communication, PC 16(3): 113-116, 178, September, 1973. [Journal economics.]

0554   Christ, C. W., Jr. "Microfiche: A Study of User Attitudes and Reading Habits," In: American Society for Information Science Journal, 23(1): 30-35, January-February, 1972. [Technical reports.]

0555   Claridge, P. R. P. "Microfiching of Periodicals from the Users' Point of View," In: Aslib Proceedings, 21(8): 306-311, August, 1969.

0556   Currie, J. D. Microforms in DSIS—An Information Center's Experience
        with Microforms. Ottawa (Ontario), Canada, Defense Scientific Informa-
        tion Service, July, 1972, 28p. AD 749 274. [Microfiche.]

0557   Grausnick, R. K., and J. P. Kottenstette. A Performance Evaluation:
        Microfiche vs. Hardcopy, Final Report. Denver, Colo., Denver Univer-
        sity, Colorado Research Institute, May, 1971, 62p. ED 056 483.

0558   Kaback, S. M. "User Benefits from Secondary Journals on Microfilm,"
        In: Journal of Chemical Documentation, 10(1): 7-8, February, 1970.
        [Microfilm cartridge.]

0559   Kottenstette, J. P. "Student Reading Characteristics: Comparing Skill-
        Levels Demonstrated on Hardcopy and Microform Presentations," In:
        Proceedings of the American Society for Information Science. Westport,
        Conn., Greenwood, 1969, Vol. 6, pp. 345-352.

*0560   Kuney, J. H. "The Role of Microforms in Journal Publication," In: Jour-
        nal of Chemical Documentation, 12(2): 78-80, May, 1972. [American
        Chemical Society; Dual publication.]

0561   Lewis, R. W. "User's Reaction to Microfiche: A Preliminary Study." In:
        College & Research Libraries, 31(4): 260-268, July, 1970.

0562   Lyon, C. C. "Some Current Uses of Microform for Scientific and Tech-
        nical Research Information," In: NMA Journal, 2(4): 129-131, Summer,
        1969. [U.S. Naval Weapons Laboratory; Journals; Technical reports.]

0563   Morrison, A. B., ed. Conference on Microform Utilization: The Academic
        Library Environment. Denver, Colo., University of Denver, April, 1971,
        241p. ED 048 901.

0564   Resnick, A. "The 'Information Explosion' and the User's Need for Hard
        Copy," In: Proceedings of the American Documentation Institute.
        Washington, American Documentation Institute, 1964, Vol. 1, pp. 315-
        318. [IBM Selective Dissemination of Information System; Hardcopy
        accessibility.]

*0565   Spigai, F. G. The Invisible Medium: The State of the Art of Microform
        and a Guide to the Literature. Washington, ERIC Clearinghouse on
        Library and Information Science, March, 1973, 38p. ED 075 029.
        [Computer output microfilm; Libraries; Microfiche; Microfilm; Micro-
        form readers and printers.]

0566   Starker, L. N. "User Experience with Primary Journals on 16mm.
        Microfilm," In: Journal of Chemical Documentation, 10(1): 5-6,
        February, 1970. [Microfilm cartridge.]

0567 Swinburne, R. E., Jr. "Microfilmed Catalog Services," In: Journal of Chemical Documentation, 10(1): 17-20, February, 1970. [Trade catalogs; Microfilm cartridge; Bell Telephone Laboratory.]

0568 Teplitz, A. Microfiche for Technical Information Dissemination: A Cost-Benefit Analysis. Santa Monica, Calif., System Development Corp., December 2, 1968, 23p. PB 184 365. [Book microfiche.]

*0569 Texas A&M University. The Role of Micrographics in Modern Information Systems. College Station, Texas A&M University, June, 1969, 117p. PB 185 423. [Microtechnology in the research library; Microfilm in information centers; Legality of microfilm; Computer-micrographics interface.]

0570 Van Oot, J. G. "Patents and Patent Guides on Microforms," In: Journal of Chemical Documentation, 10(1): 9-13, February, 1970. [U.S. Patent Office.]

*0571 Veaner, A. B. "Micropublication," In: Advances in Librarianship. Edited by M. J. Voigt. New York, Seminar Press, 1971, Vol. 2, pp. 165-186. [History; Formats; User reactions; Cost; Future developments.]

0572 Vessey, H. F. The Use of Microfiche for Scientific and Technical Reports. Paris, France, North Atlantic Treaty Organization, Advisory Group for Aerospace Research and Development, August, 1970, 17p. AD 711 258 or N70-39851. [Microfiche standards; Economics of microfiche; User acceptance; Readers and printers.]

0573 Weil, B. H., et. al. "Esso Research Experiences with *Chemical Abstracts* on Microfilm," In: Journal of Chemical Documentation, 5: 193-200, 1965.

0574 Weil, B. H., and L. N. Starker. "Experiences, Problems, and Plans of Microfilm Users," In: Journal of Chemical Documentation, 10(1): 3-4, February, 1970. [Microfilm cartridge; Microfiche; Aperature cards.]

*0575 Wooster, H. "Microfiche 1969—A User Survey," In: Journal of Chemical Documentation, 10(1): 13-17, February, 1970. (Also as AD 695 049) [Department of Defense libraries; Impact of DDC user charge; Government libraries; Microfiche quality and format; Microfiche readers and printers.]

Primary Sources

Journals—Manuscript Processing

*0576   Axelby, G. S. "Problems and Procedures in Editing a Professional Technical Journal," In: IEEE Transactions on Professional Communication, PC 16(3): 54-56, September, 1973.

0577   Bondi, A. "Design of Papers for Error Minimization," In: Journal of Chemical Documentation, 9(9): 7-10, February, 1969. [Error detection; Error prevention; Paper format; Chemistry.]

*0578   Bowen, D. D., R. Perloff, and J. Jacoby. "Improving Manuscript Evaluation Procedures," In: American Psychologist, 27(3): 221-225, March, 1972. [Psychology; Multiple reviews; Review appeal procedures; Anonymity of referees.]

0579   Brackbill, Y., and F. Korten. "Journal Reviewing Practices: Authors' and APA Members' Suggestions for Revision," In: American Psychologist, 25(10): 937-940, October, 1970. [American Psychological Association; Psychology.]

0580   Branscomb, L. M. "The Misinformation Explosion: Is the Literature Worth Reviewing?" In: Scientific Research, 3(11): 49-55, 1968. [Literature growth; Quality control.]

0581   Chambers, J. M., and A. M. Herzberg. "A Note on the Game of Refereeing," In: Applied Statistics, 17(3): 260-263, 1968.

0582   Chase, J. M. "Normative Criteria for Scientific Publication," In: The American Sociologist, 5(3): 262-264, August, 1970. [Manuscript evaluation; Social sciences; Natural sciences.]

0583   Coe, R. K., and I. Weinstock. "Editorial Policies of Major Economic Journals," In: Quarterly Review of Economics and Business, 7(4): 37-43, Winter, 1967.

*0584   Crane, D. "The Gatekeepers of Science: Some Factors Affecting the Selection of Articles for Scientific Journals," In: The American Sociologist, 2(4): 195-201, November, 1967. [Anonymity of referees; Academic characteristics of authors and editors.]

*0585   Culliton, B. J. "Dual Publication: 'Ingelfinger Rule' Debated by Scientists and Press," In: Science, 176(4042): 1403-1405, June 30, 1972. [Medical news media; Press releases of medical advances.]

0586 Cummings, M. M. "Publication—Progress or Pollution?" In: American Scientist, 61: 163-166, March-April, 1973. [Literature growth; Quality control.]

*0587 Dahlberg, I. A., and C. W. Petersen. "Predocumentation—Easier Information," In: Proceedings of the American Society for Information Science. New York, Greenwood, 1968, Vol. 5, pp. 21-23. [Primary literature; Author abstracts.]

0588 D'Aprix, R. M. "Quality Control for Engineering Authorship," In: IEEE Transactions on Engineering Writing and Speech, 8(1): 15-17, June, 1965. [Editorial services of employers.]

0589 Deacon, B., and D. Hamilton. "The Editor's Role in the Survival of the Broad Technical Journal," In: IEEE Transactions on Professional Communication, PC 16(3): 60-63, September, 1973.

0590 Evans, W. H., and D. Garrin. "The Evaluator versus the Chemical Literature," In: Journal of Chemical Documentation, 10(3): 147-150, August, 1970. [Quantitative data; Quality control; Editing.]

*0591 Falk, H., and H. E. Tompkin. "Author-Assisted Indexing," In: Proceedings of the American Society for Information Science. Washington, American Society for Information Science, 1970, Vol. 7, pp. 283-290. [Predocumentation.]

0592 Forscher, B. K. "Rules for Referees," In: Science, 150(3694): 319-321, October 15, 1965. [Purpose of scientific journals; Role of journal editors; Rules for referees; Use of referee's report.]

0593 Frechette, V. D., and R. H. Condit. "A Rationale Scale of Critical Editorial Evaluation," In: Physics Today, 20(6): 53, June, 1967. [Humorous look at process of manuscript evaluation.]

0594 Gassman, M., D. Penney, and M. A. Q. Khan. "Publication Delay," In: Nature, (Letter), 237(5349): 58, May 5, 1972. [Recommendations for reducing delays.]

0595 Goudsmit, S. A. "What Happened to My Paper," In: Physics Today, 22(5): 23-27, May, 1969.

0596 Grossman, J. A. "Time Lag in the Flow of Scientific Information: A Case Study of Thomas Henry Huxley, His Life and His Writings," In: Special Libraries, 60(5): 278-284, May-June, 1969.

0597 Holroyd, G. "On the Sociology of Knowledge," In: Journal of Librarianship, 4(1): 48-56, January, 1972. [Referees; Technological gatekeepers.]

0598   Hunt, F. H. Some Views on Dual Publication. Report. East Coast Navy
        Interlaboratory Committee on Editing and Publishing, October 1, 1968,
        Monograph-5, 1968, 9p.

0599   Information Management, Inc. Survey of the Use of Source Abstracts
        and Source Index Terms in a Selected Group of Engineering Journals,
        Final Report. Burlington, Mass., Information Management, Inc., May 21,
        1968, 71p. PB 179 048.

0600   Jain, T. C., and S. P. Goyal. "A Study of the Time-Lag in the Publication
        of Research Papers in Some Selected Periodicals in Agriculture and
        Allied Sciences," In: Annals of Library Science and Documentation,
        16(1): 11-14, January, 1969.

*0601   Journal of Chemical Documentation. "Symposium on Error Control in
        the Chemical Literature," In: Journal of Chemical Documentation,
        6(3): 125-142, August, 1966. [Error prevention; Error detection; Error
        control and elimination; Error effects.]

0602   Kochen, M. "Quality Control in the Publishing Process and Theoretical
        Foundations for Information Retrieval," In: Integrative Mechanisms in
        Literature Growth. Edited by M. Kochen. Ann Arbor, Mich., University
        of Michigan, Mental Health Research Institute, January, 1970,
        pp. V/45-V/107. [Referee system.]

0603   Layton, E. "Editor-Author Relationships: Both Can Win," In: IEEE
        Transactions on Professional Communication, PC 16(3): 57-59, 172,
        September, 1973.

0604   McCrea, W. H. "Refereeing and Editing," In: Nature, (Letter), 239(5369):
        239-240, September 22, 1972.

0605   McReynolds, P. "Reliability of Ratings of Research Papers," In: Ameri-
        can Psychologist, 26(4): 400-401, April, 1971. [Psychology; Manuscript
        evaluation.]

0606   Michaelson, M. B. "Achieving a More Disciplined R&D Literature," In:
        Journal of Chemical Documentation, 8(4): 198-201, November, 1968.
        [Quality control; Paper format.]

0607   Nature. "Who Will Referee the Referees?" In: Nature, (Editorial),
        230(5288): 3, March 5, 1971.

0608   Neufeld, J. "To Amend Refereeing," In: Physics Today, 23(4): 9-10,
        1970.

0609   Newman, S. H. "Improving the Evaluation of Submitted Manuscripts,"
         In: American Psychologist, 21(10): 980-981, October, 1966.
         [Psychology.]

0610   Pao, M. A General Method to Establish Quality Filtering Systems for
         Biomedical Literatures. Ph.D. Dissertation. Cleveland, Ohio, Case West-
         ern University, 1972. (University Microfilms, Inc., Order No. 73-6329)
         [Citation analysis; Source books; Tertiary sources.]

0611   Parlee, M. B. "On Manuscript Evaluation Procedures," In: American
         Psychologist, 27(12): 1193-1194, December, 1972. [Psychology.]

0612   Patterson, C. H. "Evaluation of Manuscripts Submitted for Publication,"
         In: American Psychologist, 24(1): 73, January, 1969. [Psychology.]

0613   Pings, C. J. "Publication Delays in the Chemical Engineering Literature,"
         In: Journal of Chemical Documentation, 7(3): 179-181, August, 1967.

0614   Rodman, H. "The Moral Responsibility of Journal Editors and Referees,"
         In: American Sociologist, 5(4): 351-357, November, 1970. [Problems
         in the delay of evaluation of manuscripts.]

0615   Rodman, H. "Notes to an Incoming Journal Editor," In: American Psy-
         chologist, 25(3): 269-273, March, 1970. [Psychology; Manuscript
         evaluation.]

0616   Ryan, M., and J. W. Tankard, Jr. "Problem Areas in Science News
         Reporting, Writing, and Editing," Paper Presented at the Annual Meet-
         ing of the Association for Education in Journalism, August, 1973, 39p.
         ED 083 622.

0617   Sanford, F. B. Use of Abstracts and Summaries as Communication
         Devices in Technical Articles. Seattle, Wash., Bureau of Commercial
         Fisheries, Division of Publications, February, 1971, 16p. COM-71-00643.

0618   Schaeffer, D. L. "Do APA Journals Play Professional Favorites," In:
         American Psychologist, 25(4): 362-365, April, 1970. [Psychology;
         Manuscript evaluation.]

0619   Shephard, D. A. E. "Some Effects of Delay in Publication of Informa-
         tion in Medical Journals, and Implications for the Future," In: IEEE
         Transactions on Professional Communication, PC 16(3): 143-147,
         181-182, September, 1973.

0620   Thompson, C. W. N. "A Systems Approach to the Management of
         Scientific Journals," In: IEEE Transactions on Professional Communi-
         cation, PC 16(3): 148-155, 182, September, 1973.

0621 Whetsel, H. B. Guidelines for Reviewers and the Editors at the Nuclear Safety Information Center, Oak Ridge, Tenn. Oak Ridge National Laboratory, Nuclear Safety Information Center, January, 1970, 162p. ED 052 803 or ORNL-NSIC-17.

*0622 Wolff, W. M. "Publication Problems in Psychology and an Explicit Evaluation Schema for Manuscripts," In: American Psychologist, 28(3): 257-261, March, 1973.

0623 Wolff, W. M. "A Study of Criteria for Journal Manuscripts," In: American Psychologist, 25(7): 636-639, July, 1970. [Psychology.]

*0624 Zuckerman, H., and R. K. Merton. "Patterns of Evaluation in Science: Institutionalisation, Structure, and Functions of the Referee System," In: Minerva, 9(1): 66-100, January, 1971.

*0625 Zuckerman, H., and R. K. Merton. "Sociology of Refereeing," In: Physics Today, 24(7): 28-33, July, 1971. [*Physical Review* system; Physics.]

Journals—Role and Development

0626 Abelson, P. H. "The Coming Evolution of Scientific Journals," In: IEEE Transactions on Professional Communication, PC 16(3): 69-70, September, 1973. [Journal economics.]

*0627 Bowen, D. H. M. "The Role of Technical Magazine/Journal Hybrids," In: IEEE Transactions on Professional Communication, PC 16(3): 66-67, September, 1973. [Journal economics; Revenue sources.]

*0628 Brown, W. S., J. R. Pierce, and J. F. Traub. "The Future of Scientific Journals," In: Science, 158(3805): 1153-1159, December 1, 1967. [Selective distribution of articles; Preprint exchanges; Problems of journals.]

0629 Coats, A. W. "The Role of Scholarly Journals in the History of Economics: An Essay," In: Journal of Economic Literature, 9(1): 29-44, March, 1971.

0630 Conrad, M. "Changing Patterns of Scientific Periodical Publications," In: Bacteriological Reviews, 29: 523-533, 1965.

0631 Finniston, H. M. "The Future of the Journals," In: Nature, 214(5083): 47-48, April 1, 1967. [Institute of Metals.]

0632   Fox, T. Crisis in Communication: The Functions and Future of Medical Journals. London, England, University of London, The Athlone Press, 1965, 59p.

0633   Freeman, M. E. "Multidisciplinary Information Sources," In: Journal of Chemical Documentation, 12(2): 94-96, May, 1972.

*0634   Herschman, A. "The Primary Journal: Past, Present, and Future," In: Journal of Chemical Documentation, 10(1): 37-42, February, 1970. [Primary journal as a social institution; Primary journal as a communication medium.]

0635   Kenyon, R. "The Future of Primary Publications," In: Report given at a session on Primary Publications at a Meeting of Managing Officers of Scientific Societies, at the ACS Headquarters, Washington, October 31, 1969. [Chemistry.]

*0636   King, D. W., and N. W. Caldwell. "Alternatives to the Journal System of Transferring Scientific and Technical Information." In: Innovations in Communications Conference, April 9-10, 1970. Bethesda, Md., Westat, April, 1970, pp. 21-35. PB 192 294. [Archival role; Communication role; Social role.]

*0637   Koch, H. W. "Role of the Primary Journal in Physics," In: Symposium on the Handling of Nuclear Information. Vienna, International Atomic Energy Agency, 1970, pp. 321-334. (Also as PB 190 267 or ED 038 989) [Journal economics; Revenue sources; Page charges; Literature growth; Astronomy; Changing patterns of communication.]

*0638   Kuney, J. H. "New Developments in Primary Journal Publication," In: Journal of Chemical Documentation, 10(1): 42-46, February, 1970. [Selective distribution of articles; Microfilm publication.]

*0639   Lancaster, F. W., and A. M. Brown. Conceptual Alternatives to the Scientific Journal: Study Conducted for the American Geological Institute. Washington, Westat Research, August, 1969, 118p.

0640   Leake, C. D. "Primary Journals: Questionable Progress and Present Problems," In: Journal of Chemical Documentation, 10(1): 27-29, February, 1970.

0641   Lowe, M. C. "The Future Role of the Technical Journal," In: Electronics and Power, 18(12): 457-459, December, 1972.

0642   Marcott, C. M. "The Changing State-of-the-Art in Trade Magazines," In: IEEE Transactions on Engineering Writing and Speech, 7(3): 23-24, December, 1964.

0643   Maxwell, R. "Survival Values in Technical Journals," In: IEEE Transactions on Professional Communication, PC 16(3): 64-65, September, 1973.

0644   Pasternak, S. "Is Journal Publication Obsolescent?" In: Physics Today, 19(5): 38-43, May, 1966. [Informal communication; Preprint exchanges.]

0645   Porter, J. R. "The Scientific Journal: 300th Anniversary," In: Bacteriological Review, 28: 211-230, 1964.

0646   Rossmassler, S. A. "Modification of Dissemination Channels for Scientific Information," In: Journal of Chemical Documentation, 9(1): 17-19, February, 1969.

0647   Smailes, A. A. "The Future of Scientific and Technological Publications," In: Aslib Proceedings, 22(2): 48-54, February, 1970.

*0648   Swanson, D. R. "Scientific Journals and Information Services of the Future," In: American Psychologist, 21(11): 1005-1010, November, 1966.

*0649   Terrant, S. W. "Problems Related to Journal Subject Coverage, Formats, and Packaging," In: IEEE Transactions on Professional Communication, PC 16(3): 68, 173-174, September, 1973. [Journal economics; Subject coverage; Format patterns; Packaging.]

*0650   UNESCO. Primary Scientific Publication. Paris, France, United Nations Educational, Scientific, and Cultural Organization, 1967, 106p. [Manufacturing, distribution and processing of primary publications; Growth of primary publications.]

0651   Vlachy, J. "Physics Journals in Retrospect and Comparisons," In: Czechoslovak Journal of Physics, 20: 501-526, 1970.

0652   Vickery, B. C., and D. J. Simpson. "Future of Scientific Communication," In: Science Journal, 2(7): 80-85, 1966.

0653   Wolff, M. E. "Primary Transmission of Specific Information—Today and Tomorrow," In: Journal of Chemical Documentation, 11(3): 137-138, August, 1971. (Also as ED 049 782) [Medicinal chemistry.]

Technical Reports

*0654   American Psychological Association. "The Role of the Technical Report in the Dissemination of Scientific Information," In: APA's Project on Scientific Information Exchange in Psychology. Washington, American Psychological Association, Report 13, December, 1965, Vol. 3, pp. 181-234. PB 169 005. [Comparison of technical reports with journal articles; Relationship of technical reports to other means of information exchange.]

*0655   Brearley, N. "The Role of Technical Reports in Scientific and Technical Communication," In: IEEE Transactions on Professional Communication, PC 16(3): 117-119, September, 1973. [Relationship of technical reports to primary journals; Publication standards.]

0656   Chadbourne, H. L. Titling Technical Reports for Optimum Use and Retrieval. Corona, Calif., Interlaboratory Committee on Editing and Publishing, August, 1965, 16p. AD 624 058.

0657   Defense Documentation Center. Abstracting Scientific and Technical Reports on Defense-Sponsored RDT/E. Alexandria, Va., Defense Documentation Center, March, 1968, 19p. AD 667 000.

0658   Fuccillo, D. A., ed. The Technical Report in the Biomedical Literature: A Workshop. Bethesda, Md., National Institutes of Health, 1967.

0659   Nature. "Do Technical Reports Belong in the Literature?" In: Nature, 236(5345): 275, April 7, 1972. [Nature of communication role of technical reports.]

0660   Nature. "The Shadow Literature," In: Nature, 222(5188): 39-40, April 5, 1969. [Review of British standard for research and development reports.]

0661   Nature. "Standard Literature," In: Nature, 237(5354): 301-302, June 9, 1972.

0662   Ronco, P. G., et al. Characteristics of Technical Reports That Affect Reader Behavior: A Review of the Literature. Medford, Mass., Tufts University, Institute for Psychological Research, 1964, 196p. PB 169 409.

0663   U.S. Congress. House of Representatives, 88th Congress, 2nd Session. Select Committee on Government Research, Documentation and Dissemination of Research and Development Reports. Washington, Government Printing Office, 1964.

0664   U.S. Federal Council for Science and Technology. Committee on Scientific and Technical Information. Guidelines to Format Standard for Scientific and Technical Reports Prepared by or for the Federal Government. Washington, Committee on Scientific and Technical Information, December, 1968, 18p. PB 180 600.

*0665   U.S. Federal Council for Science and Technology. Committee on Scientific and Technical Information. The Role of the Technical Report in Scientific and Technological Communication. Washington, Committee on Scientific and Technical Information, December, 1968, 112p. PB 180 944. [Problems of dual publication; Taxonomy of technical report literature; Relationship of technical reports to primary journals.]

Secondary Sources

Abstracting and Indexing Journals

*0666   Adams, S., and D. B. Baker. "Mission and Discipline Orientation in Scientific Abstracting and Indexing Services," In: Library Trends, 16(3): 307-322, January, 1968.

0667   American Psychological Association. "A Study of *Psychological Abstracts:* Some Findings on Its Current Functions and Operation and a Proposed Plan for Innovation," In: APA's Project on Scientific Information Exchange in Psychology. Washington, American Psychological Association, APA-PSIEP Report 15, December, 1965, Vol. 2, pp. 260-292.

0668   Andry, R. G. "Existing Documentation Services in Criminology—and Future Needs," In: Aslib Proceedings, 17(2): 50-59, February, 1965.

0669   Bourne, C. P. Characteristics of Coverage by the Bibliography of Agriculture of the Literature Relating to Agricultural Research and Development. Palo Alto, Calif., Information General Corp., June, 1969, 79p. PB 185 425.

0670   Bourne, C. P. Overlapping Coverage of Bibliography of Agriculture by 15 Other Secondary Services. Palo Alto, Calif., Information General Corp., June, 1969, 94p. PB 185 069.

0671   Bourne, C. P. Study and Comparison of the Indexing of the Bibliography of Agriculture in Relation to the Indexing of 15 Other Secondary

Services. Palo Alto, Calif., Information General Corp., June, 1969, 108p. PB 188 524.

0672 Caponio, J. F., J. K. Penry, and D. J. Goode. "Epilipsy Abstracts: Its Role in Dissemination of Scientific Information," In: Bulletin of the Medical Library Association, 58(1): 37-43, January, 1970.

0673 Carroll, K. H. "An Analytical Survey of Virology Literature Reported in Two Announcement Journals," In: American Documentation, 20(3): 234-237, July, 1969. [*Biological Abstracts; BioResearch Index.*]

0674 Coates, E. J. "*British Technology Index,*" In: Encyclopedia of Library and Information Science. New York, Dekker, 1970, Vol. 3, pp. 327-341.

*0675 Cooper, M., and E. Terry. Secondary Services in Physics. New York, American Institute of Physics, Information Division, October, 1969, 45p. ID-69-2. PB 191 119 or ED 038 999. [National Physics Information System; Characteristics of secondary services.]

0676 Flanagan, C. M. "Coordination—A Detailed Review of the Relationships between the Publications and Services of BIOSIS, CAS and EI," In: Journal of Chemical Documentation, 13(2): 57-59, May, 1973. [Overlap; Editorial policies; Operational processes; BioScience Information Service of Biological Abstracts; Chemical Abstracts Service; Engineering Index, Inc.]

0677 Gilchrist, A. "Documentation of Documentation: A Survey of Leading Abstracts Services in Documentation and an Identification of Key Journals," In: Aslib Proceedings, 18(3): 62-80, March, 1966. [Library science; Information science; Coverage; Publication delay; Most frequently cited titles.]

0678 Gilchrist, A., and A. Presanis. "*Library and Information Science Abstracts*: The First Two Years," In: Aslib Proceedings, 23(5): 251-256, April, 1971.

0679 Grandbois, M."The *Nursing Literature Index*: Its History, Present Needs, and Future Plans," In: Bulletin of the Medical Library Association, 52(4): 676-683, October, 1964.

0680 Greer, R. C., and P. Atherton. Study of Nuclear Science Abstracts and Physics Abstracts Coverage of Physics Journals, 1964-1965. New York, American Institute of Physics, 1966, AIP/DRP 66-11.

*0681 Hall, A. M. User Preferences in Printed Indexes. London, Institution of Electrical Engineers, 1972, 97p. ED 071 708.

0682   Helmuth, N. A. The Use of Extracts in Information Services. Washington, ERIC Clearinghouse on Library and Information Science, 1971, 24p. ED 058 883.

0683   Jacobus, D. P., et al. "Direct User Access to the Biological Literature through Abstracts: A Cooperative Experiment in Customized Service," In: BioScience, 16(9): 599-603, September, 1966. [Project Expert; Abstract search service; Current awareness service.]

0684   Karel, L. "Selection of Journals for *Index Medicus*: A Historical Review," In: Bulletin of the Medical Library Association, 55: 259-278, 1967.

*0685   Keenan, S. "Abstracting and Indexing Services in Science and Technology," In: Annual Review of Information Science and Technology. Edited by C. A. Cuadra. Chicago, Encyclopaedia Britannica, 1969, Vol. 4, pp. 273-303. [Economics; Standardization; Product innovations.]

0686   Keenan, S., and F. G. Brickwedde. Journal Literature Coverage by Physics Abstracts in 1965. New York, American Institute of Physics, Information Division, ID-68-1, February, 1968, 126p. PB 178 211. [Journal, subject and country coverage of *Physics Abstracts*; Profile of physics journal literature.]

0687   Kiehlmann, E. "Journal Coverage by the Major Chemical Title and Abstracting Publications," In: Journal of Chemical Documentation, 12(3): 157-163, August, 1972. [*Chemical Titles*; *Current Contents*; *Science Citation Index*; *Chemischer Informationsdienst*; *Index Chemicus.*]

*0688   Klempner, I. M. Diffusion of Abstracting and Indexing Services for Government-Sponsored Research, Final Report. New York, Columbia University, 1968, 336p. AD 666 091. (Hardcopy available from Scarecrow Press, Metuchen, N.J.)

0689   Koehler, H. "The Development of *Oral Research Abstracts*, A Comprehensive Abstracting Service for Dental Researchers," In: Proceedings of the American Documentation Institute. Washington, Thompson, 1967, Vol. 4, pp. 213-217.

*0690   Library Trends. "Science Abstracting Services—Commercial, Institutional and Personal," In: Library Trends, 16(3): 303-418, January, 1968. [National Federation of Science Abstracting and Indexing Services; Physical sciences; Biological sciences; *Science Citation Index.*]

0691   Martyn, J., and M. Slater. "Tests on Abstracts Journals," In: Journal of Documentation, 20(4): 212-235, December, 1964. [*Chemical Abstracts*; *International Abstracts of Biological Sciences*; *Analytical Abstracts*; *Index Medicus*; *Biological Abstracts*; *Journal of Applied Chemistry.*]

0692   Martyn, J. "Tests on Abstract Journals: Coverage Overlap and Indexing," In: Journal of Documentation, 23(1): 45-70, March, 1967.

0693   Montgomery, R. R. "An Indexing Coverage Study of Toxicology Literature," In: Journal of Chemical Documentation, 13(1): 41-44, February, 1973. [*Chemical Abstracts*; *Biological Abstracts*; *Index Medicus*; *Science Citation Index*.]

*0694   Parkins, P. V., and H. E. Kennedy. "Secondary Information Services," In: Annual Review of Information Science and Technology. Edited by C. A. Cuadra. Chicago, Encyclopaedia Britannica, 1971, Vol. 6, pp. 247-275. [Economics; Product innovations; Standardization; Coordination.]

0695   Ring, M. E. "Fifty Years of the *Index to Dental Literature*; A Critical Appraisal," In: Bulletin of the Medical Library Association, 59(3): 463-478, July, 1971.

0696   Seigmann, P. J., and B. C. Griffith. "The Changing Role of *Psychological Abstracts* in Scientific Communication," In: American Psychologist, 21(11): 1037-1043, November, 1966.

0697   Shannon, R. L. "*Nuclear Science Abstracts*: A 21-Year Perspective," In: Symposium on the Handling of Nuclear Information. Vienna, International Atomic Energy Agency, 1970, pp. 379-384.

0698   Smith, J. R., and H. East. "Information Services in Physics," In: Communication in Science: Documentation and Automation. Edited by A. DeReuck and J. Knight. Boston, Little, Brown and Co., 1967, pp. 134-146.

0699   Somerville, B. F. "Abstract Journal Concept Being Examined," In: Chemical and Engineering News, 50(24): 16-17, June 12, 1972.

0700   Swift, D. F., et al. Investigation into Sociology of Education Abstracts: Vol. 1, Report of First Stage of Project. London, England, Office for Scientific and Technical Information, August, 1970, 276p. ED 054 780.

*0701   System Development Corporation. A System Study of Abstracting and Indexing in the United States. Washington, National Technical Information Services, December 16, 1966. PB 174 249. [Abstract and index production; Requirements for a national system; Document representation alternatives; Organizational alternatives; Bibliographic and descriptive format.]

0702   Thorpe, P. "An Evaluation of the Rheumatology Coverage of *Index Medicus*: A Preliminary Report," In: American Society for Information Science Journal, (Letter), 23(6): 406, November-December, 1972.

0703   Urquhart, D. J. "Physics Abstracting—Use and Users," In: Journal of Documentation, 21(2): 113-120, June, 1965.

0704   Whatley, H. A. A Survey of the Major Indexing and Abstracting Services for Library Science and Documentation. London, Library Association, 1966.

0705   Wilkinson, D., and S. Hollander. "A Comparison of Drug Literature Coverage by *Index Medicus* and *Drug Literature Index*," In: Bulletin of the Medical Library Association, 61(4): 431-432, October, 1973.

0706   Wood, J. L., C. M. Flanagan, and H. E. Kennedy. "Overlap in the Lists of Journals Monitored by BIOSIS, CAS, and EI," In: American Society for Information Science Journal, 23(1): 36-38, January-February, 1972. [BioScience Information Service; Chemical Abstracts Service; Engineering Index, Inc.]

Citation and Title Derivative Indexes

0707   Adams, W. M. "Relationship of Keywords in Titles to References Cited," In: American Documentation, 18(1): 26-32, January, 1967. [Objectives of an index; Search procedures; Linear programming.]

0708   Adams, W. M., and L. C. Lockley. "Scientists Meet the KWIC Index," In: American Documentation, 19(1): 47-59, January, 1968. (Also as PB 168 682) [*Seismological Society of America Bulletin*; Attitude survey; Seismologists; Effectiveness of KWIC indexes.]

0709   Bottle, R. T. "The Information Content of Titles in Engineering Literature," In: IEEE Transactions on Engineering Writing and Speech, 13(2): 41-45, September, 1970. [Title derivative indexing.]

0710   Bottle, R. T., and C. R. Seeley. "Information Transfer Limitations of Titles of Chemical Documents," In: Journal of Chemical Documentation, 10(4): 256-259, November, 1970. [Primary journals; Patents; Technical reports.]

0711   Bottle, R. T., and C. I. Preibish. "The Proposed KWIC Index for Psychology: An Experimental Test of Its Effectiveness," In: American Society for Information Science Journal, 21(6): 417-428, November-December, 1970.

0712   Bottle, R. T. "Title Indexes as Alerting Services in the Chemical and Life Sciences," In: American Society for Information Science Journal,

21(1): 16-21, January-February, 1970. [*Current Contents*; *Current Chemical Papers*; *Chemical Titles*; Problems of nomenclature.]

0713 Brodie, N. E. "Evaluation of a KWIC Index for *Library Literature*," In: American Society for Information Science Journal, 21(1): 22-28, January-February, 1970.

0714 Chonez, N. "Premuted Title or Key-Phrase Indexes and the Limiting of Documentalist Work Needs," In: Information Storage and Retrieval, 4: 161-166, June, 1968.

*0715 Feinberg, H. Title Derivative Indexing Techniques: A Comparative Study. Metuchen, N.J., Scarecrow, 1973, 307p. [Index evaluation; Permuted title indexes; KWIC indexes; KWOC indexes; Scattering of information; Innovations.]

*0716 Fischer, M. "The KWIC Index Concept: A Retrospective View," In: American Documentation, 17(2): 57-70, April, 1966.

0717 Flury, W. R., and D. Henderson. "A User Oriented KWIC Index: KWOC-ed, Tagged and Enriched," In: Proceedings of the American Society for Information Science. Washington, American Society for Information Science, 1970, Vol. 7, pp. 101-103.

0718 Garfield, E. "Citation Indexing: A Natural Science Literature Retrieval System for the Social Sciences," In: American Behavioral Scientist, 7(10):59-61, June, 1964.

0719 Garfield, E. "Communication, Engineering, and Engineers," In: IEEE Transactions on Professional Communications, PC 15(2): 49-51, June, 1972. [Citation indexing; *Current Contents*; *Science Citation Index*.]

0720 Garfield, E. "Methods and Objectives in Judging the Information Content of Document Titles," In: Journal of Chemical Documentation, 10: 260, November, 1970.

0721 Garfield, E. "*Science Citation Index*—A New Dimension in Indexing," In: Science, 144(3619): 649-654, May 8, 1964.

0722 Helbich, J. "Direct Selection of Keywords for the KWIC Index," In: Information Storage and Retrieval, 5: 123-128, 1969.

0723 Hines, T. C., and J. L. Harris. "Permuted Title Indexes: Neglected Considerations," In: American Society for Information Science Journal, 21(5): 369-370, September-October, 1970. [Human processing; Index structure.]

*0724   Hodges, T. L. Forward Citation Indexing: Its Potential for Bibliographic Control. Ph.D. Dissertation, Berkeley, Calif., University of California, 1972, 664p. (University Microfilms, Inc., Order No. 73-16,787)

*0725   Huang, T. S. Efficiency of Citation Indexing. Ph.D. Dissertation, New Brunswick, N.J., Rutgers University, 1967, 279p. (University Microfilms, Inc., Order No. 67-14,718)

0726   Jahoda, G., and M. L. Stursa. "A Comparison of a Keyword from Title Index with a Single Access Point per Document Alphabetic Subject Index," In: American Documentation, 20(4): 377-380, October, 1969. [Chemistry; Effectiveness of KWIC indexes.]

0727   Janda, K. "Keyword Indexes for the Behavioral Sciences," In: The American Behavioral Scientist, 7: 55-58, June, 1964.

0728   Juhasz, S., et al. AKWIC: Author and Key Word in Context. San Antonio, Texas, Applied Mechanics Reviews, August, 1969, 10p. PB 185 294.

0729   Kemp, D. A., et al. "Indexing—Permuted, Rotated, or Cycled," In: Journal of Documentation, 28: 67-68, March, 1972.

0730   Kaplan, N. "The Norms of Citation Behavior: Prolegomena to the Footnote," In: American Documentation, 16(3): 179-184, July, 1965. [Functions of citations; Social organization of science.]

0731   Lipetz, B. "The Effects of a Citation Index on Literature Use by Physicists," In: Proceedings of the 1965 Congress of the International Federation for Documentation. Washington, Spartan, 1966, pp. 107-115. (Also as PB 168 868)

0732   Malin, M. V. "The Science Citation Index: A New Concept in Indexing," In: Library Trends, 16(3): 374-387, January, 1968.

0733   Martino, J. P. "Citation Indexing for Research and Development Management," In: IEEE Transactions on Engineering Management, 18(4): 146-151, November, 1971.

0734   Martyn, J. "An Examination of Citation Indexes," In: Aslib Proceedings, 17(6): 184-196, June, 1965. [Science Citation Index.]

0735   Matheson, N. W. "User Reaction to Current Contents: Behavioral, Social, and Management Sciences," In: Bulletin of the Medical Library Association, 59(2): 304-321, April, 1971.

0736   Mauerhoff, G. "Journal Coverage Overlap in *Current Contents* Editions," In: American Society for Information Science Journal, (Brief Communication), 22(5): 352-353, September-October, 1971.

0737   Norden, M. "KWIC Index to Government Publications," In: Journal of Library Automation, 2: 139-147, September, 1969.

0738   Petrarca, A. E., and W. M. Lay. "The Double-KWIC Coordinate Index: A New Approach for Preparation of High-Quality Printed Indexes by Automatic Indexing Techniques," In: Journal of Chemical Documentation, 9: 256-261, November, 1969.

0739   Sedano, J. M. Keyword-in-Context (KWIC) Indexing: Background, Statistical Evaluation, Pros and Cons and Application. Pittsburgh, Pa., University of Pittsburgh, 1964, 77p. AD 443 912.

0740   Skolnik, H. "The Multiterm Index: A New Concept in Information Storage and Retrieval," In: Journal of Chemical Documentation, 10: 81-84, May, 1970.

*0741   Tagliacozzo, R. "Citations and Citation Indexes: A Review," In: Methods of Information in Medicine, 6(3): 136-142, 1967.

0742   Tocatlian, J. T. "Are Titles of Chemical Papers Becoming More Informative," In: American Society for Information Science Journal, 21(5): 345-350, September-October, 1970. [KWIC indexing; Chemistry.]

*0743   Weinstock, M. "Citation Indexes," In: Encyclopedia of Library and Information Science. New York, Dekker, 1971, Vol. 5, pp. 16-40. [Historical review; Description; Operation; Future improvements.]

0744   Yerkey, A. N. "Models of Index Searching and Retrieval Effectiveness of Keyword-In-Context Indexes," In: American Society for Information Science Journal, 24(4): 282-286, July-August, 1973.

0745   Zabriskie, K. H., Jr., and A. Farren. "The BASIC Index to *Biological Abstracts*," In: American Journal of Pharmaceutical Education, 32: 189-200, May, 1968.

Tertiary Sources

0746   Bering, E. D. "Critical Reviews: The Sponsor's Point of View," In: Journal of Chemical Documentation, 8(4): 236-237, November, 1968. [Chemistry.]

0747   Bernal, J. D. "Summary Papers and Summary Journals in Chemistry,"
        In: Journal of Documentation, 16(2): 122-127, June, 1965. [Role in
        communication system.]

0748   Cuadra, C. A., L. Harris, and R. V. Katter. Impact Study of the Annual
        Review of Information Science and Technology, Final Report. Santa
        Monica, Calif., System Development Corp., November 15, 1968, 114p.
        PB 184 227.

0749   Darby, R. L., and W. H. Veazie. "Writing a State-of-the-Art Report," In:
        Materials Research and Standards, 8: 28-32, 1968.

0750   Etzioni, A. "The Need for Quality Filters in Information Systems," In:
        Science, 171(3967): 133, January 15, 1971.

*0751   Fix, C. D., T. H. Campbell, and W. A. Creager. Some Characteristics of
        the Review Literature in Eight Fields of Science. Washington, Herner
        and Co., PB167 625. [Astronomy; Biology; Medicine; Geophysics; Chem-
        istry; Engineering; Mathematics; Meteorology; Physics.]

*0752   Goudsmit, S. A. "Is the Literature Worth Retrieving?" In: Physics Today,
        19(9): 52-55, September, 1966. [Review literature; Data compilations.]

0753   Hart, H. "Critical Reviews: The Editor's Point of View," In: Journal of
        Chemical Documentation, 8(4): 241-244, November, 1968. [Chemistry.]

0754   Herring, C. "Critical Reviews: The User's Point of View," In: Journal of
        Chemical Documentation, 8(4): 232-236, November, 1968. [Chemistry.]

0755   Herring, C. "Distill or Drown: The Need for Reviews," In: Physics Today,
        21(9): 27-33, September, 1968.

0756   Koch, H. W., and W. Grattidge. Marketing the Products and Services of
        Information Analysis Centers. New York, American Institute of Physics,
        Information Division, AIP-ID-71-2, 1971, 23p. ED 053 758. [Review
        literature; Data compilations.]

*0757   Kochen, M. "Stability in the Growth of Knowledge," In: American
        Documentation, 20(3): 186-197, July, 1969. [Role of review literature
        in stabilizing growth of knowledge.]

0758   Stern, J. "An Analysis of the Review Literature in Physics," In: Proceed-
        ings of the American Society for Information Science. Westport, Conn.,
        Greenwood Publishing Co., 1971, Vol. 8, pp. 91-96. (Also as PB 204 859)

0759   Townsend, L. B. "Critical Reviews: The Author's Point of View," In:
        Journal of Chemical Documentation 8(4): 239-241, November, 1968.
        [Chemistry.]

*0760   Virgo, J. A. "The Review Article: Its Characteristics and Problems," In: Library Quarterly, 41(4): 275-291, October, 1971. [Sciences; Annual reviews; Critical reviews; Data compilations; Role of review articles in medicine; Production of reviews; Organization of reviews; Use of reviews.]

0761   Weber, E. "Are Society Publications Adequately Serving the Needs of Their Members for State-of-theArt Literature?" In: Engineering Societies and Their Literature Programs. New York, Engineers Joint Council, 1967. [Engineering.]

DISCIPLINE ORIENTED STUDIES

SCIENCES

General

0762   Barinova, Z. B., et al. Investigation of Scientific Journals as Communication Channels: Appraising the Contribution of Individual Countries to the World Scientific Information Flow. Washington, Joint Publications Research Service, 1968, 13p.

*0763   Campbell, T. H., and J. Edmisten. Characteristics of Scientific Journals— 1962. Washington, Herner & Co., April, 1964, 70p. PB 166 088. [Age of journals; Frequency of issuance; Circulation statistics; Subscriber cost; Publication delay; Copyright; Page charges; Sources of revenue; Publication costs.]

0764   Carpenter, M. P., and F. Narin. "Clustering of Scientific Journals," In: American Society for Information Science Journal, 24(6): 425-436, November-December, 1973. [Physics; Chemistry; Molecular biology.]

0765   Carter, L. F. "The Scientific User: The Library and Informational Service Needs of Scientists," In: Libraries at Large: Tradition, Innovations, and the National Interest. New York, Bowker, October, 1969, pp. 143-151.

0766   Earle, P., and B. C. Vickery. "Subject Relations in Science/Technology Literature," In: Aslib Proceedings, 21(6): 237-243, June, 1969. [Interaction of science and technology.]

*0767   Garvey, W. D., N. Lin, and C. E. Nelson. "Communication in the Physical and Social Sciences," In: Science, 170(3963): 1166-1173, December 11, 1970. [Communication delays; Organization and effectiveness of informal communication; Prepublication dissemination of information; Publication fate.]

*0768   Garvey, W. D., and B. C. Griffith. "Scientific Communication as a
        Social System," In: Science, 157(3792): 1011-1016, September 1,
        1967. [Communication within a discipline; Social and economic dimen-
        sions of communication; Formal and informal channels of communica-
        tion; Designing innovations; American Psychological Association.]

0769   Hall, A. M., P. Clague, and T. M. Aitchison. The Effect of the Use of an
        SDI Service on the Information-Gathering Habits of Scientists and
        Technologists. London, England, The Institution of Electrical Engineers,
        1972. v.p.

0770   Kaplan, N. "Social Aspects of the Communication System of Science,"
        In: Handbook of Modern Sociology. Edited by R. E. L. Faris. Chicago,
        Rand McNally, 1964, pp. 10-17.

0771   Loening, K. L. "International Cooperation on Scientific Nomenclature,"
        In: Journal of Documentation, 10(4): 231-236, November, 1970.
        [Chemistry; International Union of Pure and Applied Chemistry.]

0772   Lowry, W. K. "Scientific Information Problems Needing Solution," In:
        American Documentation, 19(3): 352-354, July, 1968. [Role of govern-
        ment; Role of professional society; Communication problems.]

0773   Martyn, J., and A. Gilchrist. An Evaluation of British Scientific Journals.
        London, Aslib, Aslib Occasional Publication No. 1, 1968, 51p. [Citation
        study; Citation frequency; Subjects; Publishers.]

0774   Martyn, J. Report of an Investigation of Literature Searching by Research
        Scientists. London, Aslib, 1964, 20p.

*0775   Menzel, H. "The Information Needs of Current Scientific Research," In:
        Library Quarterly, 34(1): 4-19, January, 1964. [Functions of science
        information systems; Role of informal communication; Classification of
        information needs.]

*0776   Menzel, H. "Scientific Communication: Five Themes from Social Science
        Research," In: American Psychologist, 21(11): 999-1004, November,
        1966. [Communication process as a system; Channel selection; Informal
        communication; Multiple functions of system; Scientists constitute
        publics.]

0777   NATO. Advisory Group for Aerospace Research and Development.
        Scientific and Technical Information: Why, Which, Where and How.
        Lecture Series. Paris, France, Advisory Group for Aerospace Research
        and Development, AGARD-LS-44-71, February, 1971, 72p. AD 721 730.
        [Information needs; Information analysis centers; Information sources.]

0778   Narin, F., N. C. Berlt, and M. P. Carpenter. "Interrelationship of Scientific Journals," In: American Society for Information Science Journal, 23(5): 323-331, September-October, 1971. [Models of interaction; Mathematics; Physics; Chemistry; Biochemistry; Biology.]

*0779   Orr, R. H. "The Scientist as an Information Processor: A Conceptual Model Illustrated with Data on Variables Related to Library Utilization," In: Communication among Scientists and Engineers. Edited by C. E. Nelson and D. K. Pollock. Lexington, Mass., Heath Lexington Books, 1970, pp. 143-190. [Limitations of past research; Communication models.]

0780   Parker, E. B., and W. J. Paisley. "Research for Psychologists at the Interface of the Scientist and His Information System," In: American Psychologist, 21(11): 1061-1071, November, 1966. [Information use; Methods for studying information use.]

*0781   Passman, S. Scientific and Technological Communication. New York, Pergamon Press, 1969, 151p. [Primary scientific literature; Technical reports; Informal information exchange; Secondary literature; Economics of publication; Quality of technical literature; International activities.]

*0782   Price, D. J. S. "Citation Measures of Hard Science, Soft Science, Technology, and Nonscience," In: Communication among Scientists and Engineers. Edited by C. E. Nelson and D. K. Pollock. Lexington, Mass., Heath Lexington Books, 1970, pp. 3-22. [Price's Index; Citation patterns.]

0783   Price, D. J. S. "Communication in Science: The Ends—Philosophy and Forecast," In: Communication in Science: Documentation and Automation. Edited by A. DeReuck and J. Knight. Boston, Little, Brown & Co., 1967, pp. 199-209. [Function of the scientific paper; Social organization of science and technology; Function of technological paper.]

*0784   Price, D. J. S. "Networks of Scientific Papers," In: Science, 149(3683): 510-515, July 30, 1965. (Also as PB 170 769) [Citation patterns.]

*0785   Robbins, J. C. "Social Functions of Scientific Communication," In: IEEE Transactions on Professional Communication, PC 1693): 131-135, 181, September, 1973. [Surveillance function; Socialization function; Social control function.]

0786   Sender, J. W. "Some Thoughts on Scientific Communication or Who Does What and with Which and to Whom," In: Innovations in Communications Conference, April 9-10, 1970. Washington, National Technical Information Services, 1970, pp. 184-188. PB 192 294.

0787 Storer, N. W. "Modes and Processes of Communication among Scientists: Theoretical Issues and Prospects for Investigation," Paper presented at the Conference on Theoretical Issues in the Study of Science, Scientists, and Science Policy. New York, The Social Science Research Council, 1968, 23p.

*0788 Swanson, D. R. "On Improving Communication among Scientists," In: Library Quarterly, 36(2): 79-87, April, 1966.

0789 U.S. Environmental Protection Agency. National Environmental Information Symposium: An Agenda for Progress, Held at Cincinnati, Ohio, September 24-27, 1972. 2 Vols. Washington, Environmental Protection Agency, May, 1973. PB 219 271/8 and PB 220 050/9. [Information sources.]

*0790 U.S. National Academy of Sciences, National Academy of Engineering. Scientific and Technological Communication: A Pressing National Problem and Recommendations for Its Solution. (A Report by the Committee on Scientific and Technological Communication, SATCOM.) Washington, National Academy of Sciences, 1969, 322p. [Summary recommendations on scientific and technical communication; Primary, secondary and tertiary sources; Impact of new technologies; National and international activities.]

0791 Vlachy, J. "Publication Characteristics of Research Establishments," In: Czechoslovak Journal of Physics, 20: 1149-1155, 1970. [Patterns of publication output; Author collaboration; Individual productivity; Physics.]

0792 Wilcox, R. H. "Some Neglected Areas in Research on Scientific and Technical Communications," In: Communication: Concepts and Perspectives. Edited by L. Thayer. Washington, Spartan, 1967, pp. 361-372.

*0793 Wolek, F. W. The Structure of Work and the Flow of Information in Science and Engineering. D.B.A. Thesis, Harvard Business School, 1967, 130p. [Influence of situational factors on communication; Function of primary literature; Industrial context.]

Biological Sciences

0794 Anderson, P. K. "The Periodical Literature of Ecology," In: BioScience, 16(11): 794-795, November, 1966. [Yule distribution; Citation frequency.]

0795 Anderson, S., and R. G. Van Gelder. "The History and Status of the Literature of Mammalogy," In: BioScience, 20(17): 949-957, September, 1970. [Literature growth; Literature obsolescence.]

0796 Baldwin, P. H., and D. E. Oehlerts. "The Status of Ornithology Literature," In: Studies in Biological Literature and Communications, Biological Abstracts Service, 1964, Vol. 4, pp. 1-53.

*0797 Bernard, J., C. W. Shilling and J. W. Tyson. Informal Communication among Bioscientists. Washington, George Washington University, Biological Sciences Communication Project, BSCP-16-63, December, 1963, 55p. PB 167 512. [Social organization; Influence of age and sex on informal communication patterns.]

*0798 Blaxter, K. L., and M. L. Blaxter. "The Individual and the Information Problem," In: Nature, 246(5432): 335-339, December 7, 1973. [Reading habits of biologists; Social function of communication.]

0799 Foote, R. H. "American Institute of Biological Sciences: Task Force on Communication and Information Services in Biology," In: American Society for Information Science Journal, 23(4): 280-281, July-August, 1972.

0800 Institute of Biology. "Communication in the Biological Sciences," In: Institute of Biology Journal, 14: 2-23, 1967.

0801 Judd, C., et al. Science Information Requirements of Scientists: Attitudes of Basic Researchers in Biology. Silver Springs, Md., American Institutes for Research, Technical Report #4, November, 1967, 17p. ED 028 952. [Attitudes of basic researchers toward existing systems and services expected from advanced information systems; Academic environment.]

0802 Kanasy, J. E. Citation Characteristics and Bibliographic Control of the Literature of Microbiology. Ph.D. Dissertation, Pittsburgh, Pa., University of Pittsburgh, 1971, 159p. (University Microfilms, Inc., Order No. 71-22,682)

*0803 Kennedy, H. E., and P. V. Parkins. "Biological Literature," In: Encyclopedia of Library and Information Science. New York, Dekker, 1969, Vol. 2, pp. 537-551. [Characteristics of primary journals; Secondary services.]

0804 Mullins, N. C. "The Development of a Scientific Specialty: The Phage Group and the Origins of Molecular Biology," In: Minerva, 10(1): 51-82, January, 1972. [Social structure; Communication networks; Sociometric patterns.]

*0805   Mullins, N. C. "The Distribution of Social and Cultural Properties in Informal Communication Networks among Biological Scientists," In: American Sociological Review, 33(5): 786-813, October, 1968. [Social structure; Communication networks; Sociometric patterns.]

*0806   Mullins, N. C. Social-Networks among Biological Scientists. Ph.D. Dissertation, Harvard University, 1966. [Social structure; Communication networks; Sociometric patterns.]

0807   Rothman, H., and M. Woodhead. "Publication Trends in Biological Control," In: Nature, 220(5171): 1053-1054, December 7, 1968. [Literature growth.]

*0808   Shilling, C. W., and J. Bernard. Informal Communication among Bioscientists. Part II; Policies and Practices Dealing with Informal Communication as Related to Productivity and Efficiency in 64 Selected Biological Laboratories. Washington, George Washington University, Biological Sciences Communication Project, BSCP-16A-64, June, 1964, 88p. PB 167 848.

*0809   U.S. National Research Council, Division of Biology and Agriculture. Information Handling in the Life Sciences. Washington, National Research Council, February, 1970, 88p. PB 192 590 or ED 040 722. [Informal communication; Primary sources; Secondary sources; Tertiary sources; Data compilations.]

0810   Van Cott, H. P., and R. G. Kinkade. Science Information Requirements of Scientists—VII: A Feasibility Study for Determining Requirements of Biological Information Services and Systems, Final Report. Silver Springs, Md., American Institutes for Research, 1967, 20p. PB 176 898. [Assessing communication behavior.]

0811   Webb, E. C. "Communication in Biochemistry," In: Nature, 225(5228): 132-135, January, 1970. [Literature growth; Proposed solutions to communication problems.]

0812   Whitley, R. D. "Communication Networks in Science: Status and Citation Patterns in Animal Physiology," In: Sociological Review, 17(2): 219-233, July, 1969.

0813   Woodford, F. P. "Improving the Communication of Scientific Information," In: BioScience, 19(7): 625-627, July, 1969.

Chemistry

*0814   American Chemical Society. A Five Year Plan for Information Programs, 1971-1975. Washington, American Chemical Society, 1970, 127p. ED 046 477. [American Chemical Society information program.]

0815   Amick, D. J. Information Processing Behavior: An Exploratory Study at the Interface of the Sociology of Science and Information Science. Ph.D. Dissertation, Pittsburgh, Pa., University of Pittsburgh, 1970, 155p. (University Microfilms, Inc., Order No. 71-10,544) [Characteristics of elites; Comparison of communication patterns in applied science and basic science.]

*0816   Amick, D. J. "Scientific Elitism and the Information System of Science," In: American Society for Information Science Journal, 24(5): 317-327, September-October, 1973. [Comparison of communication patterns in applied science and basic science.]

*0817   Arnett, E. M. "Computer-based Chemical Information Services," In: Science, 170(3965): 1370-1376, December 25, 1970. [Information needs of research chemists; Information needs model.]

0818   Baker, D. B., F. A. Tate, and R. J. Rowlett, Jr. "Changing Patterns in the International Communication of Chemical Research and Technology," In: Journal of Documentation, 11(2): 90-98, May, 1971. [Primary sources; Patents.]

0819   Barker, D. L. Characteristics of the Scientific Literature Cited by Chemists of the Soviet Union, Ph.D. Dissertation, University of Illinois, 1966. (University Microfilms, Inc., Order No. 66-7706) [Citation characteristics.]

*0820   Bottle, R. T. "Scientists, Information Transfer and Literature Characteristics," In: Journal of Documentation, 29(3): 281-294, September, 1973. [Communication model; Role of secondary and tertiary services in transfer of chemical information.]

0821   Cahn, R. S. Survey of Chemical Publications and Report to the Chemical Society. London, The Chemical Society, 1965, 97p.

0822   Canhain, G. W. R. "Information Problems of an Inorganic Chemist," In: Journal of Chemical Documentation, 12(1): 5-6, February, 1972. [Problems of citation searches; Chemical newspaper.]

*0823   Duncan, E. E. Current Awareness and the Chemist: A Study of the Use of CA Condensates by Chemists. Metuchen, N.J., Scarecrow, 1972, 150p.

0824 Duncan, E. E. Development of a Decision Model for Acquisition of Current Periodical Titles Based on Usage of Periodical Literature by Chemical Personnel. Ph.D. Dissertation, Pittsburgh, Pa., University of Pittsburgh, 1971, 117p. (University Microfilms, Inc., Order No. 72-2050) [Bradford-Zipf distribution; Citation characteristics.]

0825 Ewing, G. J. "Citation of Articles from Volume 58 of the *Journal of Physical Chemistry*," In: Journal of Chemical Documentation, 6(4): 247-250, November, 1966. [Citation characteristics.]

*0826 Gushee, D. E. "Reading Behavior of Chemists," In: Journal of Chemical Documentation, 8(4): 191-197, November, 1968.

0827 Haiduc, I. "Some Tendencies in the Literature of Organometalic Chemistry," In: Journal of Chemical Documentation, 12(3): 175-178, August, 1972. [Literature growth.]

*0828 Holm, B. E., et al. "The Status of Chemical Information," In: Journal of Chemical Documentation, 13(4): 171-183, November, 1973. [Role of federal government; Primary and secondary sources.]

*0829 International Council of Scientific Unions, Abstracting Board, Some Characteristics of Primary Periodicals in the Domain of the Chemical Sciences. Paris, International Council of Scientific Unions, 1967, 92p.

0830 Jahoda, G. "Information-Gathering and Use Habits of Chemists," In: Journal of Chemical Documentation, 4(3): 153-156, July, 1964.

0831 Journal of Chemical Documentation. "Symposium on Information Problems in Chemical Marketing,'. In: Journal of Chemical Documentation, 5(2): 63-86, May, 1965. [Information sources; Role of federal government; Communication problems.]

*0832 Journal of Chemical Documentation. "Symposium on Methods of Alerting Chemists to New Developments," In: Journal of Chemical Documentation, 5(3): 123-172, August, 1965. [Title derivative indexes; Abstracting journals; Preprints; Tertiary sources; Conference publications.]

0833 Kean, P., and J. Ronayne. "Preliminary Communications in Chemistry," In: Journal of Chemical Documentation, 12(4): 218-220, November, 1972. [Publication fate of preliminary publications.]

0834 Kegan, D. L. "Measures of the Usefulness of Written Technical Information to Chemical Researchers,'. In: American Society for Information Science Journal, 21(3): 179-186, May-June, 1970.

0835 Kuney, J. H., and W. H. Weisgerber. "Systems Requirements for Primary Information Systems: Utilization of *The Journal of Organic Chemistry*," In: Journal of Chemical Documentation, 10(3): 150-157, August, 1970. [Reading habits of chemists.]

*0836 Menzel, H., J. Nixon, and B. Barber. Formal and Informal Satisfaction of the Information Requirements of Chemists, Final Report. New York, Columbia University, Bureau of Applied Social Research, June, 1970, 120p. PB 193 556. [Polymer chemistry; Interplay of formal and informal communication.]

*0837 Menzel, H. "Unplanned Acquisition of Information in the Experience of Polymer Chemists," In: IEEE Transactions on Professional Communication, PC 15(2): 39-48, June, 1972.

0838 Panton, D., and B. G. Reuben. "What Do Chemists Read?" In: Chemistry in Britain, 7(1): 18-22, 1971. [Reading habits.]

0839 Platau, G. O. "Documentation of the Chemical Patent Literature," In: Journal of Chemical Documentation, 7(4): 250-255, November, 1967. [Chemical Abstracts Service; Processing patents.]

0840 Smith, C. User Requirements for Chemical Information and Data System (CIDS), Final Report. Philadelphia, Frankford Arsenal Research and Development Directorate, April, 1965, 67p. AD 616 889. [Information requirements; Department of the Army; Information-seeking; Information services; Preferred formats; Response time.]

*0841 Vagianos, L. "Information Patterns of Chemists in a University Environment," In: Journal of Chemical Documentation, 11(2): 85-89, May, 1971.

0842 Wood, J. L., and J. Ronayne. "A Survey of the Use of Scientific and Technical News Periodicals by Chemists," In: Journal of Chemical Documentation, 13(3): 113-118, August, 1973. [*Chemical and Engineering News*; Use survey.]

Geosciences

0843 Aiyepeku, W. O. "The Language and Format of Geographical Literature: A Comparative Study," In: International Library Review, 5(1): 53-62, January, 1973. [Citation characteristics.]

0844 Chakrabortty, A. R. "Citation Characteristics of Marine Geology," In: Annals of Library Science and Documentation, 18(2): 88-91, June, 1971.

0845 Clayton, K. M. Periodical Literature Survey in the Fields of Geography, Geomorphology, and Geology. Norwich, England, Office of Scientific and Technical Information, OSTI Report #5057, 1969, 11p.

0846 Craig, J. E. G. "Characteristics of Use of Geology Literature," In: College and Research Libraries, 30(3): 230-236, May, 1969. [Primary sources.]

*0847 Garvey, W. D., and K. Tomita. "Scientific Communication in Geophysics," In: Transactions of the American Geophysical Union, 53(8): 772-777, August, 1972. [Information needs; Information flow process.]

0848 Shirley, H. B., and D. C. Ward III. "The Geoscience Information Society— A Forum for Specialized Scientific Communication," In: Proceedings of the American Society for Information Science. New York, Greenwood, 1968, Vol. 5, pp. 31-35. [Origin and organization; Activities.]

0849 Thuronyi, G., and M. Rigby. Qualitative—Quantitative Evaluation of Geophysical Serials. Washington, Meteorological and Geophysical Abstracts, February, 1966, 32p. PB 173 082, Appendices: PB 173 083. [Citation characteristics; *Journal of Geophysical Research.*]

Mathematics

*0850 American Mathematical Society. Conference on Communication Problems in the Mathematical Sciences, 5-7 December, 1967, Final Report. Providence, R.I., American Mathematical Society, 1969, 24p. PB 184 083 or ED 039 122. [Primary sources; Data based systems; Information centers.]

0851 Lamb, G. H. The Coincidence of Quality and Quantity in the Literature of Mathematics. Ph.D. Dissertation, Cleveland, Ohio, Case Western Reserve University, 1971, 89p. (University Microfilms, Inc., Order No. 72-66) [Bradford distribution.]

0852 May, K. O. "Quantitative Growth of the Mathematical Literature," In: Science, 154(3757): 1672-1673, December 30, 1966.

0853   Reckenbeil, R. The Mathematics Journal from a Technical Point of View. Providence, R.I., American Mathematical Society, 1970, 28p. PB 195 487.

Physics

*0854   Aines, A. A. "Survey of Information Needs of Physicists and Chemists," In: Journal of Documentation, 21(2): 83-112, June, 1965. [Information-seeking; Britain.]

0855   American Institute of Physics, Information Division. Characteristics of Journal Publications Distributed by the American Institute of Physics. New York, American Institute of Physics, Information Division, ID-68-16, December, 1968, 6p. PB 191 122. [Distribution; Cost frequency; Abstracts.]

*0856   Anthony, L. J., H. East, and M. J. Slater. "The Growth of the Literature of Physics," In: Reports of Progress in Physics, 32(2): 709-767, 1969, [Physics; Astronomy; Communication channels; Reading habits; Evolution of information system; Literature growth; National information system for physics and astronomy.]

0857   Atherton, P., and S. Keenan. Review of AIP/Documentation Research Project Studies Prepared for Physics Abstracts Staff. New York, American Institute of Physics, AIP/DRP-65-2, March, 1965, 18p. PB 167 521.

0858   Atherton, P. A Review of Work Completed and in Progress, 1961-1965. New York, American Institute of Physics, Documentation Research Project, AIP/DRP-65-3, April, 1965, 16p. PB 168 281.

0859   Atherton, P. The Role of "Letters" Journals in Primary Distribution of Information: A Survey of Authors of Physical Review Letters. New York, American Institute of Physics, AIP/DRP-64-1, 1964.

0860   Chen, C. "The Use Patterns of Physics Journals in a Large Academic Research Library," In: American Society for Information Science Journal, 23(4): 254-270, July-August, 1972.

0861   Cole, J. R., and S. Cole. "The Ortega Hypothesis: Citation Analysis Suggests That Only a Few Scientists Contribute to Scientific Progress," In: Science, 178(4059): 368-375, October 27, 1972. [Social stratification; Characteristics of cited authors; Academic physicists.]

0862   Cooper, M., and H. M. Watterson. Institutional Producers of Physics
        Research. New York, American Institute of Physics, Information Divi-
        sion, ID-69-3, October, 1969, 28p. PB 191 120 or ED 038 997. [Rate
        of publication.]

*0863   Cooper, M., and C. W. Thayer. Primary Journal Literature of Physics.
        New York, American Institute of Physics, Information Division,
        ID-69-4, December, 1969, 35p. PB 191 121 or ED 038 996. [Sponsor-
        ship; Distribution by country; Language; Frequency; Coverage by
        secondary sources.]

0864   East, H., and A. Weyman. "A Study in the Science Literature of Plasma
        Physics," In: Aslib Proceedings, 21(4): 160-171, April, 1969.

0865   Groos, O. V. "Citation Characteristics of Astronomical Literature," In:
        Journal of Documentation, 25(4): 344-347, December, 1969.

0866   Herschman, A. Information Retrieval in Physics. New York, American
        Institute of Physics, Information Analysis and Retrieval Division,
        October, 1967, 24p. PB 176 431. [National Information System for
        Physics.]

*0867   Herschman, A. "Keeping Up with What's Going On in Physics," In:
        Physics Today, 24(11): 23-31, November, 1971. [Growth rate of phy-
        sics; Communication channels and information flow; SPIN-Searchable
        Physics Information Notices.]

*0868   Information. "Dissemination and Use of the Information of Physics,"
        In: Information, Part 1, 5(4): 205-214, July-August, 1973.

*0869   International Council of Scientific Unions. Some Characteristics of
        Primary Periodicals in the Domain of the Physical Sciences. Paris, France,
        International Council of Scientific Unions, 1966, 68p.

*0870   Keenan, S., and M. Slater. "Current Awareness Needs of Physicists:
        Results of an Anglo-American Study," In: Journal of Documentation,
        24(2): 98-106, June, 1968.

0871   Keenan, S., and M. Slater. Current Papers in Physics Use Study: Cover-
        age, Arrangement, and Format. New York, American Institute of Phys-
        ics, AIP/CPP-2, May, 1968, 64p. PB 179 677.

0872   Keenan, S., and P. Atherton. The Journal Literature of Physics: A Com-
        prehensive Study Based on Physics Abstracts 1961 Issues. New York,
        American Institute of Physics, AIP/DRP-PA-1, 1964.

0873   Keenan, S., and M. Slater. Results of Questionnaire on Current Aware-
        ness Methods Used by Physicists Prior to Publication of Current Papers
        in Physics. New York, American Institute of Physics, AIP/CPP-1, Sep-
        tember, 1967, 39p.

0874   Keenan, S., and M. Slater. Use Made of Current Papers in Physics. New
        York, American Institute of Physics, AIP/CPP-3, July, 1968, 70p.
        PB 179 678.

0875   Koch, H. W. "AIP Information Program," In: Applied Spectroscopy,
        24(1): 1-4, 1970. [National Information System for Physics; American
        Institute of Physics; SPIN-Searchable Physics Information Notices.]

*0876   Koch, H. W. "Current Physics Information," In: Science, 174(4012):
        918-922, November 26, 1971. [*Current Physics Microfilm*; *Current
        Physics Advance Abstracts*; *Current Physics Titles*; SPIN-Searchable
        Physics Information Notices.]

*0877   Koch, H. W., and A. W. K. Metzner. Primary and Secondary Publication
        of Information in Physics. New York, American Institute of Physics,
        Information Division, AIP-ID-70-4, December, 1970, 7p. PB 198 331.

*0878   Libbey, M. A., and G. Zaltman. The Role and Distribution of Written
        Informal Communications in Theoretical High Energy Physics. New
        York, American Institute of Physics, AIP/SDD-1, 1967. AEC Report:
        NYO-3732-1-rev.

0879   Mauperon, A. "Publishing Habits in the Nuclear Field," In: Symposium
        on the Handling of Nuclear Information. Vienna, International Atomic
        Energy Agency, 1970, pp. 335-346.

0880   Meadows, A. J., and J. G. O'Connor. An Analysis of Selected Journals:
        A Survey in Depth of a Selected Information Field (Astronomy and
        Astrophysics), Final Report. London, Department of Education and
        Science, Office for Scientific and Technical Information, OSTI Report
        5092, 1970. [Citation characteristics.]

0881   Meadows, A. J. "The Citation Characteristics of Astronomical Research
        Literature," In: Journal of Documentation, 23(2): 28-33, March, 1967.

0882   Moravcsik, M. J. "Private and Public Communications in Physics," In:
        Physics Today, 18(3): 23-26, March, 1965. [Use of printed communica-
        tions; Referee system; Preprints.]

0883   Oliver, M. R. "The Effect of Growth on the Obsolescence of Semi-
        conductor Physics Literature," In: Journal of Documentation, 27(1):
        11-17, March, 1971.

0884   Roll, P. G. "Introductory Physics Textbooks," In: Physics Today, 21(1): 63-74, January, 1968. [Characteristics.]

0885   Silverio, M. An Analysis of Primary and Secondary Information Sources in Solid State Physics. M.A. Thesis, Chicago, University of Chicago, Graduate Library School, 1969.

0886   Small, H. "Co-Citation in the Scientific Literature: A New Measure of the Relationship Between Two Documents," In: American Society for Information Science Journal, 24(4): 265-269, July-August, 1973. [Particle physics literature.]

0887   Trueswell, R. W., G. J. Rath, and A. H. Rubenstein. An Experiment in Measuring Certain Aspects of the Information Seeking Behavior of X-Ray Crystallographers. Evanston, Ill., Northwestern University, Department of Industrial Engineering and Management Science, Technical Reports 1-2, 1965-1968.

*0888   U.S. National Academy of Sciences. Physics in Perspective. Washington, National Academy of Sciences, August, 1972, Vol. 1, 1096p. PB 212 982/3. [Dissemination and use of information in physics.]

0889   Van Cott, H. P., and A. Zavala. "Extracting the Basic Structure of Scientific Literature," In: American Documentation, 19(3): 247-262, July, 1968. (Also as PB 175 552)

0890   Zaltman, G., and B. M. Kohler. "The Dissemination of Task and Socio-emotional Information in an International Community of Scientists," In: American Society for Information Science Journal, 23(4): 225-236, July-August, 1972. [High energy physics; Impact of geopolitical and cultural factors on professional recognition and information flow.]

*0891   Zaltman, G. Scientific Recognition and Communication Behavior in High Energy Physics. New York, American Institute of Physics, Information Division, 1968, 185p. PB 179 890. [Social organization; Influence of geopolitical and cultural factors on professional recognition and information flow.]

0892   Zavala, A., and H. P. Van Cott. A Feasibility Study of the Factor Analysis of Journal Literature, Final Report, Silver Springs, Md., American Institutes for Research, July, 1966, 42p. PB 173 127.

SOCIAL SCIENCES

General

0893   Apple, J. S., and T. Gurr. "Bibliographic Needs of Social and Behavioral Scientists: Report of a Pilot Survey," In: American Behavioral Scientist, 7(10): 51-54, June, 1964. [Academic environment; Economics; Psychology; Anthropology.]

0894   Bergen, D. "The Communication System of the Social Sciences," In: College and Research Libraries, 28(4): 239-252, July, 1967. [Models of formal and informal communication.]

0895   Brittain, J. M., et al. Citation Patterns in the Social Sciences: Results of Pilot Citation Study and Selection of Source Journals for Main Citation Study. England, Bath University of Technology, University Library, October, 1972, 148p. ED 078 867. [Citation characteristics.]

*0896   Brittain, J. M. Information and Its Users: A Review with Special Reference to the Social Sciences. New York, Wiley, 1971, 208p. [Informal communication networks; Language barriers; Primary sources; Secondary sources; Literature growth.]

0897   Broadus, R. N. "The Literature of the Social Sciences: A Survey of Citation Studies," In: International Social Science Journal, 23(2): 236-243, 1971. [Citation characteristics.]

0898   Earle, P., and B. C. Vickery. "Social Science Literature Use in the U.K. as Indicated by Citations," In: Journal of Documentation, 25(2): 123-141, June, 1969. [Citation characteristics.]

0899   Freides, T. K. Literature and Bibliography of the Social Sciences. New York, Melvill Publishers, 1973, 284p. [Communication patterns.]

*0900   Garvey, W. D., and B. C. Griffith. "Informal Channels of Communication in the Behavioral Sciences: Their Relevance in Structuring of Formal or Bibliographic Communication," In: Foundation of Access to Knowledge; A Symposium. Syracuse, N. Y., Division of Summer Sessions, Syracuse University, 1968, pp. 129-146.

0901   Goldberg, A. L. "Information Needs of Social Scientists and Ways of Meeting Them," In: International Social Science Journal, 23(2): 273-284, 1971. [Soviet Union.]

0902   Guttsman, W. L. "The Literature of the Social Sciences and Provision for Research in Them," In: Journal of Documentation, 22(3): 186-194, September, 1966. [Literature access; Britain.]

0903   Lengyel, P. "The Social Science Press: Introduction," In: International Social Science Journal, 19(2): 145-161, 1967.

0904   Libaw, F. B. "Information Handling in the Behavioral Sciences: Report of a First Convocation of a Conglomerate Clan," In: American Behavioral Scientist, 10(6): 8-12, 1968.

*0905   Line, M. B. "Information Requirements in the Social Sciences: Some Preliminary Considerations," In: Journal of Librarianship, 1(1): 1-19, January, 1969. [Communication problems.]

0906   Line, M. B., J. M. Brittain, and F. A. Cranmer. Information Requirements of Researchers in the Social Sciences: Investigations into Information Requirements of the Social Sciences. Bath, England, Bath University of Technology, University Library, May, 1971, Vol. 1, 280p. ED 054 806. [Academic environment.]

0907   Line, M. B., J. M. Brittain, and F. A. Cranmer. Information Requirements of Researchers in the Social Sciences: Investigations into Information Requirements of the Social Sciences. Bath, England, Bath University of Technology, University Library, May, 1971, Vol. 2, 261p. ED 054 807. [Academic environment.]

0908   Line, M. B., J. M. Brittain, and F. A. Cranmer. Information Requirements of Social Scientists in Government Departments: Investigations into Information Requirements of the Social Sciences. Bath, England, Bath University of Technology, University Library, March, 1971, 29p. ED 049 774.

*0909   Line, M. B. "The Information Uses and Needs of Social Scientists: An Overview of INFROSS," In: Aslib Proceedings, 23(8): 412-434, August, 1971. [Information requirements of the social sciences.]

0910   Line, M. B., et al. The Relationship between Primary and Secondary Literature in the Social Sciences: A Study of Secondary Literature in Criminology. Bath, England, Bath University of Technology, University Library, 1972. 17p. ED 072 815.

0911   MacRae, D., Jr. "Scientific Communication, Ethical Argument, and Public Policy," In: American Political Science Review, 65(1): 38-50, March, 1971. [Ethical discourse; Norms of scientific communication.]

*0912 Paisley, W. J. The Flow of (Behavioral) Science Information: A Review of the Research Literature. Palo Alto, Calif., Stanford University, Institute for Communication Research, November, 1965, 206p. PB 169 065 or ED 039 783. [Information-seeking; Information use; Information flow in the research environment; Studies of communication artifacts; Flow of behavioral science information to public.]

0913 Paisley, W. J. Perspectives on the Utilization of Knowledge. Palo Alto, Calif., Stanford University, Institute for Communication Research, February 6, 1969, 28p. ED 037 094.

0914 Parker, E. B., W. J. Paisley, and D. A. Lingwood. Communication and Research Productivity in an Interdisciplinary Behavioral Science Research Area. Palo Alto, Calif., Stanford University, Institute for Communication Research, July, 1968, 90p. PB 179 569.

0915 Pemberton, J. E. "Access to Primary Materials in the Social Sciences," In: Aslib Proceedings, 22(1): 22-30, January, 1970.

0916 Roberts, S. A., et al. Characteristics of Citations in Social Science Monographs. Bath, England, Bath University of Technology, 1972, 37p. ED 072 816.

*0917 Skelton, B. "Scientists and Social Scientists as Information Users: A Comparison of Results of Science User Studies with the Investigation into Information Requirements of the Social Sciences," In: Journal of Librarianship, 5(2): 138-156, April, 1973. (Also as ED 078 866)

0918 Uytterschaut, L. "Literature Searching Methods in Social Science Research: A Pilot Study," In: American Behavioral Scientist, 9(9): 23-26, May, 1966.

0919 Whitley, R. D. "The Formal Communication System of Science: A Study of the Organization of British Social Science Journals," In: The Sociological Review Monograph, No. 16, pp. 163-179, September, 1970.

0920 Whitley, R. D. "The Operation of Science Journals: Two Case Studies in British Social Science," In: Sociological Review, 18(2): 241-258, July, 1970. [Characteristics of papers, authors, and referees.]

0921 Winn, V. A. "A Case Study in the Problems of Information Processing in a Social Science Field: The OSTI-SEA Project," In: Aslib Proceedings, 23(2): 76-88, February, 1971. [*Sociology of Education Abstracts.*]

0922 Wood, D. N., and C. A. Bower. "The Use of Social Science Periodical Literature," In: Journal of Documentation, 25(2): 108-122, June,

1969. [National Lending Library; Britain; Sociology; Education; Law; Political science; Psychology.]

Anthropology

*0923 Amsden, D. "Information Problems of Anthropologists," In: College and Research Libraries, 29(2): 117-131, March, 1968.

0924 Boggs, S. T. "Information Problems in the Field of Anthropology," In: Proceedings of the 1965 Congress of the International Federation for Documentation. Washington, Spartan, 1966, pp. 175-178.

Communication Sciences

0925 Coblans, H. "Literature of Librarianship and Documentation—The Periodicals and Their Bibliographic Control," In: Journal of Documentation, 28: 56-66, March, 1972. [Primary sources; Secondary sources.]

0926 Dansey, P. "Do Information Scientists Read about Information Science?" In: Information Science, 6(3): 107-110, September, 1972. [Reading habits of information scientists; Primary sources; Secondary sources.]

0927 Donohue, J. C. "A Bibliometric Analysis of Certain Information Science Literature," In: American Society for Information Science Journal, 23(5): 313-317, September-October, 1972. [Bradford distribution; Epidemic theory.]

0928 Fenichel, C. J. Citation Patterns in Information Science. Masters Thesis, Philadelphia, Drexel Institute of Technology, June, 1969, 52p. ED 048 864. [Citation characteristics.]

0929 Hoban, C. F. Survey of Professional Journals in the Field of Public Communication Including New Media of Education. Philadelphia, University of Pennsylvania, February, 1967, 53p. ED 014 314.

*0930 Mitchell, D., and B. Choate, eds. Conference on the Bibliographic Control of Library Science Literature, April 19-20, 1968. State University of New York at Albany, 1970, 126p. ED 050 738. [Primary sources; Secondary sources.]

*0931   Rowland, G. E., et al. The Process of Professional Information Exchange among Science Information Specialists, Final Report. Haddonfield, N.J., Rowland & Co., June 1, 1967, 89p. PB 175 568.

0932   Taylor, L. J. "Library Science Literature: Some Problems of Information about Information," In: Aslib Proceedings, 23(9): 465-480, September, 1971. [Bibliographic control.]

0933   Windsor, D. H., and D. M. Windsor. "Citation of the Literature by Information Scientists in Their Own Publications," In: American Society for Information Science Journal, 24(5): 377-381, September-October, 1973.

Economics

0934   Coats, A. W. "The American Economics Association's Publications: An Historical Perspective," In: Journal of Economics Literature, 7(1): 57-68, March, 1969.

0935   Dunn, E. S., Jr. "Information Needs in the Field of Economics," In: Proceedings of the 1965 Congress of the International Federation for Documentation. Washington, Spartan, 1966, pp. 205-207.

0936   Fletcher, J. "A View of the Literature of Economics," In: Journal of Documentation, 28(4): 283-295, December, 1972. [Literature growth; Literature characteristics.]

0937   Handovsky, F. L. A. "Collection and Utilization of Economic Information—Some of Its Problems," In: Aslib Proceedings, 21(2): 71-74, February, 1969.

0938   Holt, C. C., and W. E. Schrank. "Growth of the Professional Literature in Economics and Other Fields, and Some Implications," In: American Documentation, 19(1): 18-26, January, 1968. [Literature growth; Economics; Psychology; Biology; Physics; Electrical engineering; Measuring exponential growth.]

0939   Swann, D. "Primary Sources in Economics," In: Aslib Proceedings, 23(4): 167-174, April, 1971.

*0940   White, M. D. Communication Behavior of Academic Economists. Ph.D. Dissertation, University of Illinois, 1971, 171p. (University Microfilms, Inc., Order No. 72-12,432)

Education

0941 Barron, P., and F. Narin. Analysis of Research Journals and Related Research Structure in Education. Final Report. Chicago, Computer Horizons, Inc., 1972, 68p. ED 072 787. [Cluster analysis; Interdisciplinary relationships.]

0942 Baugham, R. C. Survey of Information Needs of Educational Information Specialists. College Park, Md., University of Maryland, School of Library and Information Services, May 31, 1972, 31p. ED 068 101. [Educational extension agent programs; Educational information specialists.]

0943 Bayer, A. E., and J. Folger. "Some Correlates of a Citation Measure of Productivity in Science," In: Sociology of Education, 39: 381-390, Fall, 1966.

*0944 Clemens, T. Information Transfer and Research Utilization in Education. Washington, ERIC, October, 1969, 24p. ED 039 005. [Instructional materials centers; Information needs; Information networks; Information services; Teachers; Principals.]

0945 Erickson, D. K., and A. E. Blackhurst. "Information Resources for Special Education," In: Focus on Exceptional Children, 2(7): 1-13, December, 1970.

*0946 Farr, R. S. Knowledge Linkers and Flow of Educational Information. Palo Alto, Calif., ERIC Clearinghouse on Educational Media and Technology, Stanford University, September, 1969, 17p. ED 032 438. [Information centers; Information needs; Information sources; Gatekeepers.]

*0947 Garvey, W. D., C. E. Nelson, and N. Lin. "A Preliminary Description of Scientific Information Exchange in Educational Research," In: The Educational Research Community: Its Communication and Social Structure. Edited by R. A. Dershimer. Washington, Office of Education, April, 1970, pp. 69-104. ED 057 275. [Publication patterns; Information flow; National meetings.]

0948 Hemphill, J. K. "Information Needs in Education," In: Proceedings of the 1965 Congress of the International Federation for Documentation. Washington, Spartan, 1966, pp. 185-187.

0949 Herner, S., et al. Study of Periodicals and Serials in Education. Washington, Herner & Co., June 28, 1968, 120p. ED 017 747. [Coverage of secondary sources; *Education Index*; *Psychological Abstracts*; *Educational Administration Abstracts*; Use of secondary services.]

0950   Kamil, B. L. The Information-Seeking Behavior of New and Experienced
        Researchers in Special Education. Ph.D. Dissertation, Syracuse, New
        York, Syracuse University, 1974, 187p. (University Microfilms, Inc.,
        Order No. 74-10,150)

0951   Lingwood, D. A. "Interpersonal Communication, Scientific Productivity,
        and Invisible Colleges: Studies of Two Behavioral Research Areas," In:
        Colloquium on Improving the Social and Communication Mechanism in
        Educational Research. Washington, American Educational Research
        Association, 1968.

0952   McCracken, J. D. Information Needs of State Directors of Vocational
        and Technical Education. Columbus, Ohio, Ohio State University, Center
        for Vocational and Technical Education, March, 1973, 103p. Ed 078 129.

*0953   Marron, H., and P. Sullivan. "Information Dissemination in Education;
        A Status Report," In: College and Research Libraries, 32(4): 286-294,
        July, 1971. [Primary sources; Secondary sources; Tertiary sources;
        Communication patterns.]

0954   Mersel, J., and J. C. Donohue. "Information Transfer in Educational
        Research," In: Proceedings of the American Documentation Institute.
        Los Angeles, Adrianne Press, 1966, Vol. 3, pp. 89-98. [Information
        needs; Information use.]

0955   Narin, F., and D. Garside. "Journal Relationships in Special Education,"
        In: Exceptional Children, 38: 695-704, May, 1972. [Interdisciplinary
        relationships; Primary journals.]

*0956   Nelson, C. E. Scientific Communication in Educational Research, Final
        Report. Tampa, Fla., University of South Florida, November, 1972, 38p.
        ED 073 793. [Communication problems; Primary sources; Information
        use; Information flow; Communication delays.]

0957   Paisley, W. J. Developing a "Sensing Network" for Information Needs
        in Education. Palo Alto, Calif., Stanford University, Institute for
        Communication Research, September, 1971, 34p. [Monitoring changing
        information needs.]

0958   Rittenhouse, C. H. "Educational Information Uses and Users," In:
        AV Communication Review, 19(1): 76-88, Spring, 1971. [Diffusion of
        innovations.]

*0959   Rittenhouse, C. H. Innovation Problems and Information Needs of Edu-
        cational Practitioners. Menlo Park, Calif., Stanford Research Institute,
        May, 1970, 87p. ED 040 976. [Information use.]

0960   Robinson, B. F., Jr. Gatekeepers in Vocational Education. M.S. Thesis, College Park, Md., University of Maryland, 1971, 145p. ED 055 226. [Information dissemination; Information needs; Information networks; Information use; Agriculture.]

*0961   Trapp, M. Knowledge Utilization in Education: A Review of Significant Theories and Research. Iowa City, Iowa, University of Iowa, Center for the Advanced Study of Communication, January 15, 1972, 48p. ED 061 468. [Information dissemination; Information use; Diffusion of innovations.]

*0962   Wolf, W. C., Jr., and A. J. Fiorino. A Study of Educational Knowledge Diffusion and Utilization. Philadelphia, Temple University, 1972, 125p. ED 061 772. [Information dissemination; Information needs; Information-seeking; Information use; Diffusion of innovations.]

0963   Wright, K. "Social Science Information Characteristics with Particular Reference to the Educational Resources Information Center (ERIC)," In: American Society for Information Science Journal, 24(3): 193-204, May-June, 1973.

Language Sciences

0964   Griffith, B. C., and L. Ouyang. A Preliminary Interview Study of Scientifically and Scholarly Active Linguists. Washington, Center for Applied Linguistics, 1969. 12p.

*0965   Griffith, B. C., and L. O. Engstrom. Professional Characteristics and Information Practices of Members of the Linguistic Society of America. Washington, Center for Applied Linguistics, Language Information Network and Clearinghouse System, October, 1971, 31p. PB 206 504.

0966   Hood, R. A., and A. G. Woyna. Experiment in Fast Dissemination of Research in Selected Fields in Linguistics, Final Report. Washington, Bureau of Libraries and Educational Technology, August, 1972, 31p. [Rapid distribution of abstracts; Microfiche.]

*0967   Hood, R. A. "The System of Communication in the Language Sciences: Present, and Future," In: Communication among Scientists and Engineers. Edited by C. E. Nelson and D. K. Pollock. Lexington, Mass., Heath Lexington Books, 1970, pp. 293-306. [Social organization; Information sources.]

*0968 Levy, M. M., and B. C. Griffith. Information Flow in the Language Sciences: An Exploratory Case Study of the Washington, D.C., Area. Washington, Center for Applied Linguistics, LINCS Project Document Series, 1969, 103p. ED 043 869.

0969 Rappaport, M. W. Citation Patterns in Selected Core Journals for Linguistics. Washington, Center for Applied Linguistics, Language Information Network and Clearinghouse System, February, 1971, 28p. ED 047 322.

0970 Zisa, C., et al. A Survey of Journals in the Language Sciences. Washington, Center for Applied Linguistics, Language Information Network and Clearinghouse System, September, 1969, 18p. PB 186 111.

Political Science and Law

*0971 Deutsch, K. W. "Information Needs of Political Science," In: Proceedings of the 1965 Congress of the International Federation for Documentation. Washington, Spartan, 1966, pp. 199-203.

0972 Harris, M. H. "Behavioralism in Political Science: A Guide to Reference Material," In: R. Q., 7:30-35, 1967. [Citation characteristics.]

0973 Intrama, N. Some Characteristics of the Literature of Public Administration. Ph.D. Dissertation, Bloomington, Indiana University, 1968, 109p. (University Microfilms, Inc., Order No. 68-11,391) [Citation characteristics.]

0974 Jacob, R. "Information Problems and the Law," In: The Information Scientist, 6(1): 3-13, March, 1972. [Statute law.]

0975 Marx, S. M. "Citation Networks in the Law," In: Jurimetrics Journal, 10(4): 121-137, June, 1970.

0976 Patton, P. C., and E. A. Schneider. "Information System in Local Government and the Integrated Criminal Justice Data Base," In: Proceedings of the American Society for Information Science. Westport, Conn., Greenwood, 1971, Vol. 8, pp. 331-339.

0977 Rush, M. "Primary Materials in Politics and Political Science," In: Aslib Proceedings, 23(4): 175-186, April, 1971.

0978   Stewart, J. L. "The Literature of Politics: A Citation Analysis," In: International Library Review, 2(3): 329-354, July, 1970. [Citation characteristics.]

Psychology

*0979   American Psychological Association. "The Discovery and Dissemination of Scientific Information among Psychologists in Two Research Environments," In: APA's Project on Scientific Information Exchange in Psychology. Washington, American Psychological Association, APA-PSIEP #11, December, 1965, Vol. 2, pp. 39-125. PB 169 005. [Academic environment; Governmental laboratory environment.]

*0980   American Psychological Association. "Information Exchange Activities Involved in Psychological Work," In: APA's Project on Scientific Information Exchange in Psychology. Washington, American Psychological Association, APA-PSIEP #19, January, 1969, Vol. 3, pp. 161-227. PB 182 962.

*0981   American Psychological Association. "Networks of Informal Communication among Scientifically Productive Psychologists: An Exploratory Study," In: APA's Project on Scientific Information Exchange in Psychology. Washington, American Psychological Association, APA-PSIEP #21, January, 1969, Vol. 3, pp. 233-261. PB 182 962.

0982   American Psychological Association. "A Preliminary Study of Information Exchange Activities of Foreign Psychologists and a Comparison of Such Activities with Those Occurring in the United States," In: APA's Project on Scientific Information Exchange in Psychology. Washington, American Psychological Association, APA-PSIEP #10, December, 1965, Vol. 2, pp. 1-38. PB 169 005.

*0983   American Psychological Association. "The Use of Books as a Medium for the Dissemination of Scientific Information," In: APA's Project on Scientific Information Exchange in Psychology. Washington, American Psychological Association, APA-PSIEP #14, December, 1965, Vol. 2, pp. 235-259. PB 169 005.

0984   American Psychological Association. "The Use of Scientific Information in the Undergraduate Teaching of Psychology," In: APA's Project on Scientific Information Exchange in Psychology. Washington, American Psychological Association, APA-PSIEP #17, January, 1969, Vol. 3, pp. 61-94. PB 182 962.

0985   Ball, P. J., J. G. Harpur, and D. Mack. "The Role of Minor Publications in Solving Communication Difficulties," In: Papers in Psychology, 2(2): 59, 1968. [Publication delays.]

*0986   Brayfield, A. H. "Scientific Communication in Psychology: Recent History and Context," In: American Psychologist, 25(4): i-iv, April, 1970.

0987   Cotton, M. C., and W. P. Anderson. "Citation Changes in the *Journal of Counseling Psychology*," In: Journal of Counseling Psychology, 20(3): 272-274, May, 1973.

0988   Crawford, S. Y. "Communication Centrality and Performance," In: Proceedings of the American Society for Information Science. Washington, American Society for Information Science, 1970, Vol. 7, pp. 45-48. [Communication networks; Psychophysiological research of sleep; Invisible college; Informal communication; Social organization.]

0989   Crawford, S. Y. Informal Communication among Scientists in Sleep and Dream Research. Ph.D. Dissertation, Chicago, University of Chicago, 1970, 160p. [Communication networks; Invisible college; Social organization.]

*0990   Crawford, S. Y. "Informal Communication among Scientists in Sleep Research," In: American Society for Information Science Journal, 22(5): 301-310, September-October, 1971. [Communication networks; Invisible college; Social organization.]

0991   Darley, J. G. "Information Exchange Problems in Psychology," In: Proceedings of the 1965 Congress of the International Federation for Documentation. Washington, Spartan, 1966, pp. 179-183.

*0992   Garvey, W. D., and B. C. Griffith. "Communication and Information Processing within Scientific Disciplines: Empirical Findings for Psychology," In: Information Storage and Retrieval, 8(3): 123-136, June, 1972. [Ziman's consensual model of science.]

0993   Garvey, W. D., and B. E. Compton. "A Program of Research in Scientific Information Exchange: Orientation, Objectives, and Results," In: Social Sciences Information, 6(2/3): 213-238, April-June, 1967. [American Psychological Association, Project on scientific information exchange in psychology.]

*0994   Garvey, W. D., and B. C. Griffith. "Scientific Communication: Its Role in the Conduct of Research and Creation of Knowledge," In: American Psychologist, 26(4): 349-362, April, 1971. [Informal communication; Dissemination patterns; Journal publication; Transfer of information from informal to formal domain.]

*0995   Garvey, W. D., and B. C. Griffith. "Scientific Information Exchange in Psychology," In: Science, 146(3651): 1655-1659, December 25, 1964. [Prepublication dissemination; Journal publication; Information flow.]

0996   Garvey, W. D., and B. C. Griffith. "The Structure, Objectives and Findings of a Study of Scientific Information Exchange in Psychology," In: American Documentation, 15(4): 258-267, October, 1964. [American Psychological Association, Project on Scientific Information Exchange in Psychology.]

0997   Gurman, A. S. "Institutional Sources of Articles in the *Journal of Consulting and Clinical Psychology*: 1951-1968," In: Journal of Consulting and Clinical Psychology, 36(1): 133-135, February, 1971.

0998   Horrocks, J. E., and J. D. Hogan. "A Survey and Interpretation of Article Characteristics: The *Journal of General Psychology*: 1945-1969," In: General Psychology Monographs, 87(1): 3-31, February, 1973. [Authorship; Institutional affiliation; Publication content.]

0999   Jakobovits, L. A., and C. E. Osgood. "Connotations of Twenty Psychological Journals to Their Professional Readers," In: American Psychologist, 22(9): 792-800, September, 1967.

1000   Lawler, E. E., and C. O. Lawler. "Who Cites Whom in Psychology?" In: Journal of General Psychology, 73: 31-36, 1965.

1001   Levine, N., C. Worboys, and M. Taylor. "Psychology and the 'Psychology' Textbooks: A Social Demographic Study," In: Human Relations, 26(4): 467-478, August, 1973.

1002   McCollom, I. N. "Psychology Classics: Older Journal Articles Frequently Cited Today," In: American Psychologist, 28(4): 363-365, April, 1973.

1003   Myers, C. R. "Journal Citations and Scientific Eminence in Contemporary Psychology," In: American Psychologist, 25(1): 1041-1048, November, 1970.

1004   Vockell, E. L., and S. B. Bennett. "Sources of Information in Child Psychology Literature," In: Psychological Reports, 32(2): 407-410, April, 1973.

1005   Xhignesse, L. V., and C. E. Osgood. "Bibliographic Citation Characteristics of the Psychological Journal Network in 1950 and 1960," In: American Psychologist, 22(9): 778-791, September, 1967. [Citation characteristics.]

1006 Ziman, J. M. "Information, Communication, Knowledge," In: American
Psychologist, 26(4): 338-345, April, 1971. [National Information System for Psychology; Referee system; Informal communication; Primary
sources.]

Sociology

1007 Benson, R. E., M. F. Johnson, and R. H. McMahan, Jr. Information
Requirements for Public Welfare Programs. Honolulu, Hawaii, Tempo,
General Electric Co., October, 1970, 142p. PB 198 399. [Citation
characteristics.]

1008 Broadus, R. N. "A Citation Study for Sociology," In: American Sociologist, 2(1): 19-20, February, 1967.

1009 Crawford, E. T., and A. D. Biderman. "Paper Money: Trends of
Research Sponsorship in American Sociology Journals," In: Social
Science Information, 9(1): 51-77, February, 1970.

1010 Glenn, N. D. "American Sociologists' Evaluations of Sixty-Three Journals," In: American Sociologist, 6(4): 298-303, November, 1971.

1011 Groenman, S., and G. J. A. Riesthuis. "Documentary Behavior of
Demographers," In: Social Science Information, 6(2/3): 239-245,
April-June, 1967. [Information-seeking; Communication patterns.]

1012 Guha, M. "Literature Use by European Sociologists," In: International
Library Review, 3(4): 445-452, October, 1971. [Citation characteristics.]

1013 Hoffer, J. R. "The Communication of Innovations in Social Welfare—
The Role of the Specialized Information Centers," In: Proceedings of
the American Society for Information Science. New York, Greenwood,
1968, Vol. 5, pp. 25-27.

1014 Hoffer, J. R. "Information Exchange in Social Welfare: A Myth or a
Reality?" In: Special Libraries, 60(4): 193-201, April, 1969. [Docu-
mentation problems.]

1015 Lin, N., and C. E. Nelson. "Bibliographic Reference Patterns in Core
Sociological Journals, 1965-1966," In: American Sociologist, 4(1):
47-50, February, 1969. [Citation characteristics.]

*1016   Lin, N., and W. D. Garvey. "The Formal Communication Structure in Science," In: Annual Meeting of the American Sociological Association. Denver, 1971. Washington, American Sociological Association, 1971, 45p.

*1017   Line, M. B., J. M. Brittain, and F. A. Cranmer. The Information Needs of Social Workers: Investigation into Information Requirements in the Social Sciences. Bath, England, Bath University of Technology, University Library, February, 1971, 17p. ED 049 776.

1018   Oromaner, M. J. "The Most Cited Sociologists: An Analysis of Introductory Text Citations," In: The American Sociologist, 3(2): 124-126, May, 1968.

1019   Yoels, W. C. "Destiny or Dynasty—Doctoral Origins and Appointment Patterns of Editors of American Sociological Review, 1948-1968," In: American Sociologist, 6: 134-139, May, 1971.

TECHNOLOGY

General

1020   Aslib. Accelerating Innovation: Papers Given at a Symposium Held at the University of Nottingham, March, 1969. London, Aslib, 1970, 64p. [Information transfer; Role of communication in technological innovation.]

*1021   Berul, L., et al. DoD User-Needs Study, Phase I, Final Technical Report. Philadelphia, Auerbach Corp., Report #1151-Tr-3, May 14, 1965, 2 vols. AD 615-501—AD 615-502. [Bibliography of use studies; Department of Defense; Characteristics of DoD personnel; Interview guide handbook.]

1022   Brookes, B. C. "Communicating Research Results," In: Aslib Proceedings, 16(1): 7-21, January, 1964. [Interaction of science and technology; Communication problems.]

*1023   Goodman, A. F., et al. DoD User-Needs Study, Phase II: Flow of Scientific and Technical Information within the Defense Industry, Volume II: (A) Technical Description; (B) Technical Appendices, Final Report. Anaheim Calif., North American Aviation, Inc., Autonetics Division, November 30, 1966, 501p. AD 647 112.

*1024   Goodman, A. F., et al. DoD User-Needs Study, Phase II; Flow of Scientific and Technical Information within the Defense Industry, Volume III: (A) Frequency Distributions and Correlations; (B) Relationships and Comparisons, Final Report. Anaheim, Calif., North American Aviation, Inc., Autonetics Division, November 30, 1966, 543p. AD 649 284.

*1025   Goodman, A. F., J. D. Hodges, Jr., and F. G. Allen. DoD User-Needs Study, Phase II: Flow of Scientific and Technical Information within the Defense Industry, Volume I: Overview, Final Report. Anaheim, Calif., North American Aviation, Inc., Autonetics Division, November 30, 1966, 67p. AD 647 111. [Summary conclusions; Recommendations; Review of study methodology.]

 1026   Goodman, A. F. "User Needs Study, Phase 2, Structure for the Flow of Scientific and Technical Information within the Defense Industry," In: Proceedings of the American Documentation Institute. Los Angeles, Adrianne Press, 1966, Vol. 3, pp. 283-298. [Review of study methodology.]

*1027   Goodman, A. F. Flow of Scientific and Technical Information: The Results of a Recent Major Investigation, Revised Edition. Huntington Beach, Calif., Douglas Aircraft Co., Inc., Missile and Space Systems Division, September 1, 1967, 60p. AD 657 558.

*1028   McLaughlin, C. P., R. S. Rosenbloom, and F. W. Wolek. Technology Transfer and the Flow of Technical Information in a Large Industrial Corporation. Cambridge, Mass., Harvard University, March, 1965, 2 vols. PB 173 457 and PB 173 455. [Information use; Information-seeking; Information sources; Significant personal and situational variables; Communication barriers.]

 1029   North American Aviation, Inc. Analysis of Scientific and Technical Information Requirements of FAA, Final Report. Downey, Calif., North American Aviation, Inc., Space and Information Division, October 25, 1965, 123p. PB 173 090.

 1030   Slater, M. Technical Libraries: Users and Their Demands. London, Aslib Research Department, 1964, 126p.

*1031   Slater, M., and P. Fisher. Use Made of Technical Libraries. London, Aslib, Occasional Paper No. 2, 1969, 89p.

Agriculture

*1032   Allen, T. J., J. M. Piepmeier, and S. Cooney. "The International Techno-
        logical Gatekeeper," In: Technology Review, 73(5): 36-43, March, 1971.
        [Communication networks; Informal communications; International
        transfer of technology.]

 1033   Allen, T. J., J. M. Piepmeier, and S. Cooney. "Technology Transfer to
        Developing Countries: The International Technological Gatekeeper,"
        In: Proceedings of the American Society for Information Science.
        Washington, American Society for Information Science, 1970, Vol. 7,
        pp. 205-211. [Communication networks; Informal communications;
        International transfer of technology.]

*1034   Allen, T. J. Technology Transfer to Developing Countries: The Inter-
        national Technological Gatekeeper. Cambridge, Massachusetts Institute
        of Technology, Sloan School of Management, February, 1971, 29p.
        ED 052 796. [Communication networks; Informal communications;
        International transfer of technology.]

 1035   Blanton, L. H., et al. Opinion Leadership and Communication Linkages
        among Agricultural Educators, Final Report. Columbus, Ohio State
        University, Center for Vocational and Technical Education, 1971, 79p.
        ED 056 172.

 1036   Buntrock, H. "A Statistical Analysis of the Literature of Agricultural
        Economics and Rural Sociology," In: International Association of
        Agricultural Librarians and Documentalists Bulletin, 16(1): 15-28,
        1972. [Citation characteristics.]

 1037   Hazell, J. C., and J. N. Potter. "Information Practices of Agricultural
        Scientisits," In: Australian Library Journal, 17(5): 147-159, June,
        1968. [Reading habits.]

 1038   Hein, D. "Sources of Literature Cited in Wildlife Research Papers," In:
        Journal of Wildlife Management, 31(3): 598-599, July, 1967. [Citation
        characteristics.]

 1039   Journal of Chemical Documentation. "Symposium on Problems of the
        Pesticide Literature and Some Solutions," In: Journal of Chemical
        Documentation, 4(4): 195-233, October, 1964.

 1040   Lawani, S. M. "Periodical Literature of Tropical and Subtropical Agri-
        culture," In: UNESCO Bulletin for Libraries, 26(2): 88-93, March-
        April, 1972.

 1041   Littleton, I. T. The Bibliographic Organization and Use of the Literature
        of Agricultural Economics. Ph.D. Dissertation, Urbana-Champaign, Ill.,
        University of Illinois, 1968, 231p. (University Microfilms, Inc., Order No.

68-12,153) [Citation characteristics; Secondary sources; *Bibliography of Agriculture.*]

1042   Lowry, C. D., and R. Cocroft. "Literature Needs of Food Scientists," In: Journal of Chemical Documentation, 8(4): 228-230, November, 1968.

1043   Mann, E. J. "Report on International Survey of the World Literature of Food Science and Technology," In: Dairy Science Abstracts, 28: 603-606, 1966.

Engineering

*1044   Allen, T. J. "Communication in the Research and Development Laboratory," In: Technology Review, 70(1): 31-37, October/November, 1967. [Technological gatekeeper; Communication networks; Impact of social status on communication.]

1045   Allen, T. J. "Communication Networks in R&D Laboratories," In: R&D Management, 1(10): 14-21, October, 1970. [Technological gatekeeper; Impact of organization on communication; Communication roles in the laboratory.]

1046   Allen, T. J., and P. G. Gerstberger. Criteria for Selection of an Information Source. Cambridge, Massachusetts Institute of Technology, Sloan School of Management, Report #284-67, 1967, 26p. PB 176 899.

*1047   Allen, T. J. "The Differential Performance of Information Channels in the Transfer of Technology," In: Factors in the Transfer of Technology. Edited by W. H. Gruber and D. G. Marquis. Cambridge, Massachusetts Institute of Technology Press, 1969, pp. 137-154.

1048   Allen, T. J., and D. G. Marquis. Factors Influencing Technical Quality of R&D Proposals. Cambridge, Massachusetts Institute of Technology, Sloan School of Management, Working Paper #196-66, June, 1966, 28p. [Communication patterns and their influence.]

1049   Allen, T. J., and S. I. Cohen. Information Flow in an R&D Laboratory. Cambridge, Massachusetts Institute of Technology, Sloan School of Management, Report #217-66, August, 1966, 28p. PB 173 524. [Social organization.]

*1050   Allen, T. J., and S. I. Cohen. "Information Flow in Research and
        Development Laboratories," In: Administrative Science Quarterly,
        14(3): 12-19, March, 1969. [Influence of the organization; Sociometric
        patterns; Social status; Technological gatekeeper.]

*1051   Allen, T. J. Managing the Flow of Scientific and Technological Informa-
        tion, Final Report. Cambridge, Massachusetts Institute of Technology,
        Sloan School of Management, September, 1966, 298p. PB 174 440.
        [R&D laboratories; Social organization.]

 1052   Allen, T. J. Meeting the Technical Information Needs of Research and
        Development Projects. Cambridge, Massachusetts Institute of Technol-
        ogy, Sloan School of Management, Working Paper #431-69, November,
        1969, 21p. ED 047 748.

*1053   Allen, T. J. "Organizational Aspects of Information Flow in Technology,"
        In: Aslib Proceedings, 20(11): 433-454, November, 1968. [Information
        sources; R&D laboratories; Social organization; Work group structure;
        Technological gatekeeper.]

 1054   Allen, T. J. "Performance of Information Channels in the Transfer of
        Technology," In: Industrial Management Review, 8: 87-98, 1966.
        [R&D laboratories.]

 1055   Allen, T. J., A. A. Gerstenfeld, and P. G. Gerstberger. The Problem of
        Internal Consulting in Research and Development Organizations.
        Cambridge, Massachusetts Institute of Technology, Sloan School of
        Management, Working Paper #319-68, 1968. [Communication
        patterns.]

 1056   Allen, T. J. "The Problem Solving Process in Engineering Design," In:
        IEEE Transactions on Engineering Management, EM 13(2): 72-83,
        1966. [Information sources.]

 1057   Allen, T. J. Problem Solving Strategies in Parallel Research and Develop-
        ment Projects. Cambridge, Massachusetts Institute of Technology, Sloan
        School of Management, Working Paper #126-65, June, 1965, 27p.
        N66-12989 or PB 168 429. [Information sources.]

 1058   Allen, T. J., and P. G. Gerstberger. Report of a Field Experiment to
        Improve Communications in a Product Engineering Department: The
        Nonterritorial Office. Cambridge, Massachusetts Institute of Technol-
        ogy, Sloan School of Management, Working Paper #579-71, December,
        1971.

*1059   Allen, T. J. "Roles in Technical Communication Networks," In: Com-
        munication among Scientists and Engineers. Edited by C. E. Nelson and
        D. K. Pollock. Lexington, Mass., Heath Lexington Books, 1970,

pp. 191-208. [Impact of organization; Characteristics of gatekeepers; Communication isolates; Departmental liaisons; Communication roles.]

1060   Allen, T. J. Sources of Ideas and Their Effectiveness in Parallel R&D Projects. Cambridge, Massachusetts Institute of Technology, Sloan School of Management, Working Paper #130-65, July, 1965, 28p. PB 168 430 or N66-12194. [Information sources.]

1061   Allen, T. J. "Sources of Ideas in Parallel R&D Projects," In: Conference on Research Program Effectiveness, Proceedings. Edited by M. C. Yovits, et al. New York, Gordon and Breach, 1966. [Information sources.]

1062   Allen, T. J. Studies of the Problem Solving Process in Engineering Design. Cambridge, Massachusetts Institute of Technology, Sloan School of Management, 1965, 36p. PB 168 431. [Information sources.]

1063   Allen, T. J., and M. P. Andrien, Jr. Time Allocation among Three Technical Information Channels by R&D Engineers. Cambridge, Massachusetts Institute of Technology, Sloan School of Management, Report #131-65, August, 1965, 23p. N66-14577.

1064   Allen, T. J. The Utilization of Information Sources during R&D Proposal Preparation. Cambridge, Massachusetts Institute of Technology, Sloan School of Management, Working Paper #97-64, October, 1964, 34p. PB 167 317 or N65-26415.

1065   American Concrete Institute. Conference on International Exchange of Information on Cement and Concrete Research, London, March 2-6, 1970. Detroit, American Concrete Institute, March, 1970, 37p. PB 198 649.

1066   Askew, W. G. "The Offer You Can't Refuse: The Engineering Periodical," In: IEEE Transactions on Professional Communication, PC 16(3): 97-99, 176, September, 1973.

1067   Baker, N. R., J. Siegmann, and A. H. Rubenstein. "The Effects of Perceived Needs and Means on the Generation of Ideas for Industrial Research and Development Projects," In: IEEE Transactions on Engineering Management, EM 14(4): 156-162, December, 1967. [Communication patterns.]

1068   Bartkus, E. P. "Major Sources of Information for Engineering Educators," In: Engineering Education, 60(5): 377-380, January, 1970.

1069   Beardsley, C. W. "Keeping on Top of Your Field," In: IEEE Spectrum, 9(12): 68-71, December, 1972. [Information sources; Electrical engineers.]

1070 Bishop, D. "Information Flow in the Construction Industry: A Study and the Development of Its Recommendations," In: Aslib Proceedings, 24(2): 79-95, February, 1972.

1071 Cairns, R. W. "Communication in a Scientific and Engineering Society," In: Chemical and Engineering News, 46(1): 5-6, 1968.

1072 Carlson, W. M. "Needs of Practicing Engineers," In: Proceedings of the National Engineering Information Conference. Edited by F. Y. Speight. New York, Engineers Joint Council, 1969, pp. 7-12. [Information needs; Influence of work role.]

1073 Cohen, S. I. Technical Information Flow within an R&D Laboratory. S.M. Thesis, Cambridge, Massachusetts Institute of Technology, Sloan School of Management, 1966.

1074 Coile, R. C. "Information Sources for Electrical and Electronics Engineers," In: IEEE Transactions on Engineering Writing and Speech, 12(3): 71-78, October, 1969. [Citation characteristics.]

1075 Conrath, D. W. "The Role of the Informal Organization in Decision Making in R&D," In: IEEE Transactions on Engineering Management, EM 15(3): 109-119, September, 1968. [Informal communication.]

1076 Davies, R. A. "How Engineers Use Literature," In: Chemical Engineering Progress, 61(3): 30-34, March, 1965. [Relative use of different document forms.]

1077 Dorrance, D. "SDI and the Gatekeeper," In: Special Libraries, 59(10): 803-804, December, 1968.

1078 Douds, C. F. The Effects of Work-Related Values on Communication between R&D Groups. Ph.D. Dissertation, Evanston, Ill., Northwestern University, August, 1970, 2 vols. N72-18984 and N72-18985.

1079 Fidoia, A. Technological Gatekeepers and Their Role in R&D Laboratories. M.S. Thesis, Cambridge, Massachusetts Institute of Technology, 1968.

1080 Frischmuth, D. S. Interaction between Technical Information Sources and the Problem Solving Process in Systems Research and Development. S.M. Thesis, Cambridge, Massachusetts Institute of Technology, Sloan School of Management, 1966.

1081 Frischmuth, D. S., and T. J. Allen. "A Model for the Description and Evaluation of Technical Problem Solving," In: IEEE Transactions on Engineering Management, EM 16(2): 58-63, May, 1969.

1082 Frost, P., and R. Whitley. "Communication Patterns in a Research Laboratory," In: Research and Development Management, 1(2): 71-79, February, 1971.

1083 Gerstberger, P. G., and T. J. Allen. "Criteria for Selection of an Information Source," In: Industrial Management Review, 8(1): 87-98, 1966.

*1084 Gerstberger, P. G., and T. J. Allen. "Criteria Used by Research and Development Engineers in the Selection of an Information Source," In: Journal of Applied Psychology, 52(4): 272-279, August, 1968.

1085 Gerstberger, P. G. An Investigation of the Criteria Used in Information Channel Selection by R&D Engineers. S.M. Thesis, Cambridge, Massachusetts Institute of Technology, Sloan School of Management, 1967.

1086 Gerstberger, P. G. The Preservation and Transfer of Technology in Research and Development Organizations. Ph.D. Dissertation, Cambridge, Massachusetts Institute of Technology, Sloan School of Management, June, 1971, 271p. [Communication patterns.]

1087 Grant, J. Information for Industry—A Study in Communications. Petoria, Republic of South Africa, Council for Scientific and Industrial Research, CSIR Research Report 229, 1964, 74p.

1088 Hall, R. W. An Investigation into the Information Habits of Scientists and Engineers in Industry. Bloomington, Indiana University, Aerospace Research Applications Center, October, 1969, 16p. N70-11582. [Information sources; Reading habits.]

*1089 Hall, R. W. "Technical Information Habits of Engineers," In: Chemical Engineering Progress, 69(3): 67-71, March, 1973. [Information sources; Communication patterns; Technological gatekeeper.]

1090 Hinricks, J. R. "Communication Activities of Industrial Research Personnel," In: Personnel Psychology, 17(2): 193-204, Summer, 1964.

1091 Hodges, J. D., Jr., and B. W. Angalet. "The Prime Technical Information Source: The Local Work Environment," In: Human Factors, 10(4): 425-429, 1968. [Department of Defense study.]

1092 Hyslop, M. R. "The Role of Technical Societies in the Field of Technical Information," In: Journal of Paint Technology, 42(546): 63A-66A, July, 1970.

1093 Janning, E. A., R. B. Smith, and J. C. Wurst. Information Needs of the Ceramic Industry: A Users-Need Study. Dayton, Ohio, Dayton University, May, 1968, 74p. PB 179 672.

1094   Kanno, M. Effect on Communication between Labs and Plants of the Transfer of R&D Personnel. S.M. Thesis, Cambridge, Massachusetts Institute of Technology, Sloan School of Management, 1968.

1095   Klein, S. "The Information Goals of Engineers Joint Council," In: Special Libraries, 55(3): 143-147, March, 1964.

1096   Levy, N. P. "A Survey of the Information Practices of Engineers at Western Electric," In: American Documentation, 15(2): 86-88, April, 1964.

1097   Lufkin, J. M., and E. H. Miller. "The Reading Habits of Engineers—A Preliminary Survey," In: IEEE Transactions on Education, 9(4): 179-182, 1966.

*1098   Marquis, D. G., and T. J. Allen. "Communication Patterns in Applied Technology," In: American Psychologist, 21(11): 1052-1060, November, 1966. [Interaction of science and technology; Information flow; Impact of the organization on communication patterns.]

1099   Massachusetts Institute of Technology. Study of Information Requirements for Research and Development, Annual Report. Cambridge, Massachusetts Institute of Technology, Sloan School of Management, August, 1968, 79p. PB 179 538.

1100   Moore, J. R. "On Interrelationships of the Sciences and Technology as Expressed by a Categorized List of Journals and Modified by a Classification System," In: American Society for Information Science Journal, 24(5): 359-367, September-October, 1973.

1101   Mote, L. J. B. "Personal Patterns of Information Use in an Industrial Research and Development Laboratory," In: Journal of Documentation, 27(3): 200-204, September, 1971.

1102   O'Gara, P. W. Physical Location as a Determinant of Communication Possibility among R&D Engineers. S.M. Thesis, Cambridge, Massachusetts Institute of Technology, Sloan School of Management, 1968.

1103   Perrucci, R., and R. A. Rothman. "Obsolescence of Knowledge and the Professional Career," In: The Engineers and the Social System. Edited by R. Perrucci and J. E. Gerstl. New York, Wiley, 1969, pp. 247-276.

*1104   Price, D. J. S. "Is Technology Historically Independent of Science? A Study in Statistical Historiography," In: Technology and Culture, 6(4): 553-568, 1965. [Interaction of science and technology; Role of formal communication.]

1105 Robertson, A. "Information Flow and Industrial Innovation," In: Aslib Proceedings, 25(4): 130-139, April, 1973.

1106 Rosenberg, V. "Factors Affecting the Preferences of Industrial Personnel for Information Gathering Methods," In: Information Storage and Retrieval, 3(3): 119-127, July, 1967.

1107 Rosenbloom, R. S., and F. W. Wolek. Studies of the Flow of Technical Information. I: A Survey in Selected Industrial Laboratories; II: A Survey of Selected Members of the Institute of Electrical and Electronics Engineers; III: Studies of Decision-Making in Developmental Projects, Interim Report. Cambridge, Mass., Harvard University, Graduate School of Business, January, 1966, 26p. PB 169 327 and PB 175 714.

*1108 Rosenbloom, R. S., and F. W. Wolek. Technology, Information, and Organization: Information Transfer in Industrial R&D. Cambridge, Mass., Harvard University, Graduate School of Business Administration, June, 1967, 252p. PB 175 959.

1109 Rubenstein, A. H., and C. F. Douds. "A Program of Research on Coupling Relations in Research and Development," In: IEEE Transactions on Engineering Management, EM 16(4): 137-143, November, 1969. [Interaction of science and technology; Diffusion of ideas.]

1110 Sarasohn, H. M. "The Technical Journal—Who Needs It?" In: IEEE Transactions on Professional Communication, PC 16(3): 179-180, September, 1973. [Role of professional journals in appraising quality of laboratory output.]

1111 Saunderson, K. M. "Patents as a Source of Technical Information," In: Aslib Proceedings, 24(4): 244-254, April, 1972.

1112 Shotwell, T. K. "Information Flow in an Industrial Research Laboratory—A Case Study," In: IEEE Transactions on Engineering Management, EM 18(1): 26-33, February, 1971. [Impact of geographical and demographic factors on information flow.]

1113 Speight, F. Y., and N. E. Cottrell. The EJC Engineering Information Program, 1965-1967, Progress Report. New York, Engineers Joint Council, February, 1967, 50p. PB 174 424.

1114 Speight, F. Y. Proceedings of the National Engineering Information Conference Held at Washington, D. C., June 24-25, 1969. New York, Engineers Joint Council, 1969, 139p. PB 189 505.

*1115 Taylor, R. S., ed. Information Management in Engineering Education. Bethlehem, Pa., Lehigh University, 1966.

1116 van Houten, R. Technical Information for Industry: Short Report on Industry's Needs for Technical Information in General and in the Field of Electronics in Particular. Pretoria, South Africa, Council for Scientific and Industrial Research, Information Research Services, 1966, 29p.

1117 Waldhart, T. J. The Relationship between the Citation of Scientific Literature and the Institutional Affiliation of Engineers. Ph.D. Dissertation, Bloomington, Indiana University, 1973, 193p. (University Microfilms, Inc., Order No. 73-12,355) [*Engineering Index*; Citation characteristics; Interaction of science and technology; Communication patterns.]

*1118 Wolek, F. W. "The Engineer: His Work and Needs for Information," In: Proceedings of the American Society for Information Science. Westport, Conn., Greenwood, 1969, Vol. 6, pp. 471-476.

1119 Wood, D. N., and D. R. L. Hamilton. The Information Requirements of Mechanical Engineers—Report of a Recent Survey. London, Library Association, 1967.

Medicine

1120 Bauer, R. A., and L. H. Wortzel. "Doctor's Choice: The Physician and His Sources of Information about Drugs," In: Journal of Marketing Research, 3(1): 40-47, February, 1966.

1121 Becker, M. H. "Factors Affecting Diffusion of Innovations among Health Professionals," In: American Journal of Public Health, 60(2): 298-304, February, 1970.

1122 Bowden, C. L., and V. M. Bowden. "A Survey of Information Sources Used by Psychiatrists," In: Medical Library Association Bulletin, 59(4): 603-608, October, 1971.

1123 Cannan, R. K. "Communication Problems in Biomedical Research: Introduction and Report," In: Federation Proceedings, 23: 1117-1132, September-October, 1964.

*1124 Coleman, J. S., E. Katz, and H. Menzel. Medical Innovation: A Diffusion Study. Indianapolis, Ind., Bobbs-Merrill, 1966, 246p. [Communication patterns.]

1125   Cummings, M. M. "The Biomedical Communications Problem," In:
       Communication in Science: Documentation and Automation. Edited by
       A. DeReuck and J. Knight, Boston, Mass., Little, Brown & Co., 1967,
       pp. 110-123.

1126   Davis, J. M. "The Transmission of Information in Psychiatry," In: Pro-
       ceedings of the American Society for Information Science. Washington,
       American Society for Information Science, 1970, Vol. 7, pp. 53-56.

1127   Frick, B. F., and J. M. Ginski. "Cardiovascular Serial Literature: Char-
       acteristics, Productive Journals, and Abstracting/Indexing Coverage,"
       In: American Society for Information Science Journal, 21(5): 338-344,
       September-October, 1970.

1128   Friedlander, J. "Clinician Search for Information," In: American Soci-
       ety for Information Science Journal, 24(1): 65-69, January-February,
       1973. [Role of library; Accessibility; Informal communication.]

1129   Friedlander, J. Physicians Use of a Medical Library. Ph.D. Dissertation,
       Cleveland, Ohio, Case Western Reserve University, 1970, 152p. (Univer-
       sity Microfilms, Inc., Order No. 71-169)

*1130 Herner, S., et al. "User Practices Based on a Review of User Studies,"
       In: A Recommended Design for the United States Medical Library and
       Information System, Washington, Herner & Co., July, 1966, Vol. 2,
       pp. V1-V56. PB 172 924/Wzz.

1131   Ingelfinger, F. J. "Medical Literature: The Campus without Tumult,"
       In: Science, 169(3948): 831-837, August 28, 1970.

1132   Jablonski, S. "The Biomedical Information Explosion: From the Index
       Catalogue to MEDLARS," In: Bulletin of the Medical Library Associa-
       tion, 59(1): 94-98, January, 1971.

1133   Leith, J. D. "Biomedical Literature: Analysis of Journal Articles Col-
       lected by a Radiation and Cell-Biologist," In: American Documenta-
       tion, 20(2): 143-148, April, 1969.

1134   Lieberman, J. "Biomedical Communication: Crisis and Plan for Action,"
       In: American Journal of Veterinary Research, 26: Supplement, 1582-
       1586, November, 1965.

1135   McLaughlin, C. P., and R. Penchansky. "Diffusion of Innovations in
       Medicine: A Problem of Continuing Medical Education," In: Journal of
       Medical Education, 40(5): 437-447, May, 1965.

1136   McMutray, F., and J. M. Ginski. "Citation Patterns of the Cardiovascular Serial Literature," In: American Society for Information Science Journal, 23(3): 172-175, May-June, 1972.

1137   Magee, M. How Research Biochemists Use Information: An Analysis of Use of Information from Cited References. Masters Thesis, Chicago, University of Chicago, Graduate Library School, June, 1966, 36p. [Citation characteristics.]

*1138   Menzel, H. "Sociological Perspectives on the Information-Gathering Practices of the Scientific Investigator and the Medical Practitioner," In: Bibliotheca Medica: Physicians for Tomorrow; Dedication of the Countway Library of Medicine. Edited by D. McCord. Boston, Mass., Harvard University, Medical School, 1966.

1139   Miller, L. B., and E. N. Rathbun. "Growth and Development of Nursing Literature," In: Bulletin of the Medical Library Association, 52(2): 420-426, April, 1964.

1140   Montgomery, R. R. "Productivity in Toxicity Papers," In: American Society for Information Science Journal, (Brief Communication), 24(5): 402-403, September, 1973.

*1141   Morris, W. C. The Information Influential Physician: The Knowledge Flow Process among Medical Practitioners. Ph.D. Dissertation, Ann Arbor, Mich., University of Michigan, 1970, 210p. (University Microfilms, Inc., Order No. 71-4686) [Technological gatekeeper.]

1142   Morton, L. T. "British Medical Periodicals: 1868-1968," In: The Practitioner, 201(1201): 224-230, July, 1968.

1143   Orr, R. H., et al. "The Biomedical Information Complex Viewed as a System," In: Federation Proceedings, 23: 1133-1145, September-October, 1964.

1144   Orr, R. H., and A. Leeds. "Biomedical Literature: Volume, Growth and Other Characteristics," In: Federation Proceedings, 23: 1310-1331, November-December, 1964.

1145   Orr, R. H., et al. "Generation of Information: Published Output of U.S. Biomedical Research," In: Federation Proceedings, 23: 1297-1309, November-December, 1964.

1146   Orr, R. H. "Trends in Oral Communication among Biomedical Scientists: Meetings and Travel," In: Federation Proceedings, 23: 1146-1154, September-October, 1964.

1147 Raisig, L. M., et al. "How Biomedical Investigators Use Library Books," In: Bulletin of the Medical Library Association, 54: 104-107, April, 1966.

1148 Raisig, L. M. "World Biomedical Journals, 1951-60: A Study of the Relative Significance of 1388 Titles Indexed in *Current List of Medical Literature*," In: Bulletin of the Medical Library Association, 54: 108-125, April, 1966.

1149 Rath, G. J., et al. A Field Experiment in Information-Seeking by Medical Researchers. Atlanta, Ga., Institute of Management Sciences, 1969.

1150 Rath, G. J., and D. J. Werner. "Infosearch: Studying the Remote Use of Libraries by Medical Researchers," In: Proceedings of the American Documentation Institute. Washington, Thompson, 1967, Vol. 4, pp. 58-62. [Implementation and evaluation of telephone reference service.]

1151 Rehder, R. R. "Communication and Opinion Formation in a Medical Community: The Significance of the Detail Man," In: Academic Management Journal, 8: 282-291, 1965.

1152 Roland, C. G. "Thoughts about Medical Writing, VII: Loaded Language," In: Anesthesia and Analgesia (Cleveland), 50: 936-937, 1971. [Rhetorical *vs*. scientific use of language.]

*1153 Rubenstein, A. H., et al. "Explorations on the Information Seeking Style of Researchers," In: Communication among Scientists and Engineers. Edited by C. E. Nelson and D. K. Pollock. Lexington, Mass., Heath Lexington Books, 1970, pp. 209-232. [X-ray crystallographers; Medical researchers; Influence of work role; Environmental and organizational constraints.]

1154 Rubenstein, A. H., et al. "Some Preliminary Experiments and a Model of Information-Seeking Style of Researchers," In: Proceedings of the 20th National Conference on the Administration of Research. Denver, Colo., University of Denver, Denver Research Institute, 1967, pp. 93-110.

1155 Sengupta, I. N. "Factors Determining Changes in Ranking of Scientific Periodicals: A Study in Relation to Biomedical Journals during the Post-War Period," In: International Library Review, 3(3): 271-286, June, 1971. [Citation frequency.]

1156 Sengupta, I. N. "Growth of Biochemical Literature," In: Nature, 244(5411): 75-76, 118, July 13, 1973.

1157   Sengupta, I. N. "Impact of Scientific Serials on the Advancement of Medical Knowledge: An Objective Method of Analysis," In: International Library Review, 4(2): 169-195, April, 1972. [Citation frequency.]

1158   Sengupta, I. N. "Recent Growth of the Literature of Biochemistry and Changes in Ranking of Periodicals," In: Journal of Documentation, 29(2): 192-211, June, 1973. [Citation frequency; Bradford distribution.]

1159   Shephard, D. A. E. "New Information in Medical Journals: Excretory or Secretory Process," In: Mayo Clinic Proceedings, 47(6): 415-432, June, 1972.

1160   Sherrington, A. M. "An Annotated Bibliography of Studies on the Flow of Medical Information to Practitioners," In: Methods of Information in Medicine, 4(1): 45-57, March, 1965.

1161   Shilling, C. W., and H. Benton. Pharmacology, Toxicology, and Cosmetics Serials: Their Identification and an Analysis of Their Characteristics. Washington, George Washington University, Biological Sciences Communication Project, BSCP-22-65, 1965. [Citation characteristics.]

1162   Shilling, C. W., and H. Benton. Serials Related to Biochemistry and Endocrinology: Their Identification and Analysis of Their Characteristics. Washington, George Washington University, Biological Sciences Communication Project, BSCP-21-65, 1965. [Citation characteristics.]

1163   Stangl, P., and F. G. Kilgour. "Analysis of Recorded Biomedical Book and Journal Use in the Yale Medical Library: Part I, Date and Subject Relations," In: Bulletin of the Medical Library Association, 55: 290-300, 1967.

1164   Stangl, P. and F. G. Kilgour. "Analysis of Recorded Biomedical Book and Journal Use in the Yale Medical Library: Part II, Subject and User Relations," In: Bulletin of the Medical Library Association, 55: 301-15, 1967.

1165   Stokes, J., and R. M. Hayes. "A Commentary on the Biomedical Information System," In: Journal of Medical Education, 45(4): 245-249, April, 1970. [Communication model.]

1166   Tishler, M. "What Information Does the Medicinal Chemist Really Need? Projections for the Future," In: Journal of Chemical Documentation, 11(3): 134-137, August, 1971.

*1167   Trueswell, R. W., and A. H. Rubenstein. Information Searching Behavior of Physicians, Evanston, Ill., Northwestern University, Department of Industrial Engineering and Management Science, October, 1966, 19p. ED 026 100.

1168   University of Western Ontario, London. Medical Information Network for Ontario: Determination of Information Need. London, Ontario, School of Library and Information Science, 1973, 398p. ED 081 436.

1169   Vaillancourt, P. M. Bibliographic Control of the Literature of Oncology, 1800-1960. D.L.S. Dissertation, New York, Columbia University, 1968, 330p. (University Microfilms, Inc., Order No. 71-17,627)

1170   Walsh, M. C. "Bradford's Law" and the Literature of Opthalmology, Masters Thesis, Chicago, University of Chicago, June, 1967, 33p.

1171   Warren, K. S., and W. Goffman. "The Ecology of the Medical Literature," In: American Journal of Medical Science, 263(4): 267-273, April, 1972. [Bibliometric analysis; Bradford distribution; Mathematical model; Epidemic theory.]

1172   Werner, D. J. A Study of the Information-Seeking Behavior of Medical Researchers. M.S. Thesis, Evanston, Ill., Northwestern University, December, 1965, 102p.

*1173   Werner, D. J. A Theoretical and Empirical Investigation of the Relationships between Some Measures of Information Related Behavior and the Characteristics of the Individual's Task, Person, Organizational Environment, and Professional Environment. Ph.D. Dissertation, Evanston, Ill., Northwestern University, 1969, 356p. (University Microfilms, Inc., Order No. 70-6547)

1174   Wilson, P. T. "Psychiatric Information Exchange Programs," In: Hospital and Community Psychiatry, 20(7): 209-212, July, 1969.

1175   Wood, D. N., and C. A. Bower. "Survey of Medical Literature Borrowed from the National Lending Library for Science and Technology," In: Bulletin of the Medical Library Association, 57: 47-63, January, 1969.

1176   Wood, D. N., and C. A. Bower. "The Use of Biomedical Periodical Literature at the National Lending Library for Science and Technology," In: Methods of Information in Medicine, 9(1): 46-53, January, 1970.

COMMUNICATION BARRIERS—
LANGUAGE, MESSAGE STRUCTURE AND SECURITY

1177   Abdian, A. G., and P. Klinefelter. "Transfer of Security-Classified Information," In: Journal of Chemical Documentation, 9(4): 224-226, November, 1969. [Defense Documentation Center; Information dissemination; Information control.]

*1178   Basu, R. N. "Barriers to Effective Communication in the Scientific World," In: IEEE Transactions on Professional Communication, PC 15(2): 30-33, June, 1972. [International information transfer; Language; Literature volume; Jargon; Dissemination delays; Cost.]

1179   Bross, I. D. J., P. A. Shapiro, and B. B. Anderson. "How Information Is Carried in Scientific Sub-Languages," In: Science, 176(4041): 1303-1307, June 23, 1972. [Linguistics; Jargon.]

*1180   Cade, J. A. "Aspects of Secrecy in Science," In: Impact of Science on Society, 21(2): 181-190, April-June, 1971. [Pros and cons of secrecy in science.]

1181   Cavanagh, J. M. A. "Information Transfer across National Boundaries," In: Proceedings of the American Society for Information Science. New York, Greenwood, 1968, Vol. 5, 10p. [International information transfer; Proprietary interests; Defense secrecy.]

*1182   Cox, B. G., and C. G. Roland. "How Rhetoric Confuses Scientific Issues," In: IEEE Transactions on Professional Communication, PC 16(3): 140-142, September, 1973. [Persuasion in scientific literature.]

1183   Crisman, T. L. "In-House Publications—Can They Endanger Rights in Technical Information?" In: Journal of the Patent Office Society, 49: 549-565, 1967. [Proprietary interests.]

*1184   Downie, C. S. Barriers to the Flow of Technical Information: Limitation Statements—Legal Basis. Arlington, Va., Office of Aerospace Research, May 7, 1969, 19p. AD 692 400. [Distribution limitations; Proprietary interests; Security classified information; Administrative Procedure Act, Public Information Section; "Freedom of Information Law."]

1185 Downie, C. S. "Legal and Policy Impediments to Federal Technical Information Transfer," In: Proceedings of the American Society for Information Science. Westport, Conn., Greenwood, 1969, Vol. 6, pp. 411-416. [Distribution limitations; Proprietary interests; Security classified information: Administrative Procedure Act, Public Information section; "Freedom of Information Law."]

1186 Durrain, S. A. "Jargon and Scientific Communication," In: Nucleus, 7(4): 215-220, October, 1970.

1187 Foo-Kune, C. F. "Japanese Scientific and Technical Periodicals: An Analysis of Their European Language Content," In: Journal of Documentation, 26(2): 111-119, June, 1970.

*1188 Gaston, J. C. "Secretiveness and Competition for Priority of Discovery in Physics," In: Minerva, 9(4): 472-492, October, 1971. [Social structure.]

1189 Gilinski, V. "Proposed A.E.C. Rules on Private Restricted Data," In: Federal Register, 32(250): 20868-20880. December 28, 1968. [Distribution limitations; Nuclear science; Proprietary interests; Security classified information.]

1190 Gonod, P., and J. Beverly. "Constraints on the International Flow of Information in Latin America," In: Proceedings of the American Society for Information Science. Westport, Conn., Greenwood, 1972, Vol. 9, pp. 219-228. [Organization of American States, Technological development program.]

1191 Hutchins, W. J., L. J. Pargeter, and W. L. Saunders. The Language Barrier: A Study in Depth of the Place of Foreign Language Materials in the Research Activities of an Academic Community. University of Sheffield, Postgraduate School of Librarianship and Information Science, 1971, 306p. [Sciences; Social sciences; Technology.]

*1192 Hutchins, W. J., L. J. Pargeter, and W. L. Saunders. "University Research and the Language Barrier," In: Journal of Librarianship, 3(1): 1-25, January, 1971. [Sciences; Social sciences; Technology.]

*1193 Klempner, I. M. "The Concept of 'National Security' and Its Effect on Information Transfer," In: Special Libraries, 64(7): 263-269, July, 1973. [Security classified information.]

1194 Klempner, I. M. "Secrecy; Or the Cost of Withholding Information," In: Proceedings of the American Society for Information Science. Westport Conn., Greenwood, 1973, Vol. 10, pp. 111-113. [Security classified information.]

1195 Lufkin, J. M., and S. C. Krantz. "Cultural Barriers to Interprofessional Communication," In: IEEE Transactions on Professional Communication, PC 15(2): 26-29, June, 1972. [Jargon; Individual viewpoint; Message complexity.]

*1196 Luger, H. P., and R. J. Bosser. Classified Information and Technical Libraries, Final Report. Bethesda, Md., Control Data Corporation, Howard Research Division, January, 1967, 34p. AD 812 521. [Handling of classified information.]

1197 Magaha, E. P., Jr. Dissemination of Scientific and Technical Information Produced by or for the Federal Government: A Study of Distribution Controls within the Department of Defense. Frederick, Md., Army Biological Defense Research Center, March, 1966, 105p. AD 730 927. [Distribution limitations; International information transfer; Proposed system for Department of Defense.]

1198 Mannheim, F. T. Foreign Literature and Translations in Earth Science. Woods Hole Oceanographic Institution, Mass., September, 1972, 42p. PB 214 086/1.

*1199 Mead, M., et al. "Secrecy and Dissemination in Science and Technology," In: Science, 163(3869): 787-790, February 21, 1969. [Effects of secrecy on research.]

1200 Munster, J. H., and J. C. Smith. "The Care and Feeding of Intellectual Property," In: Science, 148(3671): 739-742, May 7, 1965. [Proprietary interests; Intellectual property; Statutory protection.]

1201 National Security Industrial Association. Barriers to Scientific and Technical Information. 2 Parts. Washington, National Security Industrial Association, September, 1969, 294p. AD 716 542. [Regulatory control of literature and data; Security controls; Proprietary interest.]

1202 Nature. "Secrecy in Science," In: Nature, 241(5387): 231, January 26, 1973.

1203 Rae, J. C. Development of Criteria and Procedures for Management of Classified Document Collection. Waltham, Mass., Information Management, Inc., April 14, 1966, 55p. AD 687 482. [Microforms; Handling of security classified information.]

1204 Saunders, W. L. "The Foreign Language and Translation Problems of the Social Sciences," In: Aslib Proceedings, 24(4): 233-243, April, 1972.

1205   Simpson, G. S., and J. W. Murdock. "Dollars and Secrets," In: American Documentation, (Letter), 18(2): 110-111, April, 1967. [Proprietary interests; National security.]

1206   Syracuse University, Research Institute. A Study of the Frequency with Which Russian, French, and German Scientific Articles are Cited in Selected American Scientific Journals. New York, Syracuse University, Research Institute, June, 1966, 83p. PB 170 620.

1207   Taylor, R. L. Classification Management: An Analysis of the Need for Such Programs in Defense-Oriented Companies. Masters Thesis, Columbus, Ohio State University, 1966.

1208   U.S. Federal Council for Science and Technology. Policies Governing the Foreign Dissemination of Scientific and Technical Information by Agencies of the U.S. Federal Government. Washington, Office of Science and Technology, 1968. [International information transfer.]

*1209   Vasilakis, M. "Classified Material (Security)," In: Encyclopedia of Library and Information Science. New York, Dekker, 1971, Vol. 5, pp. 174-185.

*1210   Wolek, Francis W. "The Complexity of Messages in Science and Engineering: An Influence on Patterns Communication," In: Communication among Scientists and Engineers. Edited by C. A. Nelson and D. K. Pollock. Lexington, Mass., Heath Lexington Books, 1970, pp. 233-265.

1211   Wood, D. N. "Foreign Language Problems Facing Scientists and Technologists in the United Kingdom: Report of a Recent Survey," In: Journal of Documentation, 23: 117-130, 1967.

COMMUNICATION INNOVATIONS

GENERAL

1212   American Psychological Association. "Innovations in Scientific Communication in Psychology," Report No. 16, December, 1966, In: APA's Project on Scientific Information Exchange in Psychology. Washington, American Psychological Association, January, 1969, Vol. 3, pp. 1-60. PB 182 962. [Listing titles and authors of manuscripts accepted by journals with long publication lags; Preconvention publication of contributed papers of annual APA convention.]

1213   American Psychological Association. "Theoretical and Methodological Considerations in Undertaking Innovations in Scientific Information Exchange," Report No. 12, January, 1965, In: APA's Project on Scientific Information Exchange in Psychology. Washington, American Psychological Association, December, 1965, Vol. 2, pp. 127-180. PB 169 005. [Effects of innovation on dissemination process; Effects of conference presentations on subsequent scientific activities.]

*1214   Garvey, W. D., and B. C. Griffith. "Communication in a Science: The System and Its Modification," In: Communication in Science: Documentation and Automation. Edited by A. DeReuck and J. Knight. Boston, Little, Brown & Co., 1967, pp. 16-30.

*1215   Garvey, W. D., and B. C. Griffith. "Scientific Communication: The Dissemination System in Psychology and a Theoretical Framework for Planning Innovations," In: American Psychologist, 20(2): 157-164, February, 1965.

*1216   Garvey, W. D., and B. C. Griffith. "Studies of Social Innovations in Scientific Communication in Psychology," In: American Psychologist, 21(11): 1019-1036, November, 1966.

*1217   Griffith, B. C., and W. D. Garvey. "Systems in Scientific Information and the Effects of Innovation and Change," In: Proceedings of the American Documentation Institute. Washington, American Documentation Institute, 1964, Vol. 1, pp. 191-200.

1218 Herbert, E. "Innovations in Communication: Shortening the Feedback Loop among Humans," In: Innovations in Communications Conference, April, 9-10, 1970. New York, Innovation Group, 1970, pp. 170-183. PB 192 294. [Informal communication; Video tapes.]

1219 Priest, W. C. "Restructuring Communication in Science and Technology," In: IEEE Transactions on Professional Communication, PC 15(2): 20-22, June, 1972.

INFORMATION EXCHANGE GROUPS

1220 Abelson, P. H. "Information Exchange Groups," In: Science, (Editorial), 154(3750): 727, November 11, 1966.

*1221 Albritton, E. C. The Information Exchange Group—An Experiment in Communication. Washington, Institute on Advances in Biomedical Communication, American University and George Washington University, March 9, 1965.

1222 Confrey, E. A. "Information Exchange Group No. 5 To Be Discontinued," In: Science, (Letter), 154(3751): 843, November 18, 1966. [Immunopathology.]

1223 Doermann, A. H., et al. "Information Exchange Groups—Some Evaluations," In: Nature, (Letter), 154(3747): 334, October 21, 1966.

1224 Dray, S. "Information Exchange Group No. 5," In: Science, (Letter), 153(3737): 694-695, August 12, 1966. [Immunopathology.]

1225 Green, D. E. "Death of an Experiment," In: International Science and Technology, 82-84, 86, 88, May, 1967.

1226 Green, D. E. "An Experiment in Communication: The Information Exchange Group," In: Science, (Letter), 143(3604): 309, January 24, 1964.

1227 Green, D. E. "Information Exchange Group No. 1," In: Science, (Letter), 148(3677): 1543, June 18, 1965. [Electron transfer and oxidative phosphorylation.]

1228 Green, D. E. "Information Exchange Groups—Some Evaluations," In: Science, (Letter), 154(3747): 335-336, October 21, 1966.

*1229   Heenan, W. F., and D. C. Weeks. Informal Communication among
         Scientists: A Study of the Information Exchange Group Program,
         Part I. Washington, George Washington University, Biological Sciences
         Communication Project, January, 1971, 62p. AD 726 650. [Member-
         ship; Review of program; Preprints; Costs; National Institutes of
         Health.]

1230   Herron, E. W. "Psychological Communication—A Radical Proposal," In:
         American Psychologist, 23(5): 369-370, May, 1968.

1231   Jukes, T. H. "Information Exchange Groups—Some Evaluations," In:
         Nature, (Letter), 154(3747): 334-335, October 21, 1966.

1232   Nature. "Four Years of Information Exchange," In: Nature, 211(5052):
         904-905, August 27, 1966.

1233   Nature. "Secret College End," In: Nature, 212(5065): 865-866,
         November 26, 1966.

1234   Siekevitz, P. "Information Exchange Groups—Some Evaluations," In:
         Nature, (Letter), 154(3747): 333-334, October 21, 1966.

1235   Thorpe, W. V. "Biological Journals and Exchange Groups," In: Nature,
         213(5076): 547-548, February 11, 1967. [Journal publication policies;
         Commission of Biological Editors.]

1236   Thorpe, W. V. "International Statement on Information Exchange
         Groups," In: Science (Letter), 155(3767): 1195-1196, March 10, 1967.

1237   Woodruff, M. "Unpublished Literature," In: Nature, (Letter), 211(5049):
         560, August 6, 1966. [Physics Information Exchange System.]

METHODS, MEDIA, AND PUBLICATION FORMS

1238   Aries Corporation. Interferon Scientific Memoranda: A Report on the
         Feasibility of Increasing the Efficiency and Effectiveness of Scientific
         Research through the Use of New Communications Media. McLean,
         Va., Aries Corporation, 1969, 43p. PB 184 650. [*Interferon Scientific
         Memoranda*; Informal communication; National Institutes of Health.]

1239   Aries Corporation. Interferon Scientific Memoranda: A New Communi-
         cation Media for Increasing the Efficiency and Effectiveness of Scien-
         tific Research, Annual Progress Report—1970. McLean Va., Aries
         Corporation, March, 1970, 31p. PB 195 722.

1240 Baum, H. "A Clearinghouse for Scientific and Technical Meetings: Organizational and Operational Problems," In: American Documentation, 17(1): 28-32, January, 1966.

*1241 Baum, H. "Current Awareness Service Based on Meetings: The Need, the Coverage, the Service," In: Journal of Chemical Documentation, 13(4): 187-188, November, 1973. [Current Programs.]

1242 Baum, H. "A Registry of World Meetings in Science, Technology, and Medicine," In: Proceedings of the American Documentation Institute. Washington, Thompson, 1967, Vol. 4, pp. 233-237. [Technical Meetings Index; Organization; Format.]

1243 Bernier, C. L. "Condensed Technical Literature," In: Journal of Chemical Documentation, 8(4): 195-197, November, 1968. [Critical summaries.]

*1244 Bernier, C. L. "Terse Literature: I. Terse Conclusions," In: American Society for Information Science Journal, 21(5): 316-319, September-October, 1970. [Critical summaries.]

1245 Bernier, C. L. "Terse-Literature Viewpoint of Wordage Problems—Amount, Language, and Access," In: Journal of Chemical Documentation, 12(2): 81-83, May, 1972. [Critical summaries.]

*1246 Bever, A. T. "The Duality of Quick and Archival Communication," In: Journal of Chemical Documentation, 9(1): 3-6, February, 1969. [Preprint exchanges; National Institutes of Health; Information exchange groups.]

1247 Beyer, R. E. "Bioenergetics: Birth of a Bulletin," In: Science, 162 (3855): 750-751, November 15, 1968. [Informal scientific memorandum for fast communication.]

*1248 Block, L., and R. E. Schmidt. "Demand Publishing," In: Journal of Micrographics, 5(2): 81-82, November/December, 1971. [Out-of-print publications; Microforms.]

1249 Bloomfield, M. "Current Awareness Publications," In: Special Libraries, 60(8): 514-520, October, 1969. [NASA's SCAN; Current Contents; Costs; Orientation.]

1250 Bottle, R. T. "A User's Assessment of Current Awareness Services," In: Journal of Documentation, 21(3): 177-189, September, 1965. [Current awareness journals.]

*1251 Broer, J. W. "Abstracts in Block Diagram Form," In: IEEE Transactions on Engineering Writing and Speech, 14(3): 64-67, December, 1971.

1252   Chemical and Engineering News. "ACS Conducting Experimental Pub-
        lication Research Projects," In: Chemical and Engineering News,
        49(10): 55, March 8, 1971. [American Chemical Society; Microform
        edition of journals; Single article announcement program; Dual version
        journal.]

*1253   Comptroller General of the U.S. Effectiveness of Smithsonian Science
        Information Exchange Hampered by Lack of Complete Current
        Research Information. Washington, Comptroller General of U.S.,
        March 1, 1972, 38p. ED 066 164.

1254   Cooper, M. "Current Information Dissemination—Ideas and Practices,"
        In: Journal of Chemical Documentation, 8(4): 207-218, November,
        1968. [Review.]

1255   Crombie, L. "*Specialist Periodical Reports* of the Chemical Society
        (SPR): A Major New Development in the Literature of Chemistry,"
        In: Chemistry and Industry, 1971, pp. 1122-1124. [Critical Reviews.]

1256   Diaz, A. J. "On-Demand Publishing—The Clearinghouse Concept," In:
        Proceedings of the American Documentation Institute. Washington,
        Thompson, 1967, Vol. 4, pp. 238-243. [Sociology; *Sociological
        Abstracts*.]

1257   Dopkowski, P. The News Publication as a Medium of Scientific Commu-
        nication. Washington, George Washington University, Biological
        Sciences Communication Project, 1964.

1258   Downie, C. S., et al. Technological Barriers Documentation Project of
        the Office of Aerospace Research. Arlington, Va., Office of Aerospace
        Research, June, 1968, 31p. AD 674 050. [Proposes development of
        "knowledge want ads" to encourage person-to-person interaction.]

*1259   Dugger, G. L., R. F. Bryans, and W. T. Morris, Jr. "AIAA Experiments
        and Results on SDD, Synoptics, Miniprints, and Related Topics," In:
        IEEE Transactions on Professional Communication, PC 16(3): 100-106,
        178, September, 1973. [American Institute of Aeronautics and Astro-
        nautics; Selective Dissemination of Documents.]

1260   Dugger, G. L. "Results of the Questionnaire on Publication," In:
        Astronautics and Aeronautics, 10(10): 70-75, October, 1972. [Ameri-
        can Institute of Aeronautics and Astronautics; Journal usage; Author-
        ship patterns; Journal structure and format; Selective Dissemination
        of Documents.]

1261   Dugger, G. L. "What Journal Changes Would Best Serve You While
        Countering Rising Publications Cost?" In: Astronautics and Aeronautics,

10(4): 56-59, April, 1972. [American Institute of Aeronautics and Astronautics; Miniprints; Page charges; Journal revenue; Synoptics.]

1262   Fitzpatrick, W. H., and M. E. Freeman. "The Science Information Exchange: The Evolution of a Unique Information Storage and Retrieval System," In: Libri, 15(2): 127-137, 1965. [Research-in-progress.]

1263   Freeman, M. E. "The Science Information Exchange as a Source of Information," In: Special Libraries, 59(2): 86-90, February, 1968. [Research-in-progress.]

1264   Grey, J. "Selective Dissemination of Technical Papers (SDD): A Brief Description of Some Possible Features," In: Astronautics and Aeronautics, 10(4): 59, 80, April, 1972. [American Institute of Aeronautics and Astronautics; Selective Dissemination of Documents.]

1265   Gordon, I., R. L. K. Carr, and C. L. Bernier. "Utilization of Terse Conclusions in an Industrial Research Environment," In: Journal of Chemical Documentation, 12(2): 86-88, May, 1972. [Critical summaries.]

1266   Hanford, W. E., R. E. Maizell, and M. Chernoff. "Chemical News via Audio Tapes: Chemical Industry News," In: Journal of Chemical Documentation, 12(1): 3-4, February, 1972. [Continuing education.]

1267   Hanford, W. E., et al. "The Industrial Chemist and Chemical Information: The Human Ear as a Medium," In: Journal of Chemical Documentation, 11(2): 68-69, May, 1971. [Audio tapes.]

*1268   Kuney, J. H., and V. E. Doughery. "An Experiment in Selective Dissemination: The ACS Single Article Service," In: Journal of Chemical Documentation, 11(1): 9-11, February, 1971. [American Chemical Society; Costs; Resource requirements.]

1269   Mead, M., and P. Byers. The Small Conference: An Innovation in Communication. Paris, France, Mouton, 1968, 126p. [Social sciences; Conference process; Communication barriers; Small group interaction.]

*1270   Moore, J. A. "An Inquiry on New Forms of Primary Publications," In: Journal of Chemical Documentation, 12(2): 75-78, May, 1972. [Dual edition system; Quick and archival communication.]

1271   Moravcsik, M. J. "Pro: Physics Information Exchange—A Communication Experiment (A Debate on Pre-Print Exchange)," In: Physics Today, 19(6): 62, 65, 66-67, 69, June, 1966.

1272   Moravcsik, M. J. "The Status-Discussion Meeting as an Antidote to Super Conferences," In: Physics Today, 21: 48-49, 1968.

1273   Nature. "Preprints Galore," In: Nature, (Letter), 211(5052): 897-898, August 27, 1966. [Physics information exchange; Information exchange groups.]

1274   Nature. "Preprints Made Outlaws," In: Nature, 212(5057): 4, October 1, 1966. [Commission of Biological Editors; Information exchange groups.]

1275   Nature. "Unpublished Literature," In: Nature, (Editorial), 211(5047): 333-334, July 23, 1966. [Physics information exchange; Preprints.]

*1276   Omoerha, T. "Rapid Preliminary Communications in Science and Technology," In: UNESCO Bulletin for Libraries, 27(4): 205-207, July-August, 1973. [Publication delays; Preview series; Advanced abstract series; Preprint exchange; Communication and letters series.]

*1277   Paisley, W. J. Clustering Scientific Articles to Form "Mini-Journals"—Preliminary Considerations. Palo Alto, Calif., Stanford University, Institute for Communication Research, March, 1971, 61p.

1278   Pasternak, S. "Con: Criticism of the Proposed Physics Information Exchange (A Debate on Preprint Exchange)," In: Physics Today, 19(6): 63, 65-67, 69, June, 1966.

1279   Riva, J. P., Jr. "Smithsonian Science Information Exchange," In: Journal of the Marine Technology Society, 4(2): 56-61, March-April, 1970, [Research-in-progress.]

1280   Rosenfeld, A., et al. "Preprints in Particles and Fields," In: Symposium on the Handling of Nuclear Information. Vienna, International Atomic Energy Agency, 1970, pp. 405-416.

*1281   Searle, S. R. "On Publishing Extended Abstracts and Reviews," In: American Statistician, 27(4): 155-157, October, 1973.

1282   Spaet, T. "Preprints Galore," In: Nature, (Letter), 212(5059): 226, October 15, 1966. [Information exchange groups.]

*1283   Staiger, D. L. "Separate Article Distribution as an Alternative to Journal Publication," In: IEEE Transactions on Professional Communication, PC 16(3): 107-112, 177, September, 1973. [Separate article distribution and its effect on communication system.]

*1284   Tebbutt, A. V. "Barter System for Researchers: A Proposal," In: American Society for Information Science Journal, 21(6): 422-426, November-December, 1970. [Speculative system for linking researchers with common interests.]

1285   Whidden, S. B. "The Mathematical Offprint Service," In: Innovations
        in Communications Conference. New York, American Mathematical
        Society, April, 1970, pp. 46-59. PB 192 294.

1286   Wilson, J. H., Jr. "International High-Energy Physics Preprint Network
        Emphasizes Institutional Exchange," In: American Society for Infor-
        mation Science Journal, 21(1): 95-97, January-February, 1970.

1287   Wyatt, H. V. "Research Newsletters in the Biological Sciences—A
        Neglected Literature Service," In: Journal of Documentation, 23(4):
        321-325, December, 1967.

1288   Yates, B. "Pilkington Technical Communications System—A Formaliza-
        tion of Role of Technological-Gatekeeper," In: Aslib Proceedings,
        22(10): 507-510, October, 1970.

AUTHOR INDEX

Abdian, A. G., 1177
Abelson, P. H., 626, 1220
Adams, M. O., 150
Adams, S., 205-206, 666
Adams, W. M., 707-708
Aines, A. A., 151, 240, 854
Aitchison, T. M., 769
Aiyepeku, W. O., 843
Albritton, E. C., 1221
Album, H. H., 250
Allen, F. G., 1025
Allen, T. J., 1, 1032-1034, 1044-1064,
  1081, 1083-1084, 1098
Alt, F. L., 152, 273
American Chemical Society, 814
American Concrete Institute, 1065
American Geological Institute, 274-275
American Institute of Physics, 276-278,
  855
American Mathematical Society, 482, 850
American Psychological Association, 352-
  353, 654, 667, 979-984, 1212-1213
Amick, D. J., 815-816
Amsden, D., 923
Anderson, B. B., 1179
Anderson, P. K., 794
Anderson, S., 795
Anderson, W. P., 987
Andrade, C., 481
Andrews, F. M., 110
Andrien, M. P., Jr., 1063
Andry, R. G., 668
Angalet, B. W., 1091
Anthony L. J., 856
Apple, J. S., 893
Aries Corporation, 1238-1239
Arnett, E. M., 817
Arutjunov, N. B., 239
Askew, W. G., 1066
Aslib, 1020
Atherton, P., 680, 856-859, 872
Atkin, P., 2
Axelby, G. S., 576

Bailey, C. A., 8
Bailey, L. J., 551
Baker, D. B., 522, 666, 818
Baker, G. L., 335
Baker, N. R., 1067
Baldwin, P. H., 796
Baldwin, T. S., 551
Ball, P. J., 985
Banks, E., 301
Barber, A. S., 41
Barber, B., 836
Barinova, Z. B., 762
Barker, D. L., 819
Barnes, R. C. M., 3
Barnes, S. B., 73
Barr, K. P., 523
Barron, P., 941
Bartkus, E. P., 1068
Basu, R. N., 1178
Bates, M. J., 4
Bauer, R. A., 1120
Baugham, R. C., 942
Baughman, J. C., 524
Baum, H., 354-355, 1240-1242
Baumol, W. J., 483
Bayer, A. E., 943
Beardsley, C. W., 1069
Beaulnes, A., 241
Beaver, D. B., 477
Beck, L. N., 525
Becker, M. H., 1121
Bell, C. G., 153
Bennett, S. B., 1004
Benson, R. E., 1007
Benton, H., 1161-1162
Berg, S. V., 484-487
Bergen, D., 894
Bering, E. D., 746
Berlt, N. C., 778
Bernal, J. D., 747
Bernard, J., 797, 808
Bernier, C. L., 42, 1243-1246, 1265
Berul, L., 43, 1021

Bever, A. T., 1246
Beverly, J., 1190
Beyer, R. E., 1247
Biderman, A. D., 1009
Bilboul, R., 488
Bisco, R. L., 154-156, 173
Bishop, D., 1070
Blackhurst, A. E., 945
Blackman, S., 157
Blanton, L. H., 1035
Blau, J. R., 74
Blaxter, K. L., 798
Blaxter, M. L., 798
Block, L., 1248
Bloomfield, M., 1249
Blum, A. R., 290
Blume, S. S., 75
Boalt, G., 76
Boffey, P. M., 302, 489
Boggs, S. T., 924
Bondi, A., 577
Booz-Allen and Hamilton, Inc., 303
Borenius, G., 44
Borgeson, E. C., 304
Bosser, R. J., 1196
Bottle, R. T., 710-712, 820, 1250
Bourne, C. P., 490, 669-671
Boutry, G. A., 526
Bovee, W. G., 552-553
Bowden, C. L., 1122
Bowden, V. M., 1122
Bowen, D. D., 578
Bowen, D. H. M., 627
Bower, C. A., 922, 1175-1176
Boyer, C. J., 5
Brackbill, Y., 579
Bracken, M. C., 336
Brady, E. L., 158-161
Brahlek, R. E., 133
Branscomb, L. M., 580
Brayfield, A. H., 305, 986
Brearly, N., 655
Bree, R., 207
Brickwedde, F. G., 686
Brittain, J. M., 45, 895-896, 906-908, 1017
Broadus, R. N., 897, 1008
Brodie, N. E., 713
Broer, J. W., 1251
Brookes, B. C., 429-432, 527-528, 1022
Bross, I. D. J., 1179
Brown, A. M., 506, 639
Brown, H., 162, 208
Brown, J. E., 242
Brown, W. S., 628
Bryan, H., 529
Bryans, R. F., 1259

Bryum, J. D., 163
Buckland, M. K., 433-434
Buntrock, H., 1036
Burchinal, L. G., 306
Byers, P., 1269

Cade, J. A., 1180
Cahn, R. S., 821
Cairns, R. W., 1071
Caldwell, N. W., 314, 636
Caless, T. W., 279
Campbell, A., 164
Campbell, H. C., 165, 209
Campbell, T. H., 748, 763
Canhain, G. W. R., 822
Cannan, R. K., 1123
Caponio, J. F., 672
Carlson, W. M., 280, 1072
Carpenter, M. P., 764, 778
Carr, R. L. K., 1265
Carroll, K. D., 281, 289
Carroll, K. H., 673
Carter, L. F., 243-244, 765
Castore, C. H., 141
Cavanagh, J. M. A., 1181
Cawkell, A. E., 435
Center for Applied Linguistics, 307
Chadbourne, H. L., 656
Chaison, G. N., 468
Chakrabortty, A. R., 844
Chambers, J. M., 581
Chapanis, A., 120
Chase, J. M., 582
Chemical Abstracts Service, 210
Chemical Engineering News, 1252
Chen, C., 860
Chernoff, M., 1266
Chernyi, A. I., 46
Choate, B., 930
Chonez, N., 714
Christ, C. W., Jr., 554
Clague, P., 769
Claridge, P. R. P., 555
Clark, K. E., 308
Clarke, B. L., 469-470
Clayton, F. W., 337
Clayton, K. M., 845
Clemens, T., 944
Coates, E. J., 674
Coats, A. W., 629, 934
Coblans, H., 211, 925
Cocroft, R., 1042
Coe, R. K., 583
Cohen, S. I., 1050, 1073
Coile, R. C., 1074

Cole, J. R., 47, 77-78, 80-81, 861
Cole, S., 47, 78-81, 861
Coleman, J. S., 1124
Colton, M. C., 987
Compton, B. E., 356-359, 369, 993
Comptroller General of the United States, 1253
Condit, R. H., 593
Confrey, E. A., 1222
Conrad, M., 630
Conrath, D. W., 1075
Converse, P. E., 166-167, 183
Cook, E. B., 415
Cooke, G. A., 246
Cooney, S., 1032-1033
Cooper, M., 675, 862-863, 1254
Coover, R. W., 48
Corwin, R. G., 82
Cottrell, N. E., 1113
Cox, B. G., 1182
Craig, J. E. G., 846
Crane, D., 6, 83-85, 121, 212, 471, 530, 584
Cranmer, F. A., 906-908, 1017
Cravens, D. W., 122
Crawford, E. T., 86, 1009
Crawford, S. Y., 7, 988-990
Creager, W. A., 297, 309, 748
Crisman, T. L., 1183
Crombie, L., 1255
Crowder, T., 491
Crum, J. K., 492
Cuadra, C. A., 748
Culliton, B. J., 493, 585
Cummings, M. M., 586, 1125
Currie, J. D., 556

Dahlberg, I. A., 587
Danilov, V. J., 502
Dansey, P., 926
D'Aprix, R. M., 588
Darby, R. L., 749
Darley, J. G., 991
Davies, R. A., 1076
Davis, J. M., 1126
Davis, R. A., 8
Davis, R. M., 338
Deacon, B., 589
Defense Documentation Center, 657
Dennis, J., 150, 168
Deutsch, K. W., 169, 971
DeWeese, L. C., 9
Diaz, A. J., 1256
Doebler, P. D., 416
Doermann, A. H., 1223
Dolby, R.G.A., 73
Donohue, J. C., 436, 927, 954

Dopkowski, P., 1257
Dorrance, D., 1077
Douds, C. F., 1078, 1109
Dougherty, V. E., 1268
Douglas, I. A., 437
Downie, C. S., 1184-1185, 1258
Dray, S., 1224
Dugger, G. L., 1259-1261
Duncan, E. E., 823-824
Dunn, E. S., Jr., 935
Durrain, S. A., 1186

Earle, P., 766, 898
East, H., 698, 856, 864
Echols, H., 87
Edmisten, J., 763
EDUCOM, 339-340
El-Hadidy, A. R., 213
Emrich, B. R., 531
Engineering Education, 341
Engstrom, L. O., 965
Erickson, D. K., 945
Etzioni, A., 750
Evans, H. W., 590
Everett, W., 143
Ewing, G. J., 825
Eyring, H. B., 88

Fairbairn, R. E., 170
Fairthorne, R. A., 123, 438-439
Falk, H., 591
Farquhar, J. A., 342
Farr, R. S., 10, 946
Farren, A., 761
Farris, G. F., 89
Feinberg, H., 715
Fenichel, C. J., 928
Fidell, L., 472
Fidoia, A., 1079
Finniston, H. M., 631
Fiorino, A. J., 962
Fischer, M., 716
Fishenden, R. M., 11
Fisher, P., 1031
Fitzpatrick, W. H., 1262
Fix, C. D., 751
Flanagan, C. M., 676, 706
Fletcher, J., 936
Flury, W. R., 717
Folger, J., 943
Foo-Kune, C. F., 1187
Foote, R. H., 799
Forscher, B. K., 592
Fox, T., 632
Frechette, V. D., 593
Freeman, M. E., 633, 1262-1263

Freeman, P., 304
Freeman, R. R., 417
Freides, T. K., 899
Frick, B. F., 1127
Friedlander, J., 1128-1129
Friedrichs, R. W., 90
Frischmuth, D. S., 1080-1081
Frohman, M. A., 12
Frost, P., 1082
Fuccillo, D. A., 658
Funkhouser, G. R., 171

Gannett, E. K., 418
Garfield, E., 49-51, 718-721
Garrett, R., 60
Garrin, D., 590
Garrison, W. A., 172
Garside, D., 955
Garvey, W. D., 23, 358, 360-365, 367-369,
404-405, 767-768, 847, 900, 947, 992-
996, 1016, 1214-1217
Gassman, M., 594
Gaston, J. C., 91-93, 1188
George Washington University, 494
Gerstberger, P. G., 1046, 1055, 1058, 1083-
1086
Gerstenfeld, A. A., 1055
Gilchrist, A., 677-678, 773
Gilinski, V., 1189
Ginski, J. M., 1127, 1136
Glaser, W., 173
Glass, B., 214
Glenn, N. D., 174, 1010
Goffman, W., 440-449, 1171
Goldberg, A. L., 901
Goldstein, K. M., 157
Gomperts, M. C., 450
Gonod, P., 1190
Goode, D. J., 672
Goodman, A. F., 1023-1027
Gordon, I., 1265
Gordon, R. E., 282
Goudsmit, S. A., 495, 595, 752
Goyal, S. P., 600
Graham, W. R., 13
Grandbois, M., 679
Grant, D. A., 310
Grant, J., 1087
Grausnick, R. K., 557
Green, D. E., 1225-1228
Green, J. C., 532
Greenwood, P. W., 311
Greer, R. C., 680
Grey, J., 1264
Griffith, B. C., 14, 94, 124, 325, 361, 368-
369, 452, 696, 768, 900, 964-965, 968,
992, 994-996, 1214-1217

Groenman, S., 1011
Groos, O. V., 451, 865
Grossman, J. A., 596
Grundfest, H., 496
Guerrero, J. L., 125
Guha, M., 1012
Gulick, M. C., 175
Gurman, A. S., 997
Gurr, T., 893
Gushee, D. E., 497, 826
Guttsman, W. L., 902
Guyer, L., 472

Hagstrom, W. O., 95-99, 126, 419
Haiduc, I., 827
Hall, A. M., 52, 681, 769
Hall, R. W., 1088-1089
Hamelman, P. W., 498-499
Hamilton, D., 589
Hamilton, D. R. L., 1119
Hammer, D. P., 245
Handovsky, F. L. A., 937
Hanford, W. E., 1266-1267
Hanson, C. W., 15
Hargens, L. L., 100
Harmon, G., 127, 445
Harpur, J. G., 985
Harris, J. L., 723
Harris, L., 745
Harris, M. H., 972
Hart, H., 753
Harte, R. A., 500
Hastings, P. K., 176
Havelock, R. G., 16-18
Hayes, R. M., 1165
Hazell, J. C., 1037
Heaps, D. M., 246
Heenan, W. F., 1229
Heilprin, L. B., 501
Hein, D., 1038
Helbich, J., 722
Helmuth, N. A., 682
Hemphill, J. K., 948
Henderson, D., 717
Henderson, M. M., 247
Herbert, E., 1218
Herner, M., 19
Herner, S., 19, 343, 949, 1130
Herring, C., 502-503, 754-755
Herron, E. W., 1230
Herschman, A., 273, 283-284, 289, 634,
866-867
Herwald, S. W., 504
Herzberg, A. M., 581
Hillinger, C., 533
Hillis, R. E., 128
Hillman, D. J., 502

Hills, J., 20
Hindle, A., 433-434
Hindricks, J. R., 1090
Hines, T. C., 723
Hirsch, W., 101, 473
Hoban, C. F., 929
Hodges, J. D., Jr., 1025, 1091
Hodges, T. L., 724
Hoffer, J. R., 1013-1014
Hogan, J. D., 998
Holland, W. E., 129
Hollander, S., 705
Holm, B. E., 828
Holroyd, G., 597
Holt, C. C., 938
Holt, R. R., 312
Hood, R. A., 966-967
Hookway, H. T., 248
Horrocks, J. E., 998
Hoshovsky, A. G., 249-250
Huang, T. S., 725
Huden, G., 55
Hunt, F. H., 598
Hurd, E. A., 420
Hutchins, W. J., 1192
Hutchisson, E., 300
Hyslop, M. R., 1092

Industrial Research, 505
Information, 216, 868
Information Management, Inc., 285-286, 599
Ingelfinger, F. J., 1131
Institute of Biology, 800
International Council of Scientific Unions, 829, 869
Intrama, N., 973
Irick, P., 217
Ivanov, K., 177

Jablonski, S., 1132
Jacob, R., 974
Jacobus, D. P., 683
Jacoby, J., 578
Jahn, M. J., 124
Jahoda, G., 21, 726, 830
Jain, T. C., 600
Jakobovits, L. A., 999
Janda, K., 727
Janning, E. A., 1092
Jenkins, J. J., 313
Johns Hopkins University, 370-403
Johnson, M. F., 1007
Jones, S. D., 178
Jordan, M. P., 130
Jorer, S. I., 259

Journal of Chemical Documentation, 601, 831-832, 1039
Judd, C., 801
Judge, A. J. N., 218
Judge, P. J., 251
Juhasz, S., 728
Jukes, T. H., 1231

Kaback, S. M., 558
Kadushin, C., 102
Kahn, M. A. Q., 594
Kamil, B. L., 950
Kanasy, J. E., 802
Kanno, M., 1094
Kaplan, N., 729, 770
Karel, L., 684
Karlow, N., 179
Karson, A., 43
Kasson, M. S., 490
Katter, R. V., 745
Katz, E., 131, 1124
Katzin, L. I., 474
Kays, O., 292
Kean, P., 833
Keenan, S., 66, 685-686, 857, 870-874
Kegan, D. L., 834
Keith-Spiegel, P., 479
Kemp, D. A., 729
Kennedy, H. E., 694, 706, 803
Kenyon, R., 635
Kiehlman, E., 687
Kilgour, F. G., 421, 1163-1164
King, D. W., 314, 506, 636
Kinkade, R. G., 315-319, 810
Kirson, B. L., 252
Kitagawa, T., 219
Klein, S., 1095
Klempner, I. M., 688, 1194
Klinefelter, P., 1177
Knox, W. T., 253-255
Koch, H. W., 287-288, 507-508, 637, 756, 875-877
Kochen, M., 143, 602, 757
Koehler, H., 689
Kohler, B. M., 890
Komurka, M., 220
Korten, F., 579
Kottenstette, J. P., 557, 559
Kramer, D. A., 180
Krantz, S. C., 1195
Krauze, T. K., 533
Krevitt, B., 452
Kuhn, T. S., 103
Kuney, J. H., 422, 509, 560, 638, 835, 1268
Kurke, M. I., 320

Ladendorf, J. M., 22
Lamb, G. H., 851
Lancaster, F. W., 639
Landau, H. B., 53, 510
Lanzetta, J. T., 132
Lawani, S. M., 453, 1040
Lawler, C. O., 1000
Lawler, E. E., 1000
Lay, W. M., 738
Layton, E., 603
Leake, C. D., 640
Leeds, A., 1144
Lehigh University, 54
Leimkuhler, F. F., 454-455
Leith, J. D., 1133
Lengyel, P., 903
Lerner, R. G., 289
Levine, J. M., 133
Levine, M., 1001
Levy, M. M., 986
Levy, N. P., 1096
Lewis, R. W., 561
Leyman, E., 55
Libaw, F. B., 904
Libbey, M. A., 290, 878
Library Trends, 256, 690
Licklider, J. C. R., 257, 534
Lieberman, J., 1134
Lin, N., 23, 134-135, 365-367, 404-405, 767, 947, 1015-1016
Line, M. B., 45, 456, 535, 905-910, 1017
Lingwood, D. A., 914, 951
Lipetz, B., 24, 731
Liston, D. M., Jr., 138, 258, 344-346
Littleton, I. T., 1041
Lloyd, J. J., 291
Lockley, L. C., 708
Loening, K. L., 771
Loevinger, J., 321-322
London, G., 536
Lorenz, J. G., 25
Lowe, M. C., 641
Lowry, C. D., 1042
Lowry, W. K., 772
Lufkin, J. M., 1097, 1195
Luger, H. P., 1196
Lukasiewicz, J., 537
Lyon, C. C., 562

Mack, D., 985
MacRae, D., Jr., 538, 911
Maddox, J., 539
Magaha, E. P., Jr., 1197
Magee, M., 1137
Maizell, R. E., 1266
Malin, M. V., 732
Mann, E. J., 1043

Mannheim, F. T., 1198
Mantell, L. H., 540
Marcott, C. M., 642
Margolis, J., 56
Maron, M. E., 181
Marquis, D. G., 1048, 1098
Marron, H., 953
Martino, J. P., 733
Martyn, J., 136, 691-692, 734, 773-774
Marx, S. M., 975
Massachusetts Institute of Technology, 1099
Massey, R. J., 26
Matarazzo, J. M., 511
Matheson, N. W., 735
Mauerhoff, G., 736
Mauperon, A., 879
Maxwell, R., 643
May, K. O., 57, 852
Mazze, E. M., 498-499
McCollom, I. N., 1002
McCracken, J. D., 952
McCrea, W. H., 604
McLaughlin, C. P., 1028, 1135
McMahan, R. H., Jr., 1007
McMutray, F., 1136
McReynolds, P., 605
Mead, M., 1199, 1269
Meadow, A. J., 880-881
Menzel, H., 27-28, 58, 137, 775-776, 836-837, 1124, 1138
Mersel, J., 954
Merton, R. K., 104-107, 624-625
Metzner, A. W. K., 423, 877
Michaelson, M. B., 606
Miller, A. J., 14, 124
Miller, E. H., 1097
Miller, G. A., 323
Miller, L. B., 1139
Miller, W. E., 182-183
Mills, P. R., 406
Mitchell, D., 930
Montgomery, R. R., 693, 1140
Moody, D., 292
Moore, J. A., 1270
Moore, J. R., 1100
Moravcsik, M. J., 882, 1271-1272
Morris, T. G., 440
Morris, W. C., 1141
Morris, W. T., Jr., 1259
Morrison, A. B., 563
Morton, L. T., 1142
Moscatelli, E. A., 475
Mote, L. J. B., 1101
Mountstephen, B., 184
Mullins, N. C., 94, 804-806
Munster, J. H., 1200
Murdock, J. W., 138, 1205

Murphy, L. J., 457
Myatt, D. O., 259
Myers, C. R., 1003

Naranan, S., 458-459
Narayana, G. J., 515
Narin, F., 764, 778, 941, 955
Nasatir, D., 185
National Agricultural Library, 347-348
National Security Industrial Association,
 1201
NATO. Advisory Group for Aerospace
 Research and Development, 777
Nature, 512, 607, 659-661, 1202, 1232-
 1233, 1273-1275
Nelson, C. E., 367, 404-405, 407, 767,
 947, 956, 1015
Neufeld, J., 608
Newill, V. A., 441, 444
Newman, E. S., 541
Newman, S. H., 609
Nixon, J., 836
Norden, M., 737
North, J. B., 490
North American Aviation, Inc., 59, 1029

O'Connor, J. G., 880
Oehlerts, D. E., 796
O'Gara, P. W., 1102
Oliver, M. R., 883
Olsen, H. A., 513
Olsen, W. C., 293
Omerha, T., 1276
O'Neill, E. T., 460-461
Organization for Economic Cooperation
 and Development, 260
Oromaner, M. J., 108, 1018
Orr, D. B., 324
Orr, R. H., 779, 1143-1146
Osborn, A., 184, 197
Osgood, C. E., 999, 1005
Ouyang, L., 964
Over, R., 476

Paige, L. J., 514
Paisley, M. B., 409
Paisley, W. J., 29, 60, 109, 139, 408-410,
 780, 912-914, 957, 1277
Panton, D., 838
Pao, M., 610
Pargeter, L. J., 1192
Parker, E. B., 30, 60, 408, 410, 780, 914
Parkins, P. V., 694, 803
Parlee, M. B., 611
Passman, S., 781

Pasternak, S., 644, 1278
Patil, M. B., 515
Patterson, C. H., 612
Patton, P. C., 976
Paul, E., 411
Pelz, D. C., 110
Pelzer, C. W., 221
Pemberton, J. E., 915
Penchansky, R., 1135
Penna, C. V., 261
Penney, D., 594
Penry, J. K., 672
Perez-Vitoria, A., 222
Perk, L. J., 463
Perloff, R., 578
Perrucci, R., 1103
Peterson, C. W., 587
Petrarca, A. E., 738
Phelps, C. R., 294
Physics Today, 295, 516
Piepmeier, J. M., 1032-1033
Pierce, J. R., 628
Piganiol, P., 542
Pingree, S., 10
Pings, C. J., 613
Platau, G. O., 839
Porter, J. R., 645
Porter, L. W., 31
Potter, J. N., 1037
Preibish, C. I., 711
Presanis, A., 197, 678
Prescott, S., 325-327
Price, D. J. S., 111-112, 424-425, 477, 782-
 784, 1104
Priest, W. C., 1219
Pritchard, A., 61, 462
Prosser, R. T., 517

Rae, J. C., 1203
Raisig, L. M., 1147-1148
Rajagopalan, T. S., 262
Ramamrorthy, C. V., 172
Rappaport, M. W., 969
Rath, G. J., 887, 1149-1150
Rathbun, E. N., 1139
Reckenbeil, R., 853
Rehder, R. R., 1151
Resnick, A., 564
Resnikoff, H. L., 296
Reuben, B. G., 838
Rice, C. N., 349
Riesthuis, G. J. A., 1011
Rigby, M., 849
Ring, M. E., 695
Rittenhouse, C. H., 959
Riva, J. P., Jr., 1279
Robbins, J. C., 140, 785

Roberts, K. H., 31
Roberts, S. A., 916
Robertson, A., 1105
Robinson, B. F., Jr., 960
Rodman, H., 614
Rogers, E. M., 32
Rokkan, S. C., 186-187
Roland, C. G., 1152, 1182
Roll, P. G., 884
Ronayne, J., 833, 842
Ronco, P. G., 662
Rosenberg, V., 62, 1106
Rosenbloom, R. S., 1028, 1107-1108
Rosenfeld, A., 1280
Rossini, F. D., 188-189
Rossmassler, S. A., 190, 646
Rothman, H., 63, 807
Rothman, R. A., 1103
Rowe, J. S., 163
Rowland, G. E., 931
Rowlett, R. J., Jr., 426, 818
Rubenstein, A. H., 887, 1067, 1109, 1153-1154, 1167
Rubinoff, M., 263
Ruggles, N., 191
Ruggles, R., 191
Rush, M., 977
Rutgers–The State University, 33
Ryan, M., 616

Salomonsson, O., 192
Salton, G., 223, 264
Samuelson, K., 224-225
Sandison, A., 543
Sanford, F. B., 617
Saracevic, T., 463
Sarasohn, H. M., 1110
Sarett, L. H., 193
Sasmor, R. M., 328
Saunders, W. L., 1192, 1204
Saunderson, K. M., 1111
Sawamoto, T., 265
Sawyer, J., 194
Scal, M., 518
Schaeffer, D. L., 618
Schechter, H., 194
Schlessinger, B. S., 34
Schmidt, R. E., 1248
Schneider, E. A., 976
Schoene, M. L., 258
Schoenfeldt, L. F., 195
Schrank, W. E., 938
Schreider, Y. A., 464
Schwarz, S., 44
Science Communication, Inc., 196
Scott, J. T., 544
Searle, S. R., 545, 1281

Seashere, S. E., 329
Sedano, J. M., 739
Seeley, C. R., 710
Seider, M., 82
Seigmann, P. J., 696
Sender, J. W., 330, 786
Sengupta, I. N., 1155-1158
Shank, R., 427
Shannon, R. L., 697
Shapiro, P. A., 1179
Shephard, D. A. E., 619, 1159
Sherrill, P. N., 412
Sherrington, A. M., 1160
Shilling, C. W., 428, 797, 808, 1161-1162
Shipman, J., 546
Shirey, D., 64
Shirley, H. B., 848
Shoemaker, F., 32
Short, E. C., 35
Shotwell, T. K., 1112
Sieber, H. F., Jr., 65
Siegmann, J., 1067
Siekevitz, P., 1234
Silverio, M., 885
Simpson, D. J., 652
Simpson, G. S., 266, 1205
Sinclair, R., 75
Singer, J. D., 178
Singleton, J., 473
Skelton, B., 917
Skolnik, H., 740
Slater, M., 66, 136, 184, 197, 691, 870-871, 873-874, 1030-1031
Slater, M. J., 856
Smailes, A. A., 647
Small, H., 886
Smallman, S., 476
Smith, C., 840
Smith, C. G., 113
Smith, D. A., 465
Smith, F. D., Jr., 297
Smith, J. C., 1200
Smith, J. R., 226, 698
Smith, R. B., 1093
Somerville, B. F., 699
Sophar, G. J., 519
Spaet, T., 1282
Speight, F. Y., 198, 1113-1114
Spiegel, D., 479
Spigai, F. G., 565
Squires, D. F., 199
Staiger, D. L., 1283
Stangl, P., 1163-1164
Starker, L. N., 566, 574
Stern, J., 758
Stevens, M. E., 267
Stewart, J. L., 978
Stokes, J., 1165

Storer, N. W., 114-117, 547, 787
Streufert, S., 141
Stursa, M. L., 726
Sullivan, P., 953
Sutton, H., 142
Swann, D., 939
Swanson, D. R., 648, 788
Swatez, G. M., 118
Swift, D. F., 700
Swinburne, R. E., Jr., 567
Syracuse University, 1206
System Development Corporation, 701

Tagliacozzo, R., 143, 741
Tankard, J. W., Jr., 616
Tate, F. A., 426, 818
Taylor, L. J., 932
Taylor, M., 1001
Taylor, R. L., 1207
Taylor, R. S., 144, 1115
Tebbutt, A. V., 1284
Teplitz, A., 568
Terrant, S. W., 649
Terry, E., 675
Texas A&M University, 569
Thayer, C. W., 863
Thomas, S., 55
Thompson, C. W. N., 620
Thompson, J. E., 200
Thorpe, P., 702
Thorpe, W. V., 1235-1236
Thuronyi, G., 849
Tishler, M., 1166
Tocatlian, J. T., 227, 742
Tomita, K., 365-366, 407, 847
Tompkin, H. E., 591
Townsend, L. B., 759
Trapp, M., 961
Traub, J. F., 628
Trueswell, R. W., 887, 1167
Turkov, Z., 228
Tyson, J. W., 797

UNESCO, 229-230, 650
UNESCO Bulletin for Libraries, 413
U.S. Environmental Protection Agency, 789
U.S. Federal Council for Science and Technology, Committee on Scientific and Technical Information, 168-169, 664-665, 1208
U.S. House of Representatives, 88th Congress, 2nd Session, 1964, 663
U.S. House of Representatives, 89th Congress, 1st Session, 1965, 520
U.S. National Academy of Sciences, 231, 270, 790, 888

U.S. National Research Council, 809
U.S. National Science Foundation, 232
University of Western Ontario, 1168
Upton, A., 145
Urquhart, D. J., 548, 703
Uytterschaut, L., 918

Vagianos, L., 841
Vaillancourt, P. M., 1169
Vallee, J., 298
Van Cott, H. P., 331-333, 414, 810, 889, 892
Van Den Ban, A. W., 146
Van Gelder, R. G., 795
van Houton, R., 1116
Van Oot, J. G., 570
Van Valen, L., 67
Vasilakis, M., 1209
Vavrek, B. F., 36
Veaner, A. B., 571
Veazie, W. H., 746
Velke, L., 68
Vessey, H. F., 572
Vette, J. I., 179, 201
Vickery, B. C., 69, 549, 652, 766, 898
Virgo, J. A., 760
Vlachy, J., 651, 791
Vockell, E. L., 1004
Voos, H., 550

Waddington, G., 202
Waldhart, T. J., 1117
Waldo, W. H., 299
Wall, E., 350
Wallace, J. F., 147
Wallenstein, M. B., 158, 160
Walsh, M. C., 1170
Ward, D. C., III, 848
Warren, K. S., 442, 1171
Warren, S. L., 271
Watterson, H. M., 862
Way, K., 203
Webb, E. C., 811
Weber, E., 761
Weeks, D. C., 1229
Weil, B. H., 573-574
Weiler, D. M., 311
Weinstock, I., 583
Weinstock, M., 743
Weinstock, M. J., 351
Weisgerber, W. H., 835
Weisman, H. M., 204
Werner, D. J., 1150, 1172-1173
Westley, B. H., 37
Whatley, H. A., 704
Whetsel, H. B., 621

Whidden, S. B., 1285
White, M. D., 940
Whitley, R., 1082
Whitley, R. D., 812, 919-920
Whittenberg, J. A., 319, 334-335
Wigington, R. L., 272
Wilcox, R. H., 792
Wilkinson, D., 705
Wilkinson, E. A., 466
Wilkinson, W. A., 299
Williams, V. Z., 300
Wilson, J. H., Jr., 1286
Wilson, P. T., 1174
Windsor, D. H., 933
Windsor, D. M., 933
Winn, V. A., 921
Wittmore, B. J., 148
Wolek, F. W., 149, 793, 1028, 1107-1108,
  1118, 1210
Wolf, W. C., Jr., 962
Wolfe, H. C., 300
Wolff, M. E., 653
Wolff, W. M., 622-623
Wood, D. N., 38, 70, 922, 1119, 1175-1176,
  1211
Wood, J. L., 272, 426, 706, 842
Woodford, F. P., 521, 813
Woodhead, M., 63, 807
Woodruff, M., 1237

Woolston, J. E., 233-235
Wooster, H., 575
Worboys, C., 1001
Worthen, D. B., 467
Wortzel, L. H., 1120
Woyna, A. G., 966
Wright, K., 963
Wuest, F. J., 71
Wurst, J. C., 1093
Wyatt, H. V., 1287
Wysocki, A., 72, 236-238

Xhignesse, L. V., 1005

Yates, B., 1288
Yerkey, A. N., 744
Yoels, W. C., 1019
Yovits, M. C., 148

Zabriskie, K. H., Jr., 745
Zaltman, G., 878, 890-891
Zavala, A., 889, 892
Ziman, J. M., 39-40, 1006
Zisa, C., 970
Zuckerman, H., 119, 480, 624-625

SUBJECT INDEX

Abstracting
  economics of, 490, 510, 685
  innovations in, 1251, 1281
Abstracting services, 666-706
  coordination of, 669-670, 676, 680,
    687-688, 694, 705-706
  mission *vs.* discipline, 666
  national system study, 701
Academic libraries. *See also* Library use.
  bibliography on use, 2
  survey of use, 4
Aeronautics and astronautics
  communication innovations, 1259-1261,
    1264
  data activities, 196
  information exchange at meetings, 371
  literature characteristics, 1260
  postmeeting dissemination of informa-
    tion, 378, 387
Aerospace sciences. *See* Aeronautics and
  astronautics.
Agricultural economics
  bibliographic control, 1041
  literature characteristics, 1036, 1041
Agricultural science and technology information system, 234
Agricultural Sciences Information Network
  cooperative potentials, 350
  development plan, 339
  information analysis centers in, 339
  libraries in, 339
  progress report, 347
  telecommunications, 339
Agriculture
  abstracting and indexing journals, 669-
    671, 1041
  communication in, 1032-1043
  data activities, 196
  informal communication, 1032-1035
  literature characteristics, 453, 1040
  national information system, 339, 347,
    350
  reading habits in, 1037
AKWIC. *See* Author and Keyword in
  Context.
American Association of Public Opinion
  Research
    information exchange at meetings, 408,
      410

American Chemical Society
  experimental publication program, 1252,
    1268
  information program, 814
American Council of Social Science Data
  Archives
    planning, 173
American Economics Association
  information program, 934
American Educational Research Association
  information exchange at meetings, 399
  postmeeting dissemination of informa-
    tion, 391
American Geophysical Union
  information exchange at meetings, 376
  postmeeting dissemination of informa-
    tion, 382
American Institute of Aeronautics and
  Astronautics
    information exchange at meetings, 371
    postmeeting dissemination of inform-
      tion, 378, 387
American Institute of Mining, Metallurgical,
  and Petroleum Engineers
    information exchange at meetings, 400
    postmeeting dissemination of informa-
      tion, 384
American Institute of Physics
  information program, 857-858, 875
American Meteorological Society
  information exchange at meetings, 372
  postmeeting dissemination of informa-
    tion, 381, 388
American Psychological Association
  information program, 331-332, 993, 996
  journal program, 324
American Society of Heating, Refrigerating,
  and Air-Conditioning Engineers
    information exchange at meetings, 389
    postmeeting dissemination of informa-
      tion, 392
American Sociological Association
  information exchange at meetings, 373,
    398
  postmeeting dissemination of informa-
    tion, 385, 396, 404
Animal physiology
  communication in, 812
Anomy. *See* Social stratification.

Anthropology
bibliographic needs, 893
communication problems, 923-924
Archival communication. *See* Journals.
Association of American Geographers
information exchange at meetings, 401,
407
postmeeting dissemination of information, 383
Astronomy
communication in, 227, 638
data banks, 273, 298
journal economics, 637
literature characteristics, 637, 856, 865,
880-881
national information systems, 273, 276-
278, 283, 298
tertiary sources, 751
Astrophysics
literature characteristics, 880
Audiotapes. *See* Audio-visual media.
Audio-visual media
in chemistry, 1266-1267
in psychology, 302, 327
Author and Keyword in Context, 728
Author collaboration, 419, 468-480, 491
Authors
academic characteristics, 584
relation to editors, 603

Barter system, 1284
Behavioral sciences. *See* Social sciences.
Bibliography of Agriculture, 669-671, 1041
Bibliometric analysis, 61, 429-467, 1158,
1171
Biochemistry
communication in, 811
literature characteristics, 1155-1156,
1158, 1162
Biological Abstracts, 673, 691, 693, 745
Biological control
publication patterns in, 807
Biological sciences
abstracting and indexing journals, 673,
690-691, 693, 745
communication in, 794-813
communication innovations in, 1247,
1287
current awareness services, 683, 712
data activities, 196, 199, 809
factors influencing modes of publishing,
419
informal communication, 797, 808
information handling in, 809
information needs and uses, 801, 809-
810
journal economics, 500

Biological sciences (cont'd)
literature characteristics, 803, 938
national information system, 809
primary sources, 809
reading habits in, 798
secondary sources, 673, 691, 693, 745,
803, 809
social organization, 797, 804-808
tertiary sources, 751, 809
Biomedical sciences. *See* Medicine; Biological sciences.
BioResearch Index
coverage of virology, 673
BioScience Information Service of Biological Abstracts
coordination of, 676, 706
Books
in microfiche format, 568
use bibliography, 9
use in medicine, 1147
use in physics, 884
use in psychology, 983, 1001
use in sociology, 1018
Borle distribution, 460
Bradford distribution, 430-431, 436, 438,
453-455, 460-461, 463, 1171
Bradford's law, 429, 437, 440, 451, 453,
458-459, 461, 463, 1171
British Technology Index
history of, 674

Canada
national scientific and technical information system, 241-242, 246, 260
Cassettes. *See* Audio-visual media.
Chemical Abstracts, 691, 693
on microfilm, 473
Chemical Abstracts Service
coordination of, 676, 706
Chemical and Engineering News
use survey, 842
Chemical Condensates
use survey, 823
Chemical engineering
communication in, 1071
publication delays, 613
Chemical Titles, 687, 712
Chemischer Informationsdienst, 687
Chemistry
abstracting and indexing
journals, 232, 426, 473, 687, 691,
693, 712, 823
ACS information program, 814
communication in, 814-842
communication innovations in, 1252,
1255, 1266-1267
communication models, 817, 820, 840

Chemistry (cont'd)
communication problems, 822
conference proceedings, 832
current awareness needs, 823, 832
current awareness services, 687, 712
data activities, 180, 188, 197
experimental publication program, 1252, 1268
factors influencing modes of publishing, 419
informal communication, 836-837
information needs and uses, 815-817, 830, 854
international information network, 210
journal economics, 497, 509
KWIC indexing in, 710, 726, 742
literature characteristics, 522, 819-820, 824-825, 827-828
national information systems, 280, 285-286, 299
preprints, 832-833
primary communication, 232, 426, 625, 821
quality control of papers, 577, 590, 601, 606
reading habits in, 826, 835, 838
reward system, 75
role of newspapers, 822
scientific nomenclature, 771
secondary sources, 473, 687, 691, 693, 712, 820, 823, 832
social organization, 100
tertiary sources, 746-747, 751, 753-754, 759, 820, 832
title indexing, 712
world information resources, 232
Child psychology
literature characteristics, 1004
Citation analysis
application of, 60, 63, 68-69, 498-499
bibliography, 61
evaluation of, 19, 44-45, 52, 69
in journal evaluation, 49
in paper evaluation, 56
use in preparing critical reviews, 610
Citation indexes, 707-745
Citation indexing, 719, 724-725, 733-734, 741
abuses of, 57
for studying social organization, 50-51
history of, 743
Citations
use and value of, 52, 67-68, 730
Clinical psychology
information needs and uses, 325
literature characteristics, 997
CODATA. *See* Committee for Data on Science and Technology.

Collaboration. *See* Author collaboration; Work teams.
College libraries. *See* Academic libraries.
Committee for Data on Science and Technology
data activities, 188-189, 202
data centers, 170
international programs, 162
Communication. *See also* specific disciplines of interest.
as a social system, 768, 770, 776, 785, 789
impact of organization on, 1, 1050, 1059
impact of social status on, 1044
impact of work-role on, 1, 1072, 1118
role of government in, 257
role of quick *vs.* archival, 1246, 1270
Communication barriers, 1028, 1177-1211
Communication behavior
social *vs.* physical sciences, 360
Communication delays, 360, 367, 594, 600, 613, 619, 767, 985, 1178
Communication innovations, 1212-1288
Communication leaders. *See also* Gatekeepers; Technological gatekeepers.
characteristics of, 129
Communication models, 123, 131, 138, 140, 148, 779
in chemistry, 817, 820, 840
in engineering, 140, 405
in medicine, 1165, 1171
in physical sciences, 360, 367, 405
in sciences, 23, 134, 140, 425
in social sciences, 23, 360, 367, 405, 894
in technology, 23, 425
scientific *vs.* mass communication, 134
two-step flow hypothesis, 131, 134-135, 146
Communication norms
in sciences, 911
Communication research, 7, 374, 779, 792
Communication satellites
use in international communication, 209
Communication sciences
communication in, 925-933
information exchange at meetings, 408, 410
Conference proceedings, 406-407, 832
Conference. *See* National and international meetings.
Construction engineering
communication in, 1070
Contagion theory. *See* Menzel's Contagion Theory.
Conventions. *See* National and international meetings.

Copyright
    influence on communication patterns,
        519-520
    relation to national information systems,
        245, 268-269
Criminology
    abstracting and indexing journals, 668,
        910
    primary sources, 910
Critical incident technique, 19, 64
Critical summaries, 1243-1245, 1265
Crystallography
    communication in, 887, 1153-1154
Current awareness
    methods of assessing, 42, 66
Current Chemical Papers, 712
Current Contents, 687, 712, 719, 735-736,
    1249
Current information dissemination
    review of methods, 1254
Current Papers in Physics, 66, 871, 873-874
Current Physics Advance Abstracts, 876
Current physics information program, 423,
    876
Current Physics Microfilm, 876
Current Physics Titles, 876
Current Programs, 1241

DoD. See Department of Defense.
Data activities, 150-204, 809. See also Data
    banks.
Data banks. See also Social science data
    banks; Science data banks; Technical data
    banks.
    astronomy, 273, 298
    geosciences, 196, 199, 297
    impact on the social sciences, 169
    international activities, 162, 170, 185,
        187
    large scale, 181
    law, 976
    library reference, 175
    physics, 273
    privacy and security of, 172, 194
    quality control of, 177, 200
Data centers
    characteristics of, 201
    information flow in, 201
    National Data Center, 194
    National Space Science Data Center, 197
    National Standard Reference Data Sys-
        tem, 152, 158-161
    problems confronting, 201
    progress of, 170
    Roper Public Opinion Research Center,
        176
Data editing, 200

Decision-making
    role of information in, 122, 132-133,
        135, 143, 145, 148
Demand publishing, 1248, 1256
Demography
    communication in, 1011
Dentistry
    abstracting and indexing journals, 689,
        695
Department of Defense
    user needs study, 59, 1021, 1023-1025,
        1027
    user needs study methodology, 43, 65,
        1025-1026
Diaries
    evaluation of use, 19
Diffusion of innovations
    bibliography, 1160
    survey, 32
Direct observation
    evaluation of use, 19
Dissertations
    as information source, 5
Documentation. See Information science.
Drug Literature Index, 705
Dual publication, 560, 585, 598, 665, 1252,
    1270

Ecology
    literature characteristics, 794
Economics
    bibliographic needs, 893
    communication in, 485-486, 934-940
    data banks, 191
    editorial policies of journals, 583, 590
    information needs and uses, 935, 937
    journal economics, 486
    journal market, 485-486
    literature characteristics, 936, 938
    primary sources, 939
    role of journals, 629
Economics of communication, 481-521, 781
    bibliography, 20, 33, 513
Editorial activities. See also Manuscript
    evaluation; Manuscript processing.
    bibliography, 33
Editors
    academic characteristics, 584
    relation to authors, 603
    role of, 302, 589, 592, 604, 614
    rules for, 621
Education
    abstracting and indexing journals, 700
    communication in, 941-963
    communication problems, 956
    informal communication, 951
    information exchange at meetings, 399

Education (cont'd)
information needs and uses, 913, 942, 944, 946, 948, 954, 956-959, 961-962
invisible college, 109, 951
literature characteristics, 524, 941, 949
national information system, 306, 311
primary sources, 953, 955-956
postmeeting dissemination of information, 391
productivity in, 943
publication patterns, 947
role of national meetings, 947
secondary sources, 949, 953
social organization, 82, 97, 109
social roles in, 97
structure of field, 82, 97
tertiary sources, 953
Education Index, 949
Educational Administration Abstracts, 949
Educational Resources Information Centers, 306, 311, 963
Electrical engineering
information sources, 1069, 1074
literature characteristics, 938, 1074
Elitism
and communication in chemistry, 815-816
and communication in science, 112
Endocrinology
literature characteristics, 1162
Engineering. *See also* Research and development.
abstracting and indexing journals, 681, 1117
communication in, 1, 405, 793, 1044-1119
data activities, 196, 198
information exchange at meetings, 389, 400
information needs and uses, 1072, 1118
information seeking in, 1106
information sources in, 1047, 1056, 1060, 1062-1063, 1068, 1076, 1083-1085, 1088-1089, 1091
KWIC indexing, 709
literature characteristics, 938, 1047, 1117, 1260
national information system, 253, 341, 344-346
postmeeting dissemination of information, 384, 392
prepublication dissemination of information, 405
primary sources, 379, 1066
quality control of papers, 588
reading habits in, 1088, 1097
selection of information source, 1046
tertiary sources, 751, 761

Engineering (cont'd)
use of document forms, 1076
Engineering education
information management in, 1115
Engineering Index, 1117
coordination of, 676, 706
Engineers Joint Council,
information program, 1095, 1113
Environmental sciences
communication in, 789
data activities, 196
information sources in, 789
Epidemic processes
and communication, 441
Epidemic theory. *See* Goffman's Epidemic Theory.
Epilipsy Abstracts
role of, 672
ERIC. *See* Educational Resources Information Centers.
Error control. *See* Quality control.
Ethical discourse
and scientific communication, 911, 1152, 1182
FAA. *See* Federal Aviation Administration.
Federal Aviation Administration
information needs and uses, 1029
Films. *See* Audio-visual media.
Fisher distribution, 460
Food sciences
information needs and uses, 1042
literature characteristics, 1043
Formal communication
model of, 894
performance evaluation, 137
role of, 46, 84, 137, 425, 1104
structure of, 121, 425, 768
Freedom of Information Act
relation to national information systems, 268

Gatekeepers
in agriculture, 1032-1034
in education, 946
in medicine, 1141
in vocational education, 960
Geography
information exchange at meetings, 401
journals as communication channels, 393
literature characteristics, 843, 845
postmeeting dissemination of information, 383
Geology
literature characteristics, 845-846
Geomorphology
literature characteristics, 845

Geophysics
  communication in, 847
  information exchange at meetings, 376,
    407
  journals as communication channels, 380
  literature characteristics, 849
  postmeeting dissemination of informa-
    tion, 382
  tertiary sources, 751
Geoscience Information Society, 848
Geosciences
  bibliographic control in, 292
  communication in, 843-849
  communication problems, 291, 297
  data activities, 196, 199, 297
  information program, 297
  language barrier, 1198
  library network, 293
  literature characteristics, 274-275, 292
  literature needs, 274-275
  national information system, 274-275,
    291, 297
  role of libraries in national system, 293,
    297
Goffman's Epidemic Theory, 436, 441-449,
  467, 1171
Gompert's Law of Constant Citation, 435,
  450

Hardcopy
  performance relative to microfiche, 551,
    557, 559
  performance relative to oral channels,
    120

ICPR. *See* Interuniversity Consortium for
  Political Research.
Index Chemicus, 687
Index Medicus, 684, 691, 693, 702, 705
Index to Dental Literature, 695
Indexes
  user preferences in, 681
Indexing
  economics of, 490, 510, 685
Indexing services, 666-706. *See also* Title
  derivative indexing; Citation indexing.
  mission *vs.* discipline orientation, 666
  national system study, 701
India
  national information system, 256
Informal communication. *See also* Interpersonal communication; Invisible college,
  46, 776, 781, 896
  function of, 137
  grapevine, 142
  in academic environments, 126

Informal communication (cont'd)
  in agriculture, 1032-1035
  in biological sciences, 797, 808-809
  in chemistry, 836-837
  in education, 951
  in medicine, 809, 1128, 1146, 1238-
    1239
  in physics, 878
  in psychology, 328, 981, 988-990, 994,
    1006
  in sciences, 7, 22, 27, 30, 126, 360
  in social sciences, 360, 900
  in technology, 13, 22
  innovations in, 6, 23
  models of, 124, 894
  organization of, 14, 767
  performance evaluation, 137, 767
  relation to formal communication, 900,
    994
  review of research, 7, 13
  role behavior in, 142
  role of, 775, 1075
  role of convention in, 352
  social psychology of, 13
  structure of, 121, 768
Information
  defined, 148
  distribution of, 416-417, 422
  publication of, 416-417, 422
Information channels
  oral *vs.* hardcopy channels, 120
  performance in engineering, 1047-1048,
    1054, 1060-1061
Information exchange groups, 422, 1220-
  1237, 1246, 1274, 1282
  bibliography on, 33
  evaluation of, 1223, 1228-1229, 1231-
    1232, 1234, 1236
  in biomedical research, 1220-1222, 1224-
    1227, 1229, 1232-1233, 1235, 1246
  in physics, 1237, 1271, 1273
  in psychology, 1230
Information explosion. *See also* Literature
  growth.
  control of, 536, 539, 541
  in science and technology, 531, 546-549
  myth or reality, 525, 532, 536, 550
Information flow, 6. *See also* Communication; specific disciplines of interest.
  from informal to formal domain, 360,
    999
  in academic environment, 801, 841, 979
  in governmental laboratory environment,
    979
  in industrial environment, 793
  in research environment, 912
  influence of organization on, 1, 12, 1050,
    1059

Information flow (cont'd)
  influence of situational factors, 793
  influence of work team, 1
Information needs and uses. *See also*
specific disciplines of interest.
  bibliography, 8, 33, 1021
  comparison of surveys, 3, 4
  Department of Defense, 59, 65, 1021,
    1023-1025, 1027
  Department of the Army, 55
  empirical derivation of, 58
  evaluation of methods of study, 19, 48,
    58, 69
  in research and development, 1052,
    1064, 1099
  in the defense industry, 59
  methods of study, 19, 28, 41-72, 780,
    810, 912, 1021
  model of, 127
  of mission-oriented basic research, 26
  surveys of, 1, 3-4, 6, 11, 15, 19, 21-24,
    28-29, 34, 38, 46, 243, 777, 896
  taxonomy of, 775
  transformation during inquiry, 127
Information science
  abstracting and indexing journals, 677-
    678, 704
  Bradford distribution, 927
  communication in, 931
  Epidemic theory, 927
  literature characteristics, 927-928, 933
  primary sources, 925-926
  reading habits in, 926
  secondary sources, 925-926
  tertiary sources, 748
Information seeking. *See also* Communication; specific disciplines of interest.
  and channel selection, 776
  attitudes toward, 62
  behavior, 133, 139-140
  effects of SDI on, 769
  in libraries, 36, 144
Information sources
  criteria for selection of, 1046, 1083-
    1085
Information systems
  function in science, 775-776
Information uses. *See* Information needs
and uses.
Ingelfinger's rule
  and dual publication, 585
INIS. *See* International Nuclear Information System.
Innovations
  planning of, 18, 23
Interferon Scientific Memoranda, 1238-1239
*International Abstracts of Biological
Sciences*, 691

International communication
  survey of, 25
International Council of Scientific Unions,
  Committee for Data on Science and Tech-
  nology. *See* Committee for Data on
  Science and Technology.
International Data Library and Reference
  Service, 185
International information networks, 212,
  218, 224, 1032-1034, 1065
International information systems, 205-238
  future, 234
  user-system interface, 251
International information transfer, 118, 1178,
  1190, 1197, 1208
International meetings. *See* National and
  international meetings.
International Nuclear Information System,
  213, 220-221, 228, 233-235
International technological gatekeeper,
  1032-1034
Interpersonal communication. *See also*
  Informal communication.
  effects of educational similarity on, 128
  effects of socio-economic similarity on,
    128
  model, 149
  preparation for, 149
Interuniversity Consortium for Political
  Research, 154, 183
Interviews
  evaluation of, 19
  guide handbook, 59, 1021
  use of, 53
Invisible college, 1, 6-7, 24, 29, 83, 85, 94,
  112, 121, 124, 417, 425, 988-990
  bibliography, 33
  collaboration in, 477
  leadership roles, 94
  relation of library to, 130
  role of, 109
  survey, 83

Japan
  national information system, 256, 259,
    265
Jargon. *See* Language structure.
Journals. *See also* Primary communication.
  alternatives to, 636, 639
  as a communication channel, 418, 422,
    462, 781
  bibliography on, 20
  characteristics in science, 763
  characteristics of British scientific, 773
  clustering of, 764, 766, 778, 889, 892,
    941, 1100

Journals (cont'd)
  economics of, 481-482, 484, 486-487,
    501-503, 507, 626-627, 649, 763, 781,
    1261
  economics of concurrent microform
    editions, 488, 509
  estimation of number, 523, 650
  format, 422, 650
  in microfiche format, 553, 555, 562, 638
  in microfilm format, 566, 638
  integration with secondary services, 423
  management of, 620
  model of market, 484, 486, 498
  page charges, 481, 486, 494, 503, 505,
    507, 763
  pricing structure, 484, 486
  problems of, 628
  publication costs, 503, 507, 763
  quality control of, 422, 577, 586, 588,
    601-602, 606, 781
  revenue sources, 482, 503, 514, 627,
    637, 763, 1261
  role and development of, 503, 592, 626-
    653, 783, 1110, 1246, 1270
  role of microforms in, 560
  usage patterns, 460, 860

Keyword in context indexes
  searching, 744
Keyword in context indexing
  history, 716
  in biological sciences, 745
  in chemistry, 710, 726, 742
  in engineering, 709
  in library science, 713-714
  in psychology, 711
  in seismology, 708
  in social sciences, 727
  techniques, 715-717, 722, 729, 738-739
Keyword out of context indexing
  history, 716
  techniques, 715-717
Knowledge
  growth of, 83, 107
Knowledge utilization
  bibliography, 10, 16
  survey, 17, 35, 40
Knowledge want ads, 1258
KWIC. *See* Keyword in context.
KWOC. *See* Keyword out of context.

Lange's Handbook of Chemistry,
  cultural influence on design, 180
Language data
  Zipf distribution, 452

Language sciences
  communication in, 964-970
  information program, 307
  information sources, 967
  journal market, 487
  literature characteristics, 970
  national information system, 307, 309
  social organization in, 967
Language structure, 896, 1178-1179, 1182,
  1186-1187, 1191-1192, 1195, 1198, 1204,
  1206, 1211
Latin America
  national information system, 256
Law
  communication in, 974-976
  data banks, 976
  information network prospects, 304
  literature characteristics, 975
Law of Constant Citation. *See* Gompert's
  Law of Constant Citation.
"Letters" journals
  in physics, 859
Libraries
  reference interface, 36
Library and Information Science Abstracts,
  678
Library science
  abstracting and indexing journals, 677-
    678, 704
  and KWIC indexing, 713-714
  bibliographic control in, 930, 932
  Bradford distribution, 463
  literature characteristics, 939
  primary sources, 925, 939
  secondary sources, 925, 930
Library use
  bibliography, 2, 8-9
  evaluation of surveys, 41
  in medicine, 1128, 1150, 1163-1164
  in technology, 1030-1031
  survey, 4
Linguistics
  communication in, 965-966
  literature characteristics, 969
Literature characteristics
  in aeronautics and astronautics, 1260
  in agricultural economics, 1036, 1041
  in agriculture, 1040
  in astronomy, 637, 856, 865, 880-881
  in astrophysics, 880
  in biochemistry, 811, 1155-1156, 1158,
    1162
  in biological sciences, 803, 938
  in chemistry, 522, 819-820, 824-825,
    827-828
  in child psychology, 1004
  in clinical psychology, 997
  in ecology, 794

Literature characteristics (cont'd)
  in economics, 936, 938
  in education, 524, 941, 949
  in electrical engineering, 938, 1074
  in endocrinology, 1162
  in engineering, 938, 1117, 1147, 1260
  in food sciences, 1043
  in geography, 843, 845
  in geology, 845-846
  in geomorphology, 845
  in geophysics, 849
  in geosciences, 274-275
  in information science, 927-928, 933
  in language sciences, 970
  in law, 975
  in library science, 930
  in linguistics, 969
  in mammalogy, 795
  in marine geology, 844
  in mathematics, 851-853
  in medicine, 1127, 1131-1133, 1136-
    1137, 1142, 1144-1145, 1148, 1152,
    1155-1159
  in microbiology, 802
  in nursing, 1139
  in oncology, 1169
  in opthalmology, 1170
  in ornithology, 796
  in pharmacology, 1161
  in physical sciences, 869
  in physics, 526, 544, 637, 855-856, 863-
    864, 872, 883, 886, 938
  in political science, 972, 978
  in psychology, 938, 987, 998-1000,
    1003, 1005
  in public administration, 973
  in public communication, 929
  in rural sociology, 1036
  in social sciences, 895-899, 902, 916,
    963
  in social welfare, 1007
  in sociology, 538, 1008, 1012, 1015,
    1018-1019
  in toxicology, 1140, 1161
  in wildlife management, 1038
Literature growth, 522-550, 580, 586. *See
also* Bibliometric analysis; Information
explosion; Literature characteristics.
  consequences of, 117
  mathematical model, 533
  primary communication, 229
Literature obsolescence, 46, 456, 522-550.
See also Bibliometric analysis; Literature
characteristics.
Lotka distribution, 438
Lotka's Law,
  in humanities, 457
  unified with Bradford-Zipf law, 525

Mammalogy
  literature characteristics, 795
Management
  communication within, 142
Mandelbrot distribution, 438
Manuscript evaluation. *See also* Editors;
Referees.
  delays in, 614
  humor, 593
  in psychology, 578-579, 605, 609, 611-
    612, 615, 618, 622-623
  in sciences, 582, 584, 624
  in social sciences, 582, 584
Manuscript processing, 576-625. *See also*
Editors; Manuscript evaluation; Referees.
Marine geology
  literature characteristics, 844
Marine sciences
  plan for a national information system,
    279
Mass communication
  and social change, 37
Mathematical sciences
  national information system, 294, 296
Mathematics
  communication in, 850-853
  communication innovations, 1285
  communication problems in, 296, 850
  factors influencing modes of publishing,
    419
  journal economics, 481-482, 514-515,
    517
  literature characteristics, 815, 852-853
  social organization, 83, 100
  tertiary sources, 751
Matthew effect, 79, 106
Mechanical engineering
  information needs and uses, 1119
Medicinal chemistry
  primary sources, 653, 1166
Medicine
  abstracting and indexing journals, 672,
    684, 702, 705
  communication in, 336, 338, 1120-1176
  communication innovations, 1238-1239,
    1242, 1246, 1274, 1282
  communication problems, 1123, 1125,
    1134
  data activities, 196
  drug information sources, 1120
  evolution of the National Library of
    Medicine, 336
  function and future of journals, 632
  informal communication in, 809, 1128,
    1146, 1238-1239
  information needs and uses, 1130, 1137,
    1168

Medicine (cont'd)
   information seeking in, 1149, 1153-1154,
      1167, 1172-1173
   journal economics, 493
   literature characteristics, 1127, 1131-
      1133, 1136-1137, 1142, 1144-1145,
      1148, 1152, 1155-1159
   multiple authorship in, 469
   national information systems, 336, 338,
      342-343, 351
   publication delays, 619
   quality control of literature, 610
   role of technical reports in, 658
   structure of field, 338
   tertiary sources, 610, 751
   title indexes, 712
   use of libraries, 1128-1129, 1150
   use of primary sources, 1175-1176
Mental health
   national information system, 340
Menzel's Contagion Theory, 467
Message Complexity. *See* Message structure.
Message structure, 1195, 1210
Metallurgical Society
   postmeeting dissemination of informa-
      tion, 402
Metallurgy
   journals as communication channels, 375
   postmeeting dissemination of informa-
      tion, 402
Meteorology
   information exchange at meetings, 372
   journals as communication channels, 395
   postmeeting dissemination of informa-
      tion, 381, 388
   publication practices, 403
   tertiary sources, 751
Microbiology
   bibliographic control in, 802
   literature characteristics, 802
Microfiche
   economics of, 488, 553, 572
   standards, 572
   use in fact communication, 966
   user attitudes, 554-555, 561, 572, 575
Microfilm
   impact on journal costs, 509
   user attitudes, 574
Microform publishing, 422
   costs, 571
   formats, 571
   future developments, 571
   history, 571
   relation to short-run periodicals, 552
Microforms, 551-575
   and demand publishing, 1248
   bibliography, 33
   impact on page charges, 521

Microforms (cont'd)
   performance relative to hardcopy, 551,
      557, 559
   role of, 569
   state-of-the-art, 565
   use of, 556, 563, 566
Minijournals, 1277
Miniprints, 1259, 1261
Molecular biology
   communication in, 804-806
   social organization, 805-806
Multiple authorship. *See* Author collaboration.
Multiple publication, 550
Multiterm indexing, 740
Museum specimen data, 199

National Agricultural Library
   system study, 348
National and international meetings, 352-414.
   See also specific disciplines of interest.
   announcement of, 1240-1242
   organization of, 1269, 1272
National Data Center, 194
National Federation of Science
   Abstracting and Indexing Services, 690
National Information System for Psychology,
   301-303, 305, 308, 310, 312-335, 1006
National information systems, 239-272,
   416. *See also* specific disciplines of
   interest.
   alternatives for science and technology,
      243
   Canada, 241-242, 246, 256, 260
   compatibility problems, 267, 272
   copyright law, 245, 268-269
   criteria for, 284
   elements of design, 258
   elements of planning, 258, 261
   evolution of technical system, 266
   factors favoring development of, 240
   functions, 239
   governmental activities, 245
   India, 256
   intersystem compatibility, 247
   Japan, 256, 259, 265
   Latin America, 256
   legal aspects, 268
   management aspects, 259
   problem of development for science, 248
   proposals for science and technology,
      243-244, 254, 259, 271
   proprietary rights, 268, 270
   recommendations for science and tech-
      nology, 244, 254, 259-260
   requirements, 239, 243
   review of legislation, 243

National information systems (cont'd)
 review of proposals, 243, 249-250, 259,
  263-264
 role of information community in, 259
 role of libraries, 270
 role of scientific and technical community in, 259
 Scandinavia, 256
 sciences, 239, 241-244, 248, 254, 259,
  266, 273-300
 South Africa, 256
 Soviet Union, 252, 256, 262
 standardization requirements, 272
 technology, 239, 241, 243-244, 250,
  254, 259, 266
 trends and issues, 245
 United Kingdom, 256
 United States, 256
 user-system interface, 251
National Library of Medicine
 evolution of, 336
 toxicology information program, 337
National Mental Retardation Information
 and Resource Center
 developmental plan, 340
National Space Science Data Center, 179
National Standard Reference Data System,
 159-160, 188
 information handling in, 152
 plan of operation, 158
 status report, 161, 190
 survey of use, 204
News media
 in chemistry, 822, 842
 in sciences, 616, 1257
Newsletters, 1287
NISP. *See* National Information System for
 Psychology.
Nuclear science
 abstracting and indexing journals, 680,
  696
 communication innovations, 1280
 international information program, 207
 international information system, 213,
  220-221, 228, 233-235
 processing conference papers, 411
 publishing habits in, 879
Nuclear Science Abstracts, 680, 697
Nursing
 abstracting and indexing journals, 679
 literature characteristics, 1139
Nursing Literature Index, 679

Oceanography
 data activities, 196
Oncology
 bibliographic control in, 1169
 literature characteristics, 1169

Opthalmology
 literature characteristics, 1170
Optical Society of America
 information exchange at meetings, 377
 postmeeting dissemination of information, 386, 397
Oral communication. *See* Informal communication; Interpersonal communication.
Oral Research Abstracts, 689
Organizations
 communication in, 31, 142
 impact on information flow, 12, 29, 1098
Ornithology
 literature characteristics, 796
Ortega hypothesis, 861

Page charges
 effects of decline on journals, 489, 495-
  496
 historical review, 518
 in aeronautics and astronautics, 1261
 in astronomy, 637
 in biological sciences, 500
 in chemistry, 497
 in economics, 486
 in mathematics, 481, 514, 517
 in physics, 507-508, 511, 516, 637
 in sciences, 484, 494
 in social sciences, 494
 in technology, 494
 of primary journals, 503
Patents, 818-819, 1111
 growth of, 420
 in microform format, 570
Pesticides
 communication problems, 1039
Pharmacology
 abstracting and indexing journals, 705
 data activities, 196
 literature characteristics, 1161
Physical sciences
 abstracting and indexing journals, 690
 communication in, 360, 367, 405, 767
 informal communication, 767
 literature characteristics, 869
 prepublication dissemination of information, 365, 367, 405, 767
Physics
 abstracting and indexing journals, 675,
  680, 686, 698, 703
 author collaboration, 791
 characteristics of textbooks, 884
 communication in, 277, 284, 287, 637,
  854-892
 communication innovations, 1271-1273,
  1275, 1278, 1286
 competition in, 91-92

Physics (cont'd)
 current awareness services, 66, 871-874, 876
 data banks, 273
 factors influencing modes of publishing in, 419
 influence of cultural factors on communication, 891
 influence of geopolitical factors on communication, 891
 influence of recognition on communication, 891
 informal communication, 878
 information exchange at meetings, 377
 information needs and uses, 845, 888
 intellectual influence in, 77
 international transfer of information, 890
 journal economics, 507-508, 511, 516, 637
 literature characteristics, 451, 526, 544, 637, 855-856, 863-864, 872, 883, 886, 938
 marketing of information products, 506
 national information system, 273, 276-278, 281, 283-284, 287-290, 295, 300, 675, 866, 875
 postmeeting dissemination of information, 386, 397
 preprints, 882
 primary sources, 651, 860, 877
 publication patterns in, 791, 862
 referee system, 625, 882
 reward system, 79-80, 91-92
 role of "letters" journals, 859
 secondary sources, 877, 885
 social organization, 77, 79-80, 88, 91-92, 861, 891
 tertiary sources, 751-752, 755-756, 758
Physics Abstracts, 680, 686
 role in current awareness, 66
Physics Information Exchange, 1271, 1273, 1275, 1278
Political science
 abstracts of data-based research, 178
 communication in, 971-973, 977, 978
 data banks, 154
 information needs and uses, 971
 literature characteristics, 972, 978
 primary sources, 977
 social organization, 100
Predocumentation, 587, 591, 599, 617
Preprints, 365, 417, 1274, 1276, 1282
 bibliography, 33
 in biomedical research, 1246, 1275
 in chemistry, 832-833
 in mathematics, 1285
 in nuclear science, 1280

Preprints (cont'd)
 in physics, 882, 1271, 1273, 1275, 1278, 1286
 in psychology, 301-302, 320, 322
 in sciences, 419, 466, 628
Price's Exponential Growth Model, 525
Price's Index, 782
Primary communication, 20, 33, 229, 418, 426, 793, 896. *See also* Journals; Technical reports; specific disciplines of interest.
Primary literature
 definition of, 415
Priority of discovery, 91-92, 104-105, 1188
Problem solving. *See* Decision-making.
Professional societies
 as publishers, 427
 communication role of, 1, 24, 1092
 economics of publication programs, 504
Proprietary interests
 impact on communication, 268, 270, 1181, 1183-1185, 1189, 1200-1201, 1205
Psychiatry
 information needs and uses, 1122, 1126, 1174
Psychological Abstracts, 667, 696, 949
Psychology
 abstracting and indexing journals, 667, 696
 authorship in, 472-473, 476, 479
 bibliographic needs, 893
 books as a communication channel, 983, 1001
 changing national meetings, 368
 classic articles in, 1002
 communication in, 979-1006
 communication innovations, 1212-1217
 communication problems, 312, 985, 991
 communication programs, 331-332
 design of international meetings, 353
 foreign *vs.* U.S. information exchange, 982
 forms of international congresses, 414
 functions of international congresses, 414
 future market for information, 303
 informal communication, 328, 981, 988-990, 994, 1006
 information exchange at meetings, 352-353, 356, 361
 information flow in academic environment, 979
 information needs of individuals and institutions, 335
 information use in undergraduate training, 984
 international information exchange at meetings, 353, 358, 369, 389

Psychology (cont'd)
  invisible college, 988-990
  KWIC indexing, 711
  literature characteristics, 938, 987, 998-
    1000, 1003, 1005
  manuscript evaluation, 578-579, 605,
    609, 611-612, 615, 618, 622-623
  national information system, 301-303,
    305, 308, 310, 312-335
  prepublication dissemination of informa-
    tion, 995
  primary sources, 324, 994-995, 997-998,
    1006
  publication system in, 315-316, 319,
    330, 334
  referees in, 302, 1006
  social organization, 988-990
  technical reports as a communication
    channel, 654
  use of audio-visual media, 327
Public administration
  literature characteristics, 973
Public communication
  literature characteristics, 929
Public libraries
  bibliography on use, 2
Publication delays. *See* Communication
  delays.
Publication forms
  hierarchy of, 330
Publication system
  desirable characteristics, 315
Publishing
  by scientific and technical societies, 427
Publish-or-perish syndrome
  effects of, 542, 545

Quality control
  of papers, 577, 586, 588, 601-602, 606
Question negotiation
  in libraries, 36, 144
Questionnaires
  evaluation of, 19
  samples of, 53-55, 71
Quick publication
  in psychology, 301, 320-322
  role of, 1246, 1270

Rapid dissemination programs, 1247, 1276
Reading habits
  in agriculture, 1037
  in biological sciences, 798
  in chemistry, 826, 835, 838
  in engineering, 1088, 1097
  in information science, 926

Reading habits (cont'd)
  in sciences, 15, 1088
  in technology, 15
Referee system
  function of, 624
  institutionalization of, 624
  structure of, 624-625
Refereeing, 581, 604, 608
Referees, 597, 602
  anonymity of, 578, 584
  control of, 607
  rules for, 592, 621
Referee's report
  use of, 592
Regional information system
  elements of design, 258
  elements of planning, 258
Reports. *See* Technical reports.
Reprints
  in sciences, 419
Research
  social context of, 100
Research and development
  informal communication, 1075
  information needs and uses, 1052, 1064,
    1067, 1078, 1099
  information sources, 1057, 1060-1061,
    1063-1064, 1080
  problem solving, 1057, 1080
Research and development laboratories
  communication in, 1044-1045, 1049-
    1051, 1053-1055, 1059, 1073, 1082,
    1086, 1090, 1094, 1101
  communication roles in, 1045, 1051,
    1059, 1079
  consulting in, 1055
  information flow in industrial, 1107-
    1108, 1112
  social organization, 1044-1045, 1049,
    1051, 1053
Review literature. *See* Tertiary sources.
Reward system
  academic environment, 75, 84
  in chemistry, 75
  in physics, 79-80
  in sciences, 74, 84, 93, 106, 119, 424
Rhetoric in science, 911, 1152, 1182
Roper Public Opinion Research Center, 176
Royal Society of London
  position on page charges, 512
Rural sociology
  literature characteristics, 1036

SCAN, 1249

Scandinavia
national information system, 256

Science Citation Index, 47, 67, 687, 690,
693, 719, 721, 732, 734

Science data banks, 151, 184
evaluation of data, 190
survey of U.S. Activities, 196

Science Information Exchange. *See* Smithsonian Science Information Exchange.

Sciences
abstracting and indexing
journals, 666
behavior patterns in, 104
collaboration in, 470-471, 480
communication in, 762-793
communication innovation, 1240-1242,
1257, 1276
communication problems, 772, 790
communication system, 74, 106, 405,
1104
competition in, 92, 96, 98, 103-105
elitism in, 112
growth of, 103, 105, 370
information exchange at meetings, 412
information flow from international
meetings, 413
information needs and uses, 1, 4, 6, 765,
774-775, 779, 917
information sources, 1088
interaction in, 124, 778
interaction with technology, 111, 425,
766, 784, 1022, 1098, 1100, 1104,
1109, 1117
internationality of, 115
journal economics, 484, 494
language barriers, 1191-1192
literature characteristics, 527, 530, 580,
763
manuscript evaluation, 582, 624
national information systems, 239-240,
242-244, 248, 254, 259, 266, 271
prepublication dissemination of information, 405
priority of discovery, 96, 98, 104-105
publication opportunities, 106
quality control of literature, 580
quantitative data in, 184, 193
reading habits in, 15, 1088
reward system, 84, 93, 106-107
role of national meeting in communication, 362-364
role of publications in, 84
role of technical reports in, 665
social control, 98, 103
social norms, 73, 117, 424

Sciences (cont'd)
social organization, 74, 85, 87, 94, 101,
103-104, 107, 114, 116-118, 124, 782-
783
social stratification, 78, 81, 95, 103, 119
use of news media as communication
channel, 616
work teams in, 89, 96, 99

Scientific information
users *vs.* nonusers, 136

Scientific meetings. *See also* National and
international meetings.
communication at, 356, 422
documentation of, 354
role of presentations, 355, 357

Scientific nomenclature
international cooperation, 771

Scientific publication system
desirable characteristics, 315

SDI. *See* Selective dissemination of
information.

Searchable Physics Information Notices, 867,
875-876

Secondary services, 666-745. *See also*
specific disciplines of interest.
coordination of, 676, 694
economics of, 490, 694
marketing of, 506
on microfilm, 558, 573
product innovations, 685, 694
relationship with primary publications,
423, 426
standardization, 684, 694
use of microfilm cartridge, 558

Secrecy in science, 1188, 1199, 1202, 1205
pros *vs.* cons, 1180

Security classified information, 1181, 1184-
1185, 1189, 1193-1194, 1197, 1201, 1205,
1209
handling of, 1177, 1196, 1203, 1207

Seismology
use of KWIC indexes, 708

Selective dissemination of documents, 628,
638, 1252, 1259-1260, 1264, 1268, 1283

Selective dissemination of information, 417,
1077

Single article dissemination. *See* Selective
dissemination of documents.

Smithsonian Science Information Exchange,
1253, 1262-1263, 1279

Social organization, 73-119. *See also* specific discipline or environment of interest.

Social science data banks, 150, 173, 186,
195
availability and quality, 166
Canadian clearinghouse, 165
development of, 182
impact on research, 169

Social science data banks (cont'd)
  information retrieval from, 154
  international activities, 185, 187
  management of systems, 157, 171
  networks, 167
  privacy and security, 172
  relation to libraries, 168, 175
  review of developments, 155-156
  sample survey data, 176
  use of, 153, 174
Social sciences
  bibliographic needs, 893
  communication in, 86, 405, 767, 893-922
  communication problems, 905, 921
  communication programs, 360, 367
  data activities, 196
  informal communication, 767
  information handling in, 904
  information needs and uses, 896, 901, 905-909, 917
  journal economics, 494
  KWIC indexing, 727
  language barriers, 1191-1192
  literature characteristics, 895-899, 902, 916, 963
  literature searching in, 918
  manuscript evaluation, 582
  model of journal market, 499
  prepublication dissemination of information, 365, 367, 405, 767
  press, 903
  primary sources, 896, 915, 919-920, 922
  role of national meeting, 362-364
  secondary sources, 896
  social organization, 86
Social status
  impact on communication, 1044, 1050-1051, 1053
Social stratification. *See also* Social organization.
  consequences of, 95
  development of, 95
  effects on communication, 78, 95
  in academic environments, 861
  in physics, 77, 79, 861
  in sciences, 74, 78, 81
  patterns of, 78, 119
Social structure. *See* Social organization.
Social ties
  measurement of, 85, 112
Social values
  in sciences, 73, 117
  in sociology, 76
Social welfare
  communication in, 1007, 1013-1014
  information needs and uses, 1007, 1017
  literature characteristics, 1007

Sociological Abstracts, 1256
Sociology
  assessment of research quality, 47
  books as a communication channel, 1018
  communication in, 1007-1019
  communication innovations, 1256
  information exchange at meetings, 373, 398
  internationalization of, 108
  influentials in, 108
  journal evaluation, 1010
  journals as a communication channel, 394
  literature characteristics, 538, 1008, 1012, 1015, 1018-1019
  postmeeting dissemination of information, 385, 396, 404
  research role of, 76
  research sponsorship in, 1009
  research support and multiple authorship in, 473
  social organization, 76, 83, 90
Sociology of Education Abstracts, 700, 921
Solution development record
  evaluation of, 19
Source abstracting. *See* Predocumentation.
Source indexing. *See* Predocumentation.
South Africa
  national information system, 256
Soviet Union
  national information system, 256, 262
Special education
  communication in , 945, 950
Specialist periodical reports, 1255
SPIN. *See* Searchable Physics Information Notices.
State-of-the-art reports
  preparation of, 749
Statistical bibliography. *See* Bibliometric analysis.
Synoptics, 1259, 1261

Tape cassettes. *See* Audio-visual media.
Teamwork. *See* Work team.
Technical data banks, 151, 184
  survey of U.S. activities, 196
Technical meetings. *See also* National and international meetings.
  documentation of, 354
  role of presentations, 355, 357
Technical Meetings Index, 1242
Technical reports, 417, 654-665, 781
  abstracting of, 657
  characteristics affecting reader behavior, 662
  in microfiche format, 554, 562
  quality control of, 665, 781
  relation to primary journals, 654-655, 665

Technical reports (cont'd)
  role of, 654-655, 659, 665
  standards, 655, 660-661, 664
  taxonomy of, 665
  titling of, 656
Technical societies. *See* Professional
societies.
Technological gatekeepers, 34, 597, 1044-
1045, 1050-1051, 1053, 1059, 1077,
1079, 1089, 1288. *See also* Gatekeepers;
International technological gatekeepers.
Technological innovation
  role of communication in, 1020
Technology
  communication barriers in, 1028, 1191-
  1192
  communication in, 1020-1031, 1104
  communication innovations, 1240-1242,
  1258, 1276, 1288
  communication problems, 249, 790
  editing journals in, 576
  factors influencing communication in,
  1028
  information needs and uses, 1028-1029
  information sources in, 1028
  interaction with sciences, 111, 425, 766,
  782, 784, 1022, 1098, 1100, 1104,
  1109, 1117
  journal economics, 494
  library use in, 1030-1031
  national information system, 239-244,
  249-250, 254, 259, 266
  quantitative data in, 184
  role of national meeting in, 362-364
  role of technical reports, 665
  social organization, 114, 782-783
Terse conclusions, 1244, 1265
Tertiary sources, 610, 746-761
  innovations in, 1255, 1281
Textbooks. *See* Books.
Title derivative indexes, 707-745
  evaluation of, 715
Title enriched indexing, 717
Title indexes
  in biological sciences, 712
  in chemistry, 712
  in medicine, 712
Toxicology
  coverage by secondary services, 693
  information program of the National
  Library of Medicine, 337
  literature characteristics, 1140, 1161
  national information system, 349
Trade catalogs
  in microfilm format, 567
Trade magazines, 642
Transportation research
  international communication, 217

UNISIST. [World Science Information
System], 205-206, 208, 211, 214-216,
222-223, 226-227, 229-231, 236-239.
United Engineering Information Service,
341, 344-346
United Kingdom
  national information system, 256
United States
  national information system, 256
University laboratories
  social organization of, 118
University libraries. *See* Academic libraries.
Urban planning
  data banks, 192
U.S. Geological Survey
  bibliographic control system, 292
U.S.S.R. *See* Soviet Union.

VINITI [All-Union Institute of Scientific
and Technological Information]
  review of, 252, 262
Virology
  coverage by secondary services, 673
Vocational education
  gatekeepers in, 960
  information needs and uses, 952, 960

Wildlife management
  literature characteristics, 1038
Work teams
  colleague roles, 89, 118
  composition and performance, 113
  impact on information flow, 1, 29
  innovations in, 89
  social organization, 89, 96, 99, 118
  social roles, 89, 96, 99, 118
World Science Information Network System
  proposal for, 219
World Science Information System. *See*
UNISIST.

Yule distribution, 460

*Zentralstelle fur Atomkernenergie-Dokumenta-
tion*, 411
Ziman's Consensual Model of Science, 992
Zipf distribution, 429-430, 438, 452
  derivation of, 431
  library application of, 432-434, 439,
  465
Zipf's Law
  possible proof of, 464
  unified with Lotka-Bradford Law, 525